THE TAGORES OF JORASANKO

The Tagore House at Jorasanko, Calcutta

THE TAGORES OF JORASANKO

HIRONMOY BANERJEE

Translated
by
Biplab K. Mazumdar

GYAN

GYAN PUBLISHING HOUSE

New Delhi 110 002

The Tagores of Jorasanko
(Biography, Literature, Art and Culture)

ISBN 81-212-0488-7

Published 1995 in India by
Gyan Publishing House
5 Ansari Road
New Delhi 110 002

Printed at Mehra Offset Press, New Delhi

FOREWORD

While translating the original Bengali book, 'Thakurbarir Katha', I was richly captured by the atmosphere of its racy mixture of absorbing gaiety and responsibility with a buoyancy of *joie de vivre* to portray a modest smile of excellence through a colourful array of their characters. This great House of the Tagores develops an intense love for the mankind to regenerate a cosmopolitanism of culture and accelerates the wheels of our glory for the federation of mankind at the lofty dome of joy. This unputdownable House at Jorasanko, withstanding all the tardy-gaited nights of dangers and hardships, imparts to the young generation to seek the truth, to search for freedom of enquiry, to establish in them a compelling desire to live greatly and magnanimously, to ask what they must do, to say what they think, to give them the knowledge and awareness, to see and enjoy what they believe, and to inform the people what is going on throughout the world. The main aim of this House at Jorasanko is the establishment of the worship of men.

Being a virtuoso of letters equipped with a richly satisfying mark of distinctive qualities, Dr. Hironmoy Banerjee, I.C.S., former Vice-Chancellor of Rabindra Bharati University, Calcutta, entrusted me to translate his book 'Thakurbarir Katha' into English. His contributions to the welfare of Bengal are known to all and sundry. Being a beloved student of Dr. Banerjee, I was attracted by his fine-grained personality and by his charismatic administrator as a civilian during the pre- and post-independence decades of India. His untiring efforts inspired me much in translating this book.

I am grateful to pay my respect, confidence and affection to a great civilian, educationist, author, critic, etc. After his death, he still earns an accolade from the four corners of Bengal. I am also grateful to his family members to complete this work.

I am indebted to my mother and to my eldest brother for their useful advice.

Lastly, I am very grateful to Gyan Publishing House, New Delhi and to Shri Satyendra Nath Sarkar, an eternal vigilante of this publications house, for his conscientious and extraordinary interest in publishing this translated work. His keen judgement, coordinated with unflinching courage and unswerving determination, is praiseworthy with a view to disseminate the ideological phenomenon of its (the House at Jorasanko) intrinsic truth and glorification to a new horizon for a better tomorrow.

Biplab K. Majumdar

Contents

Translator's Preface

The Tagores of Jorasanko are a question of principle, of purpose, of idealism, of character. They are at bottom just, virtuous and hopeful. The roots of their house at Jorasanko are in the soil of what is lovely, pure, and clear. This house is the sweet breath of morn, and the gems of heaven. The Tagores needed Milton's famous "Give me the liberty to know, to utter, and to argue freely according to conscience, above all liberties" from the 'Areopagitica'. The tone of this house is surpassingly sweet and clear. If you stare at this house, you will feel everyman coming and going freely, swiftly living and swiftly dying, leaving a brilliant mark of brilliancy in his own field. This house is a crackling of sparks when a great fire dies out. It is an epitome of Rabindranath's poetical career, the pennant of genius streaming in his wake. The conception of his greatness is explicitly moral, as well as intellectual and aesthetic.

Rabindranath is neither ivory tower nor flowery landscape dwellers. He is concerned with his times, concerned with life and liberty and the freedom of the individual and of his world. Born in this house, he is the singer of man's emancipation. This house itself is an experience in truth. It may truthfully be called fascinating. It is an urgent, magnetic house for anyone with the faintest itch for travel in its veins. It is a most comprehensive creation, reflecting vast study and research. Full of vigour of thought and expression. Rabindranath's prose has warmth, colour, and a thrilling descriptive power. His innate love of poetry, his appreciation of beauty and his command of the apt, illumine this house. Words of the Tagores from this house fully deserve to be treasured. From this memorable house.... magnificent.... decidedly amusing....infinitely moving....Rabindranath had the full equipment of a great writer. A long and absorbing narrative of his forefathers had a gripping saga full of colour and drama....a horrifying interest. Together with the progenitors, this house marched ahead through the fields of literature, music, art and what not; and later on it binds and sustains our attention with piercing honesty.

Brilliantly apparelled with the glowing gems of Tagores and surpassingly coupled with the boundless beauty of Rabindranath's poetic genius, this house has now been a sacred place of happiness to all sections of people. Thousands and thousands of foreigners assemble together every year to fathom the aesthetic beauty of his deep-rooted philosophy. He is the wit and wisdom of the ages. Bowed by the weight of a century, it leans upon its hoe and gazes on the ground to assure the safety of its majesty and grandeur, to safeguard its dignity, and to protect the freedom of the individual; this house of Tagores, as a charioteer, rides triumphantly laurelled with the fat of the years of augustness and nobleness. It still stands alone after the silence of a century. In this age of emptiness, burdened with grieves, tongued with censure of the world's blind greed and fraught with menace to the universe, this house holds out its thousand hands to embrace the purity of man's soul and mind with the Tagores. To establish the worship of men is its sole aim.

Beyond the infinite and boundless reach, Rabindranath has set a glory to our country by his worth, his greatness, and his nobility. Breathing to his breathless excellence and tasting the pleasures of his works, we continue our resolve to such the sweets of his sweet philosophy. With his breath, he perfumes the air. Sacred and sweet is all we see in him.

Born in 1774, Rammohan Roy founded the Brahmo Samaj in India. He voiced forth against the practices and purposes of idolatry. He was in the mainstream of Indian leaders and social reformers who vehemently attacked on the insensate barbarism of 'Sutteeism'. He was the first writer of the good Bengali prose. Sister Nivedita writes: "We had a long talk on Rammohan Roy in which he (Vivekananda) pointed out three things as the dominant notes of his teacher's message—his acceptance of the Vedanta, his preaching of patriotism and the love that embraced the Mussalman equally with the Hindu. For all these things he claimed himself to have taken up the task the breadth and foresight of Rammohan Roy had mapped out." (Notes on some wanderings with Swami Vivekananda, p. 19).

After the death of Rammohan Roy, Rabindranath's grand-father, Dwarakanath Tagore shouldered the responsibility of keeping it alive. Throughout his life, he maintained a tradition of magnificence and prodigal expenditure. He visited England where he was honoured as 'Prince Dwarakanath Tagore'. He enthusiastically said: "It was England who sent out Clive and Cornwallis to benefit India by their councels and arms. It was England that sent out to that distant nation the great man who had succeeded in stablishing peace in the world, and who was the first who introduced a proper and permanent order of things in the East." (Kishori Chand Mitra : Memoir of Dwarakanath Tagore, p. 94).

The family name of the Tagores is Banerjee (Bandopadhya). The British officials used the word 'Thakur' for the Brahmins who were in their service in India. It was then anglicized as 'Tagore'.

After Dwarakanath Maharshi, Debendranath Tagore, one of the liberators of the ages, resolved to establish firmly the principles and practices of Brahmoism, on a solid ground of its glory. He succeeded. The ashram at Shantiniketan begins with the Maharshi.

Rabindranath, the youngest of seven sons, through the windows of this house, reflected the liberty of enquiry and the right of disseminating our opinions against the pernicious tyranny of the English. This independent exercise of his reflections communicated to the whole world with the energy and ingeneousness of truth. He electrified the spirit of nationalism and translated the declarations of the rights of man into definite actions. Rabindranath dedicated himself to the Swadeshi Movement. And he suddenly left it and kept himself away from this movement. Why? Ajit Chakravarty's comments in the Modern Review of July, 1917, have made it clear: "For four years since its foundation, the ashram went on humming the old forgotten strain that came from the past, from the woodlands of Aryan India of four thousand years ago. Then there burst into the country a thunder-storm. The great national movement with its trumper-blast of Bande-Mataram, its flaunting hopes and high aspirations, its riotous excitement and frantic expectancy, came. The poet became its high priest. The ashram was no longer a shadow of the benighted past, it was a reality of the dawning day. The country's consciousness surged high in the ashram. Of course, the western features of the school, e.g. self-government of the boys and the atmosphere of the freedom did suffer at this period. But the emphasis was certainly laid on the spirit of ancient India. Not simply on the spiritual side of ancient India, but on the side of social life and rules as well, which were, without question, narrow and convention bound.

Fortunately, the narrow and aggressive lines on which the whole movement was worked out, making patriotism an end into itself and efficiency the goal of all activities, grew discordant to the poet's growing spiritual life. He suddenly cut himself away from the movement. He sought solitude of spirit, he sought the universal joy of nature, he sought the hidden springs of spiritual life. It was then that many his larger Gitanjali poems were written."

Rabindranath's 'Shantiniketan' (Abode of peace) is a sacred place and a testament to our lofty educational mission on the broadway of goodfaith and goodwill. It is a creative ambassador of the East and the West for our openness and love. The ardent lovers of this place experience it by faith, by heart, and by reason. Rabindranath and his Shantiniketan spring from the same root and are close akin. They are warmly invited by their purity of soul and singleness of mind, at the holy feast where the east and the west meet together. "Man has been able to make his pursuit of power easier today by his art of mitigating the obstructive forces that come from the higher regions of his humanity. With his cult of power and his idolatry of money he has, in a great measure, reverted to his primitive barbarism, a barbarism whose path is lit up by the lurid of light of intellect." (Rabindranath Tagore : From Darkness to Light).

Rabindranath's Shantiniketan is as strong as a tower in hope, virtue, and valour couched in its eyes. It courageously heralds a means to the end of a free society where pure morals and unfettered religious sentiments may be justified irrespective of nationality, colour or religion. Let us keep the waters free. His novel has a sureness of technique and a firework brilliance of touch....both good literature and good writing.

Rabindranath lives in life, sun of undying light, And
fathoms his own heart for ways of good at Shantiniketan.

He is assembly a personage on the grand scale, in the grand manner, gloriously balanced, rounded. He toured Europe and this tour encouraged him much. He dreamt a dream of establishing an Asiatic University at Shantiniketan. And he finally translated his dream into reality. The Visva Bharati (The World University of India) was opened by Dr. Brojendranath Seal on 23rd Dec. 1921).

He was invited to pay visits to England and America, to give lectures, on the great problems of life. These lectures created tremendous impression on thoughtful minds. He was invited at Oxford. The impression of a writer in the Christian Commonwealth ran as follows:

"Nor were the expectations of the large audience disappointed. At the close of Mr. Tagore's address on 'Realisation of Love', one felt that the whole problem of modern social life had been lifted on to a plane higher than is usual, and had been dealt with in a most moving spirit of mystic insight. One saw at last the thinness of the modern money-made, and money-making civilization in the piercing lights of Tagore's gospel of the radiant joy of life and the wonderful unity between mankind and the universe.... Tagore told his audience that sin was an attitude of life thatregarded its goal as finite, and its own little self as its chief aim and object of affection...."

(*Modern Review*, April, 1917)

This house is a masterpiece both of sound and minute research and of good judgement and clear judgement, centering around the Tagores. It stands on a pregnant but fertilizing ideas of the Tagores; this house born of true tolerance, a house that combines penetration and reconciliation according to the best traditions of humanity, culture, and art. The eyes of this house are simple and serene. It does not argue. Language of this house is quiet and persuasive. Its style of standing at Jorasanko is simple and straight forward, as lucid as distilled water. It means every historical event it witnessed. The first duty of Rabindranath at Shantiniketan is to see that every child born therein shall be well housed, clothed, fed, and educated, till it attains years of discretion. He has come to a realization that one truth stands firm. All that happens in world history rests on something spiritual. If the spiritual is strong, it creates world history. If it is weak, it suffers world history.

The ashram at Shantiniketan, Bolepur, founded by Maharshi Debendranath Tagore, and started by his son, the poet Rabindranath Tagore, has awakened the interests of many people who are interested in the poet's life and works... Rabindranath thought of Shantiniketan, the place of meditation of his saintly father. It was there, under the chatim tree, with infinite solitude of space around him that the great spirit of Maharshi found.

The repose of his heart
The joy of his mind
The peace of his soul.

But the connection of the ashram with the historic poet of India, has been finely dealt with by Rabindranath in his beautiful introduction of the book, 'Shantiniketan'. The Bolepur School of Rabindranath by W.W. Pearson. It gives a bit of his autobiography and is therefore extremely interesting:

"The greatest teachers in ancient India, whose names are still remembered, were forest dwellers. By the shady border of same sacred river or Himalayan lake, they built their altar of fire, grazed their cattle, harvested wild rice and fruits fo their food, lived with their wives and children in the bosom of primeval nature, meditated upon the deepest problems of the soul, and made it their object of life to grow in sympath with all creation and in communion with the Supreme Being. There students flocked round them and had their lessons of immortal life in the atmosphere of truth, peace and freedom of the spirit... All our great classic poets in their epic verses and dramas looked back reverence upon that golden day break of the awakenment of India's soul."

(Shantiniketan. The Bolepur School of Rabindranath Tagore by W.W. Pearson)

Rabindranath is the greatest living authority on culture. From this house, he has presented an exceptionally judicious and balanced account of this period's creative writing, full of pregnant comments on the age and its literature. This house of Tagores is its own kind of masterpiece addressed to the discriminating readers as well as to the viewers. If we tell with pungency and wit, this house, an unvarnished truth, has a richly amusing story.

When Rabindranath visited America, the Detroit Times writes: "The American look upon him as more than a curious and impressive figure in an oriental garb delivering an old fashioned message...... When at the end his lecture on the Cult of Nationalism, he allows the poet..... Prophet to stand on forth in utter simplicity and dignity as he reads from his own poem, repeating and repeating his message:

My Master bids me stand at the roadside of
    ratreat,
    And sing the song of the defeated,
For she is the bride whom he woos in secret.

Those who walk on the path of pride
    Crushing the lowly life under their tread,
Spreading their footprints in blood

    Upon the tender green of the earth,
Let them rejoice, and thank thee, Lord,
    For the day is theirs.

But thou hast done well in leaving me with the humble
    Whose doom it is to suffer,
And bear the burden of power,
    And hide their faces and stifle their sobs in the dark.

For every throb of their pain
    Has pulsed in the secret depth of thy night,
And every insult has been gathered
    In thy great silence
And the morrow is theirs.

(Modern Review, 1917, Rabindranath in America)

His intellectual attainments, independence of mind, sweetness of temper, sanity of outlook, practical ability, social influence, public spirit, princely magnificence, devoted patriotism, sense of world brotherhood, judiciousness of monolithical unity amongst the world people, single-mindedness of his cosmopolitan culture at the lofty dome of joy and beauty, and his multi-dimensional personalities in all fields of thoughts and ideas make his own way equally conspicuous. He is one of the greatest poets in the sum of his works, the greatest number of the greatest ideas. The mission of his poetical thought is the expression, or rather the exploration of life. For life is very great and manifold. In the famous poem 'By Blue Ontario's Shore' Walt Whitman thus defines, the mission of the poet:

The immortal poets of Asia and Europe have done
their work and pass'd to other spheres,
A work remains, the work of surpassing all they have done.

... ...

The poet is the equable man,

... ...

He bestows on every object or quality its fit proportion,
neither more nor less
He is the arbiter of the diverse, he is the key,

... ...

In peace out of him speaks the spirit of peace, large, rich,
thrifty,
building populous towns, encouraging agriculture,
arts, commerce, lighting the study of man,
the soul, health, immortality, Government.

In war he is the best backer of war, he fetches artillery
as good as the engineers, he can make every
word he speaks draw blood,

... ...

As he sees the farthest, he has the most faith.
His thoughts are the hymns of the praise of things.
In the dispute on God and Eternity he is silent,
He sees Eternity less like a play with a prolouge
and a denouement,
He sees Eternity in men and women, he does not see
men and women as dreams or dots.

... ...

For the Great Idea,
That, O my brethren, that is the mission of poets.

The house of Tagores at Jorasanko is itself an institution for educating its citizens in all the virtues. This house without Shantiniketan is lame, Shantiniketan without this house is blind. Shantiniketan is a daughter of this house as maternity is to a woman. Both the sacred places are blended together, overlapping each other, side by side, for joy and beauty, to a new horizon, where Rabindranath and the accomplishments of his fore-fathers should be the rule of life for a universal faculty of common mind.....the nearest and surest way to the criterion of truth. We see it by faith and by the eyes of reason. Ralph Waldo Emerson, on his Phi Beta Kappa address, July 18, 1876, says: "Great men are they who see that spiritual is stronger than material force, that thoughts rule the world." Rabindranath's spiritual introspection through the sweets and sounds of nature, and his deep-seated mental vision into the age of our anxiety, negation and despair, dissociated from all ethics and philosophy, lie at the root of the great thinkers of this world.

In a remarkable poem on 'santiniketan', Rabindranath makes this starting savings.

Shantiniketan

Oh, The Shantiniketan, the darling our hearts!
Our dreams are rocked in her arms,
Her face is fresh and fair to us for ever
In the peace of her silent shadows we dwell, in the green of her fields.
Her mornings come and her evenings bringing down the caress of the sky;
The stillness of her shady paths is thrilled by the whisper of the wood;
Her amlaki groves tremble with the rapture of rustling leaves.
She is within us and around, however far we wander.
The strings of our love are strung in her own deep tunes.
She weaves our hearts in a song making us one in music.

(This song is sung in chorus in Bengali by the boys of the Shantiniketan school)

Heart-sick like Mathew Arnold, of the thousand discords on earth and of "man's fitful uproar mingling with his toil," Mr. C.F. Andrews came under Rabindranath's 'healing power'. On first reading 'Gitanjali', he felt entranced like one about to enter the inner shrine. "A still hushed presence" bound all his spirit and whispered to him.

"Weary at heart with this world's restless strife.
Here find the peace everlasting life."
(The Motherland and Other Poems: C.F. Andrews)

Under the guidance of Rabindranath, he 'beheld life's vision whole', and came to know 'How love through all His universe doth flow.'

He beheld face to face within the veil—
Love in the joy of world-embracing light,
Love in the blade of grass with sun-beams light,
Love in the baby's smile of new-born bliss,
Love in the star-crowned infinite abyss.

This perfect realisation of nature must be familiar to all who have read in Rabindranath's reminiscences of that never to be forgotten morning in Sudder Street.

In 'The Palm at Shantiniketan', Mr. Andrews gives voice to what so many of us have felt when pacing its gravel-walks. He has come under the spell of the abiding peace of that ashram, its blending of work and worship, of action and repose. The palms, studied by him at all hours, are only a material illustration of the spirit of the place; they are not lifeless; they have their toil and sleep awakening to a life of ecstasy and passionate longing when touched by the 'low moon's rosy splendour,' as it 'rises along the darkling earth.' But their enduring effect, as we stand beneath them in the still moontide when 'the morning breezes have ceased' and the palms are still hushed in enchantment, is to enfold our souls in "a dream of endless peace'. Mr. Andrews is only one of many who have felt at Bolepur.

"Tossed to and fro I had sorely striven,
    Seeking, and finding no release:
Here, by the palm-trees, came God-given
    Utter, ineffable, boundless peace.
Peace in the deep mid-air surrounding
    Peace in the sky from pole to pole,
Peace to the far horizon bounding,
    Peace in the universal soul."

Under the palms at Shantiniketan one can understand why so many of France's workers sought refuge at Port Royale, with its monastic repose and purity and unmonastic absence of rigour and regulation. Rabindranath's world-conquering poems couched in majestic words and coupled with metaphysical knowledge has culminated our glory at the lofty dome of this old house. It is by love of humanity alone that he transmute evil into good, by acceptance of it and not denial of it, by altruism and not egotistic aloofness. This house has now become great an institution, awakening the philosophy of impulses with which this house began its work into the various departments of education by which public opinion controls the lives of men and women. The value of this philosophy is not in devising but in discovering. What will it discover? In the poem entitled 'The Base of all Metaphysics', Walt Whitman says underneath all philosophies he clearly says:

> "The dear love of man for his comrade, the attraction of friend to friend,
> of the well married husband and wife, of children and parents,
> of city for city and land for land."
> That is to say the eternal verities of life.

Judged from a purely aesthetic standpoint, this significant house of Tagores, so rich in deeds, is the Indian's boast. No nation can be great without a belief in its future. It is the spirit that finds expression in:

> Rabindranath's voice and Shantiniketan's stand,
> Gitanjali's faith and Jorasanko's house trust in this our chosen land.

Mr. Henry Neuman has contributed an article under the title 'Two Nobel Prize Winners, Kipling and Tagore' to the 'Standard' of New York. He is of opinion Kipling's outlook upon life is as different from that of Rabindranath Tagore as can possibly be conceived; though both of them are recipients of the Nobel Prize.

"To Kipling the credit must always be due that he interpretated the romance of modern machinery for those who ordinarily prefer prose to poetry, but who do respond to the pulsing of piston-rods and the click of train-wheels suggested by his vigorous rhythms. And it is more than the audible rhythms of modern life that he interprets. Back of all our great construction from the steel mills to the ocean greyhounds, he hears the call of our age to severe unflinching toil."

His poems are flawless gems: his essays are the most perfect specimens of Bengali prose: his criticism contains the sanest and most crystalline interpretations: his novels mark a new era in Bengali fiction: his songs breathe the most enthralling strains—the spirit's utmost rapture and aspiration—taking us to the very verge of the infinite and letting us gaze into it: his short stories possess invention, creation, imagination, and originality and belong to the highest class of narrative. In fact, in the opinion of many persons, his tales and musical pieces constitute his most valid title to immortality.

There is scarcely a literate Bengali household where Rabindranath's name does not work like a heavenly incantation: there is scarcely a Bengali youth who has not drugged himself with his lyric verses. No age and no nation a show of an instance of a writer who has achieved such vivid and enduring and marvellous results in almost all the departments of human speech—in poetry, drama, essay, fiction, criticism, song, story, political disquisition religious discourse. This house from where he and his metaphysical knowledge were grown up is quite distinct.

In 'Janmakatha' (Birth Story), Rabindranath says:

Where have I come from. Oh where
didst thou fine me?
A baby is asking its mother:
Folding the babe to her breast.
Half crying, half laughing, she answers
'Thou wast in my heart as its desire,
My dearest darling.
'Thou wast in the dolls of my
Childhood's games,

And when I made figures of Siva in clay,
I made and unmade thee then:

(xxiii)

Thou wast enthroned
With our household God;
In His worship, I worshipped thee,
My dearest darling.
'In all sweet hopes that ever were mine,
In all my loves and desire,
In the life of my mother and in
grandmother's life hast thou lived:

In the lap of the lady
Who rules in our house
Thou hast for ages been hidden,
My dearest darling.

'When in girlhood my heart
Like a flower was opening
Thou wast a sweet fragrance about it:

Thy own tender softness
Thou gavest unknown,
To my youth form,
My dearest darling.

'Thou pet of all Shining Ones,
Thou eternal, unchanging,
Co-aged with dawn—
From the world's dream-life
Thou hast been born in a torrent of bliss
As a real thing to play with my heart,
My dearest darling.

'As I gaze on thy face
The mystery I cannot understand:
Thou belongest to all and how can'st
thou be mine?

My body I kiss in thine
Since now thou art mother' babe:
Laughing thou am'st to the world,
My dearest darling.

'Lest I should lose thee
I hold thee tight to my breast
I cry if I see thee not every moment:
I know not what snare of maya
Could entrap the world's treasure
In these slender arms of mine,
My dearest darling.

(Translated by A.K. Chakravorty & A.R. Coomarswamy)

The central idea of the Tagores of Jorasanko is that education is the greatest need of Modern India, education for the masses as well as for the classes, for men as well as for women. This house gives a valuable idea of a perfect education. It is to prepare the mind to learn, to train it to receive the impressions. The soul-striking philosophy of the Tagores, with a melodious flow of tomorrow morning, is the impartation of certain characteristic fund of ideas and concepts which is common to society as a whole, and must be imported to every individual if he is to pass as efficient. There is a road steep and thorny, and beset with perils of every kind, but yet a road, and it leads to the heart of the Tagores at Jorasanko. The realisation of this house produces the greatest amount of happiness for the human race in a way of temper serene. Breaking through the foul and ugly mists of vapours, this house stands on a terra firma like a bright metal on a sullen gound. Many good morrows to the majesty and excellency of the Tagores at Jorasanko. All are the gallant leaders of our country.

The highest prize of the Tagores and the crowning fortune of this house are the greatest happiness. The true test of this house secures its place amongst the highest order of great men. Its proceedings are just and honourable. Its peace is of the nature of conquest. By its constant touch, it drinks freely the love of the people as a whole. The grand success of its justness and right desires is a history we have in the Tagores of Jorasanko.

I am grateful to Dr. Hironmoy Banerjee I.C.S; former Vice-Chancellor of Rabindra Bharati University, Calcutta, who had entrusted me to translate this book into English—an object of proud to any author. I was a beloved student of Dr. Banerjee who inspired me, as a mentor, to translate his book, 'Thakurbarir Katha' into English.

The book reaches right down into the heart of its main character. The most celebrated work by Dr. Hironmoy Banerjee presents an unforgettable portrait of the Tagores at Jorasanko. Astonishing readability on every page. The writer's accuracy seems irreproachable. The charm, the wisdom and the all embracing human interest merge with fresh attraction. A book of great excellence which both the research scholar and the general reader will find absorbing and fascinating and instrumentive and which deserves to be widely read. A wonderfully dramatic narrative...one of the most vivid portrayals of the period we have ever read— a kind of book written by an erudite scholar whose mind played over the whole scene. A brilliant sketch of a hundred years of Tagores' history at Jorasanko—a unique combination of masterly narrative and scholarship.

Wanderlust, evidently, established full command over Rabindranath in his old age. He partly inherited this from his father who was also very fond of travelling. This was prompted partly by his desire to know other people and partly by economic consideration. The Viswa Bharati had by then been raised to the status of a University, and consequently its monetary needs had increased. The Government was then being run by a foreign power which felt little interest in the activities at Shantiniketan. Lectures tours abroad fetched money and helped to solve the problem of funds for the Viswa Bharati.

Rabindranath was very keen to his children acquainted with the contents of the Ramayana and the Mahabharata because these two epics give the best introduction to the national ethos. He has compared them to the Ganges and the Jamuna which provide food for the people. As both the

Bengali versions of the two epics by Kritibas and Kasiramdas are big in size, he felt the need for similar versions. That is why he encouraged his nephew Surendranath to produce a condensed form of the Mahabharata and entrusted Mrinalini Devi with the task of writing a short version of the Ramayana.

Thousands and thousands of visitors assemble together to hear, from this house, a wonderous melody that flows from soul to soul and star to star and the master's joy shall be theirs. Let the House of Tagores gaze at the glory of the sunrise of sunset, the mountain height, the midnight moon, the sea and skies. In starry skies over the house is all the wonders of the Tagores everywhere, in everyplace the Tagores behold the glory of their perpetual self-giving. Truth of this house is marching on to a horizon of Rabindranath's magic of meditation. Jadunath Sarkar, a distinguished historian, says: "Rabindranath agrees with Bankim Chandra, whose Anandamath is a long plan for a moral rebirth of all individuals, before the nation can truly rise. He agrees with Milton who sings—love virtue, she alone is free: "In 'My Reminiscences', Rabindranath says:

> "This world is sweet—I do not want to die.
> I wish to dwell in the everlasting life of Man."

This great house makes the Tagores all dazzlingly alive... a thumping great opus, perhaps a masterpiece. It has some claims to being a great one. It has a freshness and sharpness, an originality, which is a rare virtue in studies of the Tagores. An intelligent, knowledgeable and precise analysis of the most important and most meaningful events of the time. An excellent bit of history-in-the-making full of fascinating bits of information and sharp insights. Beautifully written, dense with feeling...a book one reads with enormous fascination and cannot easily forget. Dr. Banerjee's stunning exploration of the moral cost of the Tagores has created a furor. There is a vigour and robust reality about this house which blows like a refreshing gale of wind. The author writes with discretion and discernment of all these great ones. I have translated it into English so that the readers can read easily and naturally and the illustrations may be both delightful and appropriate. Strong personalities and golden-hearted man like Rabindranath are drawn with vigorous touch.....a book overflowing with energy and prideful tender realism.

The life and works of the Tagores inside and outside of this great house exemplify all—singleness of purpose, strength of character. The great historical synthesis of the Tagores is once considered a font of sustained and enlightened learning, an achievement which confirmed the treasured tenets of the day. It is remarkable, technically and aesthetically. It has depth as well as breadth, and offers insight and understanding as well as knowledge. A lively and attractively survey of the birth and growth of this house and its interrelationship with the Tagores. This house marshals a vast array of historical facts and offers an abundance of stimulating ideas. It is thoroughly recommended for its balance and sound judgements of the Tagores. Through this house, Rabindranath has seen the whole of life, its shallows and depths alike, in the one vision. Born in this house, Rabindranath was rich in experience and profound in personal philosophy.

It strikes our minds and sways our feelings. The true test of this house is the effect of Rabindranath and his introspection of life. His noble thought is wrapped in its garment. Its higher values and his finest thoughts are clothed in the austere dignity. This house fosters fundamental unity in diversity. When we read Hamlet, we forget that Shakespeare was only an Englishman, when we read the Divine Comedy, we do not think that Dante was an Italian, and when we study Faust, we are not worried over the German nationality of Goethe. The same is true of Gitanjali and Sadhana and their author Tagore, Rabindranath.

Romain Rolland, the French writer on international subjects, wrote a letter of reverend appreciation, inviting the poet, Rabindranath, to become one with them in a Brotherhood of the Free Spirit. Being a poet, philosopher and thinker, he has exchanged thoughts of love between the East and the West.

'Messengers with news from other lands
greet me and pass along the road.'

(Gitanjali)

To Rabindranath, the people of the world must first be sincere towards one another. This sincerity should be a potent influence from within. Nothing can be done by an organisation superimposed from without—hypocrisy written all over its surface. Heart must speak to heart. The only creative work is that of love. This is the outline of the doctrine, which the Poet sage of Bengal is intent to spread everywhere as the surest means to awaken the hitherto divided and oppressed world of humanity and to bind it into a union of brotherhood and freedom. His Shantiniketan, 'The Home of Peace' is the sign and token of a rebinding and a building up of this World Brotherhood.

It may be of service to point out how the prophetic words of Rabindranath have already penetrated the minds of the English missionaries. The poet in his address to some Japanese students said:

"If I could show you my heart, you would find it green and young, perhaps younger than that of some of you who are standing here before me. And you would find also that I am childish enough to believe in things which the grown-up people of the modern age, with their superior wisdom, have become ashamed to own." The idea of childspirit in man has been the perennial theme of song among the purest of our poets. He exhorted Europe to pay regard to the vast multitudes of Asia and Africa to raise them to the joys of Western Science and progress. 'Be afraid,' he said to us, 'to leave them to their weakness. The very strength of that weakness passively threatens to set up a barrier to civilisation and to compromise that to peace to which the universe aspires.'

The Tagore Number of 'Young India', New York, published in Dec. 1920, contains an article on Rabindranath Tagore by Mr. S.K. Ratcliff, another on 'Tagore—The Man' by J.T. Sunderland, a third on 'Tagore's Boys School', ten poems by the poet and an article of selections containing his views on 'India's Foreign Rule'. Of his religious belief, Mr. Ratcliff says: "In religious belief he holds to the position of his father, the Maharshi, and his poetic gift has been freely given to the service of the Brahmo Church. The devotional songs of Rabindranath Tagore have entered closely into religious life of the reformed Hindu community; you hear them sung in every Brahmo household."

Of his poetical genius the same writer says:

"Mr. Tagore's poetical genius appears most fresh....Upon the English reader, it may be, the main impression left by the lyrics will be that of a wonderfully clear and effortless expression of profound things. To sing dedication of life in this silent and overflowing leisure is the poet's own statement of his purpose; and as you read you are possessed by one feeling above all—the conviction that only in a large, simple and unhurried life, in an atmosphere of meditation and recollectedness, could such poems as these have come to birth at all....."

When the Second Round Table Conference in London had come to a fiasco, Gandhiji was arrested. Tumultous agitation raised all over the country. The poem 'Question' was written.

'God, again and again through the ages you have sent
messengers To this pitiless world:
They have said, 'Forgive everyone', they have said,'
Love one another.....

Rid your hearts of evil.
They are revered and remembered, yet still in these
dark days
We turn them away with hollow greetings, from outside
the doors of our houses.....'

(Translated by W. Radice)

In this Nobel Prize acceptance speech, Stockholm, December, 1950, William Faulkner says: "Our tragedy today is a general and universal physical fear so long sustained by now that we can even bear it... The basest of all things is to be afraid." Before the First World War, Mussolini's invasion of Ethiopia had perturbed his mind and heart. The horror of this experience was to him the statesman's game and the hired assassin's trade. The great poem 'Africa' was written.

'When, in that turbid first age,
The Creator, displeased with himself,
Destroyed his new creations again and again;
In those days of his shaking and shaking his head
in irritation
The angry sea
Snatched you from the breast of Mother Asia,
Africa—
Consigned you to the guard of immense trees,
To a fastness dimly lit.
There in your hidden leisure
You collected impenetrable secrets,
Learnt the arcane languages of water and earth and sky;
Nature's invisible magic.
Worked spells in your unconscious mind.
You ridiculed Horror
By making your own appearance hideous;
You cowed Fear
By heightening your menacing grandeur,
By dancing to the drumbeats of chaos'....

(Translated by W. Radice)

In the article on the Shantiniketan school, there are lengthy extracts from Mr. Ramsay Macdonald's article in the Daily Chronicle of London, in which he says: 'Into its exchequer Mr. Tagore has put not only the Noble Prize but the royalties on his books.'

From the 'Editorial Notes', we quote the following:
'Words of Cheer For India'

"What do you suppose will satisfy the soul
except to walk free and own no superior?
Liberty is to be subserved, whatever occurs."

—*Whitman*

"And what avail the plow or sail,
Or land or life, if freedom fail?"

—*Emerson*

Under the title, 'Two Nobel Prize winners, Kipling and Tagore', Mr. Henry Neuman has contributed an article to the 'Standard' of New York. He is of opinion that Kipling's outlook upon life is as different from that of Rabindranath Tagore as can possibly be conceived; though both of them are recipients of the Nobel Prize.

"To Kipling the credit must always be due that he interpreted the romance of modern machinery for those who ordinarily prefer prose to poetry, but who do respond to the pulsing of piston-rods and the click of train wheels suggested by his vigorous rhythms. And it is more than the audible rhythms of modern life that he interprets. Back of all our giant construction from the steel mills to the ocean greyhounds, he hears the call of our age to serve unflinching toil.

But just because he voices the present day ideal of the strenuous will, he typifies as well as its ethical shortcomings. He is blind to the tragedies of the masterful traits which he so glorifies. To judge from his writings, modern industry is simply a superb conquest over Nature by Titans whom this endeavour makes all the stronger. He has not a thought for the thousands who are maimed and crushed in the process.....

To grasp the teachings of Tagore it must be remembered that the mind of Indian thinkers has a passion above all things for unity. Some minds love to dwell upon the differences in a manifold universe; and on the other hand, there are those that are unhappy until they can see the oneness back of the diversity. Tagore is typical of his people in being attracted by the unifying process. Hence he thinks of his God not as a single personal being, but as the whole undying universe, the all without beginning or end. Whereas Kipling's is a magnificent individual superman, the master of all good workmen, a great captain, engineer and man of letters. Tagore's deity is not a person at all, but the depersonalised, infinite existence in every atom in the whole of things.

From this point of view the supreme business of life is self-realisation by union with this all-embracing one. 'In the music of the rushing stream,' says the poet, 'is heard the glad assurance, I shall become the sea.' The height of bliss is attained in such a bliss... The main appeal to Western readers in Tagore's writings is more likely to be found in its call to renunciation."

Rabindranath is a unique product of the East. In delicacy of character painting, in the play of personality, and in the reflection of all the light and shade of life in society, Rabindranath occupies a significant position in the Indian consciousness.

Thy call has sped over all countries of the world
and men have gathered around thy seat.
The day is come.
But where is India?

Does she still remain hidden, lagging behind?
Let her take up her burden and march with all.
Send her, mighty God, thy message of victory,
O Lord every awake!

Those who defied suffering
have crossed the wilderness of death
and have shattered their prison of illusions.
The day is come.
But where is India?

(xxxiii)

Her listless arms are idle and ashamed
and futile her days and nights, lacking in joy of life.
Touch her with thy living breath,
O Lord ever awake!

The morning sun of the new age has risen.
Thy temple hall is filled with pilgrims.
The day is come.
But where is India?

She lies on the dust in dishonour,
deprived of her seat.
Remove her shame,
and give her a place in thy House of Man,
O Lord ever awake!

The world's highroads are crowded,
resounding with the roar of thy chariot wheels.
The sky is trembling with traveller's songs.
The day is come.
But where is India?

Doors are shut in her house age-worn
feeble is her hope, her heart sunk in silence.
Send thy voice to her children who are dumb,
O Lord every awake!

Peoples there are who have felt thy strength
in their own hearts and sinews
and have earned life's fulfilment,
conquering fear.
The day is come.
But where is India?

Strike thy blow at her self-suspicion and despair!
Save her from the dread of her own
pursuing shadow,
O Lord ever awake!

(Rabindranath Tagore: The Day is Come)

Wherever Rabindranath went, he found homes open to receive him, people proud to call him their guest. Invited by the Theosophical Society and the Free Religious Community in Holland, he was received with a signal honour. The love and honour and admiration for him grew as his visit progressed. By his lectures, but even more by his personal charm, magnetic personality and charismatic leadership, at the acme of his beautiful wisdom and simple joy in life, the people of Holland were very much proud of his presence a blessing. No one had ever gone to Holland from India before, and own the hearts of his own Dutch people in such a manner. Dr. J.J. Vander Leeuw's description runs as follows:

"When the wise poet came to visit Holland, he did not find an audience strange to him and his works, but, on the contrary, thousands of enthusiastic admirers, full of joy at his coming, full of love for him and his works. In Holland, Tagore is considered as one of the representative men of the New Era; his works in English and in Dutch translations are widely read and appreciated. 'The Spirit of Tagore' is even an expression used to denominate a certain attitude in life, which is becoming more and more universal, at time goes on."

The whole book is of real distinction by the highest literary measure.... a book of that rare kind which one pick up with mild interest and furnishes with rapt attention... very skillfully constructed to give realism, and character with the minimum of words. Generations of inherited knowledge lie behind this house. It gives its many-faceted fragrance.

Let us now have a look at the history of this glorious building, 'The Tagores of Jorasanko', through the brightest and transparent glasses of hope and fulfilment.

—Dr. Biplab K. Majumdar

1

THE TAGORES OF JORASANKO

The house of the Tagores is a precious object of pride to the Bengalion. Chitpore Road[1] is the main thoroughfare which runs through this congested part of North Calcutta. It is one of the arterial roads of the metropolis city of Calcutta, and an important centre of trade and commerce. A tramway also winds its way along this road. Even so, it has lost its old prestige with the growth of vehicular traffic, on account of the lack of its width. Compared to other major roads, it looks a narrow lane. Instead of adding to its prestige, the tramway has rather impaired its utility as a means of communication. Linked to it is a street known as the Dwarakanath Tagore Lane which is even narrower. The red house standing on this lane is the house belonging to the Tagores. Though big in dimensions, this mansion can boast of no architectural distinction which impresses the mind. There are other buildings in the same locality with which it can stand no comparison. The "marble palace" built by Rajendra Lal Mullick stands close by. This mansion of the Tagores cannot claim kinship with it. It looks more or less like a building belonging to an ordinary Zamindar.

This ordinary - looking house located in this narrow lane has however attained such distinction as has never fallen to the lot of any house in India. For a full century,

1. It has been since renamed Rabindra Sarani

it functioned as the cultural centre of this country. For three successive generations, the members of this family led all the important movements of the country, in the field of religion, literature, music, education and social reforms, Dwarakanath Tagore, whose name has been linked with the lane on which this house stands, was a junior contemporary of Rammohan Roy. Both were prominent national leaders who had distinguished themselves by their command over the English language, a rarity in those days, and progressive and rational outlook. Attracted by such affinities, they became close friends. In these diverse activities, Rammohun got not only encouragement but active co-operation from Dwarakanath. Dwarakanath had an uncommon aptitude for commercial enterprise. The commercial firm he set up in partnership with an Englishman and with Englishmen as employees, was one of the most prosperous business houses of those days. He had other investments which earned him rich dividends. He was as fond of charity as entertaining guests in a lavish scale. All distinguished members of both the European and the Indian community would be invited to the dinners given by him. These dinners came to be recognised as such important social events in those days that they used to make headline news in the following day's issue of the local papers. He was equally popular among Europeans and Indians. People gave him the epithet "Prince" for his munificence and lavish style of living.

He died in England on 1, August, 1846. After his death, his commercial firms went into liquidation for lack of adequate supervision. In consequence, his sons had to face extreme distress. Even the fraction of property, which was saved due to his farsightedness, was sufficient to provide them the means to live comfortably. The prestige and position, in society, of the family was maintained thanks to the noble qualities of the eldest son, Debendranath, even though it cost its wealth.

Debendranath was endowed with qualities diametrically opposite to those of his father. Dwarakanath strove for wealth. His keen sense of business established him in the position of a rich, progressive leader. Debendranath won the heart of his countrymen in a different way. He was a pious man who had surrendered himself entirely to God. So he had no attraction for wealth. His extreme devotion to God prevented him from worshipping Him in the form of an image. So he objected to image worship. For the same reason, he could not accept the tenets of Christianity. He equally objected to imagining a man as an incarnation of God conceived as Son of God. So, maintaining his link with Hinduism, he established a new religion, by conceiving the Brahmo of the Upanishads as the monotheistic God of theism of the Upanishads. In this way, his intense devotion to God helped him to establish himself as the leader of a new religious movement in the nineteenth century. He endeared himself to his countrymen by his abstention from pleasure, by his adoption of the life of a wandering mendicant, and by his sincere devotion to God. Out of a sense of profound respect, his people decorated him with the title, 'Maharshi' (The great sage).

Rabindranath was born in this family, as the youngest son of Maharshi. The blooming of his genius not only enhanced the reputation of his family, but also lighted up the face of India. In the field of literature, he was a prodigy. He combined in himself the roles of a poet, story-writer, novelist, dramatist, literary critic and philosopher. Those who had disliked his new style in the first phase of his career and turned hostile critics, found to their amazement, that his, talents impressed the people of the West so deeply that they conferred on him the highest honour available to a writer, even as he stepped into his middle age. He won the Nobel Prize. His countrymen came to know about some new aspects of his genius, as discovered by the eyes of foreigners. They felt elated to be able to claim him as one of their own.

To their utter wonder, they discovered that Rabindranath was not only a creative writer, but a seer, a man of wisdom. His intellect enabled him to find out solutions of intricate philosophical problems and thereby won the admiration of the people of the world over again. Though a poet, he found recognition as one of the greatest philosophers of the world. He was invited by the Oxford university to deliver lectures on weighty philosophical subjects. He was given an assignment which is exclusively reserved for the world's best philosophers. He was invited to deliver the Hibbert lectures. He selected a subject which tells the story of his own religious experience through which he attained communion with God and earned his right serve Him. He named his subject 'The Religion of Man'. The substance of what he said in these lectures is that God resides in the heart of man, particularly in the heart of the down-trodden and neglected poor people. So, service of the poor is the best form of service of God. As the first poet of Bengal, he taught his fellow brothers that man is of supreme value to man the greatest poet of Bengal sang service of man is service of God, loving man is loving God.

That is why he became eager to establish bonds of love with the people of the world. He got acquainted with new people, accepted hospitality in new houses; what was distant was brought near, unknown persons became intimate friends. He travelled round the world time and again, as India's ambassador of culture to carry the message of India to the people of the world. People of all countries cordially greeted him. They accepted the bonds of friendship offered by him. He was greeted with equal warmth in both South America and Japan. East Indies and England welcomed him equally cordially. Both Russia and the United States of America loved him well. He was pleased most, he said, when he found Eastern ideas mingle with western thought. To facilitate the exchange of their spiritual wealth, he built up an institution in a calm and quiet rural setting in Bengal, after life-long sincere efforts. He called this centre "Viswa Bharati", as he visualised it as the place where Eastern and Western culture, where the cultures of the world would nestle together.

Thus a man who was once a poet of Bengal was transformed into a poet of the world. Through his thoughts and writings, he built up a bridge between different people of the world. The literature that was built up in the process was equally appreciated by Christians and Muslims, by black men and white men, and by the capitalistic and socialistic states. Rabindranath became more precious to the Bengalee than Shakespeare was to the Englishman.

It was in this house of the Tagores that such a person commanding universal respect was born. It was here that he spent his childhood and youth. Even when he selected Santiniketan as his place of work, his attraction for the paternal house persisted. Whenever he would visit Calcutta, this was the house where he would live. On such occasions, it would hum with activities focussed round him. Like the old days, it would become the venue of literary discourses, conferences and even staging of dramas. He would come here from Santiniketan, accompanied by his groups to celebrate the religious festival of the 11th 'Magh' his father had introduced. That festival found recognition, as one of the major annual festivals of Calcutta. Then again, in the evening of his life when he fell victim to a fatal disease, he returned to this house for medical treatment. It was in a room of this building that he breathed his last when medical treatment failed to save his life. From that day onwards, this house of the Tagores became a place of pilgrimage. What was once a house of a particular family came to be recognised as a house belonging to the people of the whole country, through the process of getting associated with the achievements of the different members of the family in course of generations. Its maintenance and security came to be recognised as the special responsibility of the people.

The Tagore family was then in extreme financial difficulty. In course of generations, the family had expanded, but not the prosperity it owned. In consequence, many of its branches had been afflicted with poverty. A part of Maharshibhawan which fell to the share of the sons of Hemendranath, the third son of Maharshi, had been sold to an outsider. The South-western part of the ancestral property, which fell to the share of the second brother of Maharshi, had been inherited by Abanindranath and his two brothers. To their misfortune, that property was sold to an outsider in discharge of a mortgage. The branches which had not to face such extreme distress found their income so much reduced that they were compelled to let out portions of the property owned by them. Big rooms had been partitioned and rented to different parties. Shops were set up in the rooms opening on the spacious courtyard lying to the south of the *Thakur dalan* small factories were installed in the dark rooms in the interior. Consequently, men of diverse classes started living and working here. The spacious courtyard, in front of the Thakur dalan was turned into a common passage. What contrast to the heyday when distinguished men assembled in this courtyard to see the staging of drama by the members of the Tagore family and the Magh festival was celebrated in a solemn atmosphere on the 11th Magh, to the accompaniment of vedic songs.

An account recorded by a grand-daughter of the family brings to relief the apalling contrast of this tragic transformation. On this cataclysmic change, Sarala Devi regretfully observes as follows:

"To what an abject conditions has the house of Jorasanko been brought! There was the Jorasanko of the last tossed on this waves of high thoughts, packed with intense activity, reverberating with music day and night; and to-day it stands deserted, stained with the droppings of pigeons, maintaining hardly any link with the family of Maharshi Debendranath. If any one who had once lived in this house came here and took a look around to find his eyes filled with tears, would not the house look back at him with tearful eyes? What a contrast between the house of the old days and this heap of bricks and wood of to-day. It will not be long before it collapses altogether".[2]

The poor condition of the courtyard of the *Thakur dalan* caused her no less pain. How much it was deep-seated can be guessed from the following comments :

"That courtyard has now become a highway. The share of Ritu of the youngest son of the third uncle, has been purchased by a Marawari. He has the right of way across the courtyard. When prayers and devotional songs are conducted there on 11th Magh, the smoke of the oven lighted by the Marawari housewife and the smell of spices used in cooking creep into the prayer hall through the shutters and the roof of that part of the house. The dark rooms of the ground floor opening inside are crowded with tenants, Bengalee and non-Bengalee. They observe no fixed hours for entrance and exit. They have the right to pass through the prayer meeting of the 11th Magh as and when they like and they enforce this right too." [3]

For these reasons, the preservation of the house in which Rabindranath was born and associated with the sacred memory of Tagore and his distinguished ancestors assumed the character of a national problem. A meaningful step was taken towards the solution of this problem immediately after Tagore's death. This made the people feel deeply the shock of permanent separation from the genius who was to them an object of pride, and whose writings became the magic medium of their cultural entertainment. This sorrow found expression in diverse way on traditional liaise. Luckily for us, the people found a leader who could direct this powerful emotion, to a constructive channel, in the person of Suresh Chandra Majumdar. A memorial fund was opened with him as the chairman. The appeal for

2. Sarala Devi Chowdhurani, Jibaner Jharapata. P. 9.
3. Ibid. Page-72.

funds was responded to with unbounded enthusiasm throughout the whole of undivided Bengal. Apart from Calcutta, an extensive arrangement was made for collection of funds from the headquarters of every district. There was a tremendous response to the appeal for funds throughout Bengal. Elaborate arrangements were made for collection of fund by collecting donations from individuals and staging charity shows of Tagore's dramas. Collections exceeded fifteen lakh rupees. Since collections for similar memorial funds easily total rupees fifty lakh rupees now a days, the figure may appear small; but having regard to the conditions prevailing in those days, it should not be considered small.

Our country was then a part of an empire built by a foreign power. It is the bounden duty of the people to show the respect due to the person who dies in a blaze of glory. The nation responded to this call in all sincerity, but the government did not. The foreign rulers showed no interest to respond to this call of duty. On the contrary, it was only natural for them to develop a hostile attitude to a world famous poet, who had given free expression to forthright utterances. There was an occasion when the British government honoured him with Knighthood, in recognition of the merits of this genius. But within a few years, he was so terribly shocked by the massacre at Jallianwala Bagh, that he was forced to renounce that title in protest. The party holding political power refused to discharge the duty developing on them, to show the respect due to one who had been endowed with so many virtues. It is easy to guess, therefore, how much the capacity of the people to respond to the appeal for funds had been reduced. It was not possible to visualise what huge dimensions the efforts would have attained if the political power had joined hand with the will of the people.

Suresh Chandra Majumdar displayed a farsightedness in the distribution of the money collected in this manner. Part of it was donated to the Visvabharati and the balance was allocated to the cost of acquisition of as much property of the Tagores as possible and adoption of measures to save it from collapse and decay permanently. In the meantime, the share inherited by Girindranath, second brother of Debendranath, had been sold to outsiders in discharge of debts incurred by the family. That is how premises No. 5 of Dwarakanath Tagore Lane and a small piece of land appertaining to premises No. 6/4 of Dwarakanath Tagore Lane were acquired. The Revenue Department of the Government had assessed the value of the property to be five and half lac rupees. After depositing this amount the Memorial Committee got possession of the property, which contained the three-storeyed house which used to be known as the "Baithakkhana Bari" during the time of Dwarakanath. There was extensive vacant place to its south. An auditorium was built there with the balance of the fund and the Rabindra Bharati Society was established to administer these properties.

Unfortunately, it was not possible to save the "Baithakkhana Bari" from demolition. This was indeed a great misfortune, for it was associated with the memories of a glorious period. This "Baithakkhana Bari" was one of the places where the elite of the society of Calcutta used to assemble during the days of Dwarakanath. This is where Rammohun and Dwarakanath frequently met. The dinner parties Dwarakanath gave here were attended by distinguished Government officers as well as men who led the society of the country.

After the death of Dwarakanath, this property fell to the share of Girindranath, according to the terms of his will. Girindranath died young. During the time of his eldest son, Gaganendranath, it became a cultural centre of distinction in Calcutta. He was fond of staging dramas. Under his patronage, the Bengali stage made history by its achievements. The two brothers, Gaganendra and Abanindra, who distinguished themselves as artists, were the sons of his younger brother, Gunendranath. During their time, it became a place of pilgrimage of Indian artists. There is no trace of this building now. During the Second World War, a large contingent of American Negro soldiers came to Calcutta. During this time of emergency, the Government requisitioned this building for their accommodation. But thereafter, when rationing was introduced, the building was used for storage of foodgrains. Such rough treatment proved too much for this ancient house to bear. In consequence, it became damaged to such a degree, that it became impossible to save it from collapse. Some say that it was demolished on the advice of experts. Others give a different version. The fact remains that it was pulled downs and the place where the house stood has been converted into a lawn, where the birth anniversary of Rabindranath is celebrated, in a public meeting on the 25th Vaisakh every year.

In the meantime, the Rabindra Memorial Committee was confronted with a new problem. The man, who had acquired the share of Girindranath, did not accept the award by way of compensation, made by the officer, in the relevant land acquisition case, and appealed against it. The appeal was decided in his favour by fixing a higher amount of additional compensation of three lac rupees. In the meantime, all the funds collected by the Society had been exhausted. Nobody had anticipated that new liabilities would be created in this manner. A solution of this problem was urgently needed.

Fortunately, the political condition of the country had undergone radical transformation in the meantime. The foreign rulers had left the country. A national government had been established. Bengal was partitioned and its western part had been annexed to the Indian federation. Dr. Bidhan Chandra Roy, was then the Chief Minister of West Bengal. In this situation, Suresh Chandra Majumdar approached him to help him solve the problem. It so happened that at about that time, Dr. Bidhan Chandra Roy was tying with a new idea. The Publicity Department of West Bengal Government was then conducting its activities in the traditional way. Its main technique was to publish information about governmental activities in form of an insipid account. In consequence, not many people were attracted to it and of those attracted, few found it interesting. The Chief Minister wanted that information should be dressed up in an attractive form so that it can hold the attention of the people. He wanted to introduce a new method of publicity through the medium of dance, music and drama. With this end in view, he opened a branch for popular entertainment, under the Publicity Department. Artiste are however, needed to make a success of this folk entertainment section. A good artiste cannot be produced without rigorous training. He felt deeply the need for an institution to impart training in dance, drama and music of high quality.

This gave him the clue to find a solution both for the problem confronting the Memorial Committee as well as his own problem. Through mutual discussion, it was decided that Government would pay the additional compensation for the acquisition of the property of the Tagores, and undertake the responsibility for recurring demands, like the payment of Corporation taxes and electricity bills of the Society's office. In return for that, the Government would be permitted to utilise the surplus lands of the Society to build an institution for teaching drama, dance and music. Thus came into being the Academy of Dance, Drama and Music. The building, constructed for, this purpose by the West Bengal Government, was named "Sangeet Bhavan."[4]

The year 1961 was then knocking at the door. Just a hundred years before, Rabindranath was born in this house, on the 25th Baisakh. The people of West Bengal were eagerly looking forward to an appropriate celebration of his birth centenary. The country had

4. Speech of Dr. Bidhan Chandra Roy at the first meeting of Rabindra Bharati University.

attained independence. The Head of the Republic was the leader of the people. So, the government of the people joined hands with the people of the country to provide for a homage, in keeping with the prestige of the most distinguished son of the soil, on the occasion of his birth centenary. This work that had been undertaken under the leadership of Suresh Chandra Majumder indicated what form the homage should take. The shares owned by the different members of the Tagore family were being gradually bought off by outsiders. The part that had not yet been sold was facing utter collapse, for failure of the other members to carry out essential repairs for want of resources. In this situation, the objective should be to acquire the remaining part of the house of the Tagores and to preserve it as a National Trust. It was the bounden duty of the national Government to save from destruction a house, the members of which had contributed so generously to the culture of the nation generation after generation, which gave birth to a genius commanding universal respect in the person of Rabindranath, which functioned as the centre of activities which brought about the renaissance of Bengal.

So, the Chief Minister of West Bengal took the decision that purchase and maintenance of the properties should be a part of the celebration. But then the question naturally arises how the property would be used. The house that has enjoyed the respect of the people by its diverse associations cannot be used for any ordinary purpose. It should not be used for office accommodation. So, it was felt that it should be utilised as a memorial to the men whose holy association has transformed it into a place of pilgrimage. Though he found recognition as a writer with international reputation, Rabindranath never admitted that the language of the mouth is the only medium of expression or thoughts and emotions. According to him, the media of expression are many and diverse. What cannot be expressed in language can be expressed more effectively through painting, dance, music and drama. These are not so much the language of the intellect as the language of the emotions. Unless one masters both the languages of the two principal faculties of man, the intellect and the emotion, one cannot achieve balanced development. So, it was settled that a university would be established there with a view to imparting education based on principles developed by Tagore and that it should be named after him. This is how the decision was taken by the Government to found the Rabindra Bharati University.

The house of the Tagores also claims the distinction of being the hub of the renaissance movement of Bengal. The members of this family took an active part, generation after generation, in the movements initiated in the different areas of Bengali Society, by the impact of the Western Culture, during this period. Though much younger than Rammohun, Dwarakanath was his close collaborator. His son, Debendranath, led the religious movement of the time. It was the members of this family who sowed the seeds of the nationalistic movement. A daughter-in-law of this family was the pioneer in the cause of women's emancipation. The need was felt for establishing a permanent museum to commemorate the glories of this chapter of our history. This sprawling house of the Tagores could be used for the museum. The best of the property could be suitably used for the other purposes.

These are the two ideas that gave birth to the Rabindra Bharati University. The foundation-stone of this University was laid by Jawaharlal Nehru, the then Prime Minister of India, on 25th Baisakh, 1368 of Bengali calendar. On the same auspicious day next year, the Rabindra Bharati University was established. The institution established earlier, under the leadership of Suresh Chandra Majumder, had been, however, named "Rabindra Bharati". Its office was also located in the same compound. To mark its separate identity, its name was slightly modified and it was renamed Rabindra Bharati Society. The mind of the Bengalee was thus relieved of the anxiety caused by the apprehension about the uncertain future of the house. The house of the Tagores buzzed again with activity. It now houses a cultural institution and an educational institution. It is now a property owned by the people of the country.

A question may arise : why are the people and their leaders so keen to preserve this house on a permanent basis? To say in reply, that Rabindranath Tagore was born in this house is not to say enough. It is true that his outstanding genius has brought us glory. The appearance of Rabindranath in this family was not however, a fortuitous event. Generation after generation, the family produced men who distinguished themselves in different fields. Many of his brothers and sisters were highly talented. Their devotions to and interest in different subjects built up a unique atmosphere in this house which is seldom seen elsewhere.

Dwijendranath, the eldest brother, was a poet and indifferent to worldly affairs. His childlike simplicity and poetic activities created an atmosphere of literature. His second brother, Satyendranath attained the distinction of being the first Indian to enter the Indian Civil Service as a meritorious student. He also wrote poems and cherished national feelings. His greatest achievement was his championing the cause of women's emancipation. It was through his encouragement that his wife, Jnanadanandini Devi, a daughter-in-law of this orthodox family visited the United Kingdom and broke the purdah system.* The third brother, Hememdranath, wanted to use Bengali as the medium of education. Moreover, he was keen on making the women of the family literate. He compelled the female members to take lesson from him. Jyotirindranath, his fifth brother

* Purdah System : Seclusion of women from public observation among Muslims and some Hindus esp. India.

by birth, was a highly talented person. He was equally distinguished as a poet, dramatist, composer and artist. He translated many books from Sanskrit and French into Bengali. He showered particular affection upon his younger brother, Rabindranath. Above everything else, Debendranath stood behind them. He had little attachment to domestic life. He used to spend most of his time outside home, when his older children had grown up. He, however, maintained a watchful eye to see to it that the family affairs ran smoothly. Under his general supervision, the family estates were efficiently managed and the domestic life ran smoothly. The sons enjoyed full freedom to cultivate their talents on cultural interests according to their choice. And their father would not interfere in their affairs.

This built up a unique atmosphere in the house. The whole family was as it were working to help the blossoming of a prodigy. Rabindranath has no right to claim exclusive credit for achieving worldwide reputation. There were many factors which worked towards it. The high personal qualities of the ancestors, the industry of the grand-father, the piety of the father and above all, the congenial atmosphere built up by the brothers cumulatively, contributed to the development of Rabindranath's genius.

Indeed, the house of the Tagores carries the memory of such a distinguished family without parallel. Every nook and corner of the house was associated with the memories of distinguished members of the family. The Bengalee would naturally be extremely eager to know the story of this house. People will be more eager to know about the men who invested it with fame. The object of the present book is to satisfy this curiosity. In this book, the history of the Tagores of Jorasanko will be traced through successive generations. Those who covered it with glory will receive special treatment. An account will be given of the various movements which were initiated from this house during the renaissance of Bengal. And, above all, an attempt will be made to acquaint the readers with the atmosphere built up in this house which made the development of Rabindranath's genius possible.

2

FORE-FATHERS

The ancestors of the Tagore family at Jorasanko were Brahmins belonging to Sandilya gotra. There was a time when Buddhism was dominant in the eastern region of India. To this may be attributed the change of the name of Angadesh into Bihar. The ruins of the Nalanda University bear evidence that Buddhism flourished here during the reign of Harsha Vardhan. This institution was a major centre for the diffusion of Buddhist doctrines and many scholars would come here both from the different parts of India and abroad to acquire knowledge about Buddhism. Fa-Hien came to study here from distant China. No wonder that the influence of Buddhism spread over Bengal, which is contiguous to Bihar, during this time. As a consequence, the rituals prescribed by the Vedas practically disappeared. It became difficult, therefore, to find out Brahmins who were well-grounded in vedic rituals.

A new problem, therefore, arose when Hinduism was revived in Bengal. It became a problem to trace out men who were qualified to conduct vedic sacrifices or perform ceremonies prescribed in the Grihya sutra. Adisur, who was a minor chieftain in Bengal, in the 8th century A.D. brought five Brahmins well-grounded in vedic rituals from Kanauj to solve the problem. Bhatta Narayan, who was the son of Khittish, was one of them. He was an established Literateur. The Sanskrit drama, *Veni Samhar*, written by him, on an affair touching on Draupadi, found recognition as one of the best dramas in Sanskrit literature.

Adisur made adequate provisions for their maintenance. Not only Bhatta Narayan, but each of his sons was granted a village. The descendants of each son were given surnames after the name of the village where they settled. Thus the descendants of 'Varaha', the eldest son, got the surname 'Bandhopadhyaya' as he had received the village named 'Bandyaghati'. Similarly another son, settled in the village 'Kushari', became a man of 'Kushari Gaon' and got the Surname 'Kushari'. Byomkesh Mustaffi says, in his 'Banger Jatiya Itihas' that the Tagore family descended from the branch of Kusharis. The members of the Tagore family do not accept the proposition. They consider themselve as belonging to the branch of 'Bandhopadhyas'.

The expression, 'Piralli Brahmin' has become specially associated with the Tagore family. So, it would be necessary to find out what significance it carries. With the spread of Muslim power in Bengal the Hindu community came in close contact with Muslims in many spheres. The conservative element of the Hindu society did not take it in good grace. Not unoften a Hindu family which established close relations with the muslims, without changing religion found itself confronted with derogatory accusations. They were denied the status enjoyed by a family which avoided contact with Muslims. Consequently, they found it difficult to arrange their marriages within their community. That explains why this stigma got itself attached by a stroke of bad luck to that branch of the brahmins of the Sandilya sub-groups of the Rarhi group, from which the Tagore family stems. There is more than one version of the story that is supposed to explain this. Though differing in minor details they more or less converge on the main story which is given below :—

A Muslim chief, Khan Jahan Ali, by name, established himself in the district of Jessore; and became recognised as a Nawab. There was a family of four brothers in his kingdom. Of them, the two elder brothers named Kamadeva and Jayadeva found employment, as officers of position under Khan Jahan Ali.

One day during the Ramjan fast, a gentleman presented to Khan Jahan Ali some lemons which he smelt. Kamadev and Jayadev who happened to be present there remarked jokingly that the Nawab should not have allowed himself to the indulgence of smelling the lemons as it amounted to breaking the rules of Ramjan fast. When the Nawab asked them what they meant they explained that, according to Hindus, smelling is almost as good as eating. The Nawab lacked the sense of accepting it as a joke and became so infuriated that he decided to put them in serious trouble as his subsequent conduct will show.

On a subsequent occasion, he invited some distinguished men to a festival. The two brothers among others attended the same as invitees by virtue of their positions, as two of his principal officers. A sumptuous dinner was provided. Needless to say, many meals forbidden to Hindus were served. Beef was one of them. They could not reasonably object to this as the host himself was a Muslim. During the meal, as soon as the smell of the food reached their nostrils, Khan Jahan Ali declared that Kamadev and Jayadev had forfeited their right to remain Hindus inasmuch as they had, tasted forbidden food. On that pretext, Khan Jahan Ali forcibly converted them to Islam by marking them read out the tenets of the faith.

The four brothers were then living together. Two of them suddenly found themselves converted to Islam, through the whims of the Nawab. It was not, however, possible to separate their families from those of their brothers overnight. So, the families of the converted brothers were forced to live with the families of unconverted brothers for some days. The converted brothers were compelled to pay visit to the common residence to meet their families. So, when the converted brothers, removed their families the two unconverted brothers acquired the stigmata of having lived for sometime with the converted Muslims. This was the basic reason behind the stigma of being a Piralli. In consequence, Rabideva and Sukdeva though continuing as Hindus acquired the stigmate of being 'Piralli's.[1]

Having been stained with the stigma of a Sukdeva found it difficult to procure a bridegroom for his daughter. No desirable family would agree to marry the daughter of Sukdeva Ray Choudhury. By a decree of fate however, the problem was solved through a dramatic development. It so happened that Jagannath Kushari,[1] who was scion of an affluent family was sailing along the river on business. He was still unmarried. Suddenly overtaken by a hurricane, he sought asylum in the village of Sukdeva Ray Chudhury. Finding such a respectable man in trouble Sukdeva gave him shelter in his own house. And finding Jagannath a desirable party he gave in marriage his daughter to him. In the circumstances, he was compelled to settle in the village of his father-in-law. This is how the family founded by him acquired the stigma of being a Piralli by a decree of fate.

The date of this event can be fixed more or less accurately from available data. It is a fact that Dwarakanath, the grandfather of Rabindranath was born in 1794. From that date backwards to his founding ancestor Jagannath, we get that they counted eight generations. Counting an average of twenty five years for each generation, we get two hundred years as the time that separates Jagannath from Dwarkanath. So, it appears that Jagannath acquired the stigma of being a Piralli towards the end of the sixteenth century.

Purushottam Vidyabagish was the son of Jagannath. Panchanan, who was his great-grandson, came to Calcutta in search of fortune, in the first

1. Byomkesh Mustafi, bano qatuyo its has, paut P. dcordiuf to Byomkesh mustafi gaganath descended force kushari brand. The Tagore's law oven, class that they are Bacdyo fallyajiaVidi Sadge & Times by Rabindranath Tagore, P. 2

quarter of the 18th century. The battle of Plassey had not yet been fought and the British had not won their right to rule in Bengal. Even so, the commercial activities of East India Company were firmly established. Job Charnak had founded Calcutta. Sutanity, Gobindapur and Calcutta had been purchased. A port had been built on the bank of the river "Bhagirathi". Import and export transactions with the United Kingdom were being vigorously pursued. A business relation had been established between British sailors and merchants and the Bengalees.

It was in this setting that Panchanan came to Calcutta to seek fortune. Gobindapur was the name of the village where 'Fort William' is at present situated. Panchanan settled in the same village on the bank of the river Bhagirathi. The people, however, whom he found as neighbours did not belong to the high caste. They were principally fishermen, Malos and Kaibartas by caste. They lived by catching fish and manual labour. Presumably they used to be engaged in loading and unloading of goods of ships. It may be also presumed that Panchanan came in contact with the British sailors and merchants engaged in supervising this work. It is this curious situation that won for this branch of the Sandilya gotra, the surname 'Tagore' to replace their original surname. The low-caste Hindus used to address Brahmins as 'Thakur' and that is how Panchanan came to be known as 'Thakur' to his neighbours. The Englishmen in pronouncing it distorted it into 'Tagore'. That is how this branch came to be known as the 'Tagores'. Consequently, it assumed two forms : One in Bengali and the other in English. This English version linked with the name of Rabindranath has become known all over the world.[2]

Jayaram, who was the son of Panchanan, had come into contact with the officers of the Company and got an employment under them as an Amin. Consequently, during his time the family advanced towards prosperity.

2. James Farrol, The Tagore Family

He died in 1756.[3] He was survived by four sons. Of them, two brothers are closely linked with our story. So our narration will be confined to them only. Nilmani, the second son of Jayaram, became the head of the family after the death of his father.

Due to some political development, the family had to shift their place of residence. In 1756, Siraj-ud-Daulla attacked and captured Calcutta. This adversely affected the family whose members had to run away to save their lives. Next year i.e., in 1757, the battle of Plassey brought about the downfall of Siraj-ud-Daulla. The East India Company had to undertake some protective measures. Fort William used to occupy a considerable area where the General Post office is at present situated. The Company decided to rebuild the Fort at a site located further south. So the residence of Tagores at Gobindapur, was acquired under orders of Government, compelling the Tagore family to shift its dwelling. After that, Nilmani having bought a new site further north in Sutanuty, built a new home and a temple for the family-deities. The documents covering the purchase of lands describe Nilmani as the purchaser. This house is still in occupation of the branch of the Tagore family, known as the Pathuriaghata branch.

Some accounts say that the residence was shifted from Gobindapur to Pathuriaghata, during the life of Jayaram. The account given by Byomkesh Mustaffi, however, does not support this story. He states that Jayaram died in 1756. If so, it could not be possible for him to shift the residence. It is universally accepted that he died after the invasion of Siraj-ud-Daulla. That is an historical event which took place in 1756. It was in consequence of this attack that the East India Company had to take the decisions to fortify the Fort William. That again necessitated the acquisition of the land of Gobindapur; and it was in consequence of that the Tagore family had to give up their house at

3. Banglaw Jatiya Itihas by Byomkesh Mustaffi 6th chapter.

Gobindapur. It follows that the change of residence did not take place before 1757; but after that if it be so, it was impossible for Jayaram to supervise the affairs as he was then a dead man.

There is additional evidence which can throw some light on it. Several transfer deeds were executed for purchase of the land for the house at Pathuriaghata. Details of three of them are available. Two of them were executed by Ram Chandra Kalu and Jagmohan Das as vendors. In both of them, Nilmani Thakur has been described as the vendee. These two documents definitely prove that Jayaram did not build the house at Pathuriaghata; and he was not alive then. Another fact should be mentioned in this connection. In 1757, the wife of Jayaram executed a deed donating Rs. 13,000 to the family deities which she received by selling her ornaments.[4] It follows that she was then a widow. In that case, it is not wrong to presume that at that stage, she could not personally use these ornaments. The third document of transfer was a patta which the Collector executed in favour of Nilmani. It should be mentioned in this connection that Nilmani was the second of the four sons of Jayaram and the eldest son died in an early age. If so, it was only proper that the second son should be the head of the family. Since the documents were executed in favour of Nilmani, it can be reasonably inferred that his father was not alive at that time. Of the two documents, one executed by Ramchandra Kalu was registered in 1171 B.S. corresponding to 1764, and the patta of the Company was granted on 1st January 1764. So, Jayaram had died before that.

Nilmani was a man of enterprise. He took an appointment under the East India Company. He would not hesitate to go to distant places in discharge of his duties. There is no difference of opinion that he had spent a time as the Sharistadan of an office of the Company in another country. Two diametrically opposite versions have been set up about where he had gone.

4. This story has been referred in London Times on the demise of Dwarakanath in London in 1846.

Amritalal Mukherjee says in his book, that Nilmani had gone to Chittagong in 1765, as an employee of the Company. Byomkesh Mustaffi in his book 'Banglam Jatiya Itihas' says that he took up an appointment as the sharistadan an officer in Orissa. It is difficult to say which version is correct. There is, however, some evidence which supports the second version. We know that the fore-fathers of the Tagore family acquired some landed properties in Cuttack. There is however no evidence to show whether they had acquired any property in Chittagong. The existence of landed properties in Cuttack supports the version that Nilmani Thakur had accepted service in Cuttack.

Be that as it may, there is no doubt that Nilmani was a man of enterprise. Very likely, he retired from the Company's service in 1784 and came back to the family residence at Pathuriaghata. In the meantime, his third brother, Darpanarayan, had acquired considerable wealth through commercial activities in Calcutta. It appears that such a bad feeling was generated between these two distinguished brothers that Nilmani left his paternal home and shifted elsewhere. The story that has gained currency over this affair is as follows :—

When Nilmani was abroad, he would remit his surplus income to his third brother, Darpanarayan who was both enterprising and had an aptitude for business. He carried on large-scale business activities in Calcutta. He used to invest the money remitted by Nilmani in his business. Very probably, Nilmani returned to his family residence in Calcutta after relinquishing his post in Orissa. After his arrival, he demanded a share of the wealth Darpanarayan had acquired, on the plea that the money remitted by Nilmani had been invested in his business in Calcutta. Darpanarayan, it is heard, rejected the demand of Nilmani. This shocked Nilmani so much that he left his paternal home with only the cloth on his body and took with him only the images of Lakshmi and Janardan who were the family deities.

Consequently, Nilmani became a man without shelter. Finding him in this straightened conditions, Baisnab Das Seth, a local man of affluence, made a gift of some lands to him at Jorasanko. So Nilmani started living there, after constructing a house there. That is how the house of the Tagores was shifted to Jorásanko in 1784.

This development must have naturally created a great sensation. Both the brothers were established in life and occupied a position of distinction in society. They became involved in such extreme undignified disputes over the question of sharing the family property, that one of them was compelled to leave the paternal home. It was indeed a sensational affair. It is said that, in consequence, the well-wishers and friends of both the brothers tried to bring about compromise and ultimately succeeded. On their mutual consent, it was settled that Darpanarayan would pay Nilmani Rupees one lakh in settlement of his dues. This transaction settled the dispute between the two brothers over the joint properties.

This account has been corroborated by more than one version. Bhabani Sindhu Dutta, the biographer of Debendranath supports it. He observes :

"They sat on arbitration, and decided that Darpanarayan would pay one lakh rupees to Nilmani Thakur. At that time, Baisnab Das Seth, a rich weaver, donated a few bighas of land to Nilmani to enable him to build a house at Jorasanko. Nilmani Thakur built a house on that land and lived there".[5]

James Farrol has also stated in his book on the Tagore family that the dispute between the two brothers over the joint property was settled by Darpanarayan agreeing to give one lakh rupees to Nilmani.

But Byomkesh Mustaffi has not accepted fully this version in his contribution to the book titled. Banger Jatiya Itihas. He agrees that the dispute was settled in

5. Bhabasindhu Datta, Maharshi Debendranath Tagore.

the manner indicated above but he does not however, believe that Nilmani being upset by the remarks of Darpanarayan instantaneously left the house taking with him only the cloth he wore. In support of his view, he has referred to a piece of circumstantial evidence. It has been already stated that Nilmani Thakur has been mentioned as the vendee of the deed on the land purchased at Pathuriaghata for building a dwelling place. If so, he argues there is no reason why he should give up his claim on the property at Pathuriaghata which he could legally claim as his own.

It is difficult to follow the logic of this point. For one thing, the dispute arose not over the family property but over a claim on the capital invested by Darpanarayan in his business. It cannot be predicted how under such circumstances a brother will react to a misunderstanding with his own brother. A man who is conscious of his legal rights would probably continue to live in the paternal house and then seek redress in court. On the other hand, a man who is endowed with refined emotions and delicate sensitivity will be so much shocked with the conduct of his brother that out of profound sorrow he would give up his claim on the joint property and voluntarily leave it.

There was no doubt that Nilmani was a man of enterprise. After establishing his family at Jorasanko, he managed to acquire some new properties in his old age. He faced no difficulty, therefore, in establishing himself a second time in life. It is said that the north-eastern part of the house of the Tagores at Jorasanko was built first. The thickness of the walls of this part will confirm this The width of the ground floor wall will be about three feet. So, this part was probably built in 1784. This proves that this house of the Tagores is two hundred years old. It is as old as the Asiatic society of Calcutta which was founded by Sir William Jones in the same year.

The will of Ramlochan, eldest son of Nilmani, records some evidence to indicate that Nilmani had acquired some properties, after building the house at Jorasanko. The will he executed shows his properties in two lists. One of them is the list of the self acquired property; and the other was the list of the property inherited from his father. The list of inherited properties includes the dwelling house, a house of Dharmatala, a house of Battola, a house at Janbazar, two items of Brahmottar land and three other landed properties. There is no doubt that one who could acquire so much property, after his retirement, was a man of considerable enterprise. He died in the house at Jorasanko in 1794. Ramlochan, Rammoni and Ramballabh were the three sons of Nilmani. They lived in the paternal house as members of a joint family. Ramlochan, being the eldest, functioned as the head of the family. Ramlochan and Rammoni married two sisters—Menaka Devi and Alaka Devi. Ramlochan married Alaka Devi and Rammoni Menaka Devi.

Ramlochan was blassed with only one daughter. He had no son. Rammoni was better of in this respect. Within a few years of the birth of his eldest son, Radhanath, his second son, Dwarakanath was born in 1794. In the meantime, the daughter of Alaka Devi passed away and she had to live the life of a childless mother. In this state of things, it was as natural on her part to want to adopt the second son of her sister as it was for the parents to agree to this. This is because the parents of the child were closely related to the prospective adoptive parents in two ways. The adoptive father was also the uncle. The adoptive mother was also the aunt. So, it was easy to fulfil the desire of Alaka Devi. By a decree of fate, Menaka Devi, the mother of Dwarakanath, died when he was still a baby of one year of age. In consequence, Alaka Devi shouldered all responsibilities to bring up the child. After being widowed, Rammoni married Durgamani Devi. Ramanath was the fruit of that marriage. So, he was really Dwarakanath's step-brother.

Ramlochan died on 12th December 1807. At that time, the three brothers,—Ramlochan, Rammoni and Ramballabh, lived together in the paternal house of Jorasanko. Of them, Ramlochan left no adult son. Rammoni had two sons other than Dwarakanath, of whom, Radhanath was the eldest and Ramanath the youngest. When Ramlochan died, Dwarakanath, his adopted son, was only thirteen years old. Ramlochan executed a will by which he left the administration of his property in charge of Alaka Devi, the adoptive mother of Dwarakanath and Radhanath, his elder brother. Radhanath had two sons, Mathuranath and Brojendranath. After the death of Ramlochan, the property of Jorasanko together with other properties were jointly owned by Rammoni, Ramballabh and Dwarakanath, an adopted son of Ramlochan. Afterwards, with Dwarakanath attaining prosperity, the shares of his two uncles, came to him in liquidation of loans taken on mortgage. During his life-time, he so arranged that the two sons of Radhanath and Ramanath, the youngest son of Rammoni, could live elsewhere in Calcutta, by a suitable partition of the paternal property. We get this information from the will executed by Dwarakanath. It is recorded in it that he gave the residential house at Bat Tala, to Ramanath; the house at Janbazar to Mathuranath, the first son of Radhanath and the house purchased from Kalika Brahmachari, to the younger son, Brojendranath.[6] This property was probably located at Thanthania. By this arrangement, the ownership of the house at Jorasanko devolved exclusively on Dwarkanath.

6. Will executed by Dwarakanath, on 16.8.1843.

3

DWARAKANATH

As stated earlier, Dwarakanath was born at Jorasanko, in 1794. When he was one year old, his mother died. He mother's sister, Alaka Devi, was also the wife of Ramlochan who was his father's elder brother. So, she was closely related to him in two ways. During his infancy, he was brought up by this aunt after his mother's death. So, she was as good as a real mother to Dwarakanath. He could not have retained any memory about his own mother.

Through a combination of circumstances, this foster-mother became his lawful mother. Ramlochan had no son of his own; on the other hand, Rammoni, his second brother, was blessed with more than one son. His first son, Radhanath, was older than Dwarakanath who was his second son. Then his second wife gave birth to his third son, Ramanath. The two brothers lived in the same house. Having married sisters, they became related by marriage as well. Then again Alaka Devi had brought up Dwarakanath from infancy. On this background, it was natural for Ramlochan and his wife Alaka Devi, to be inclined to have Dwarakanath as their adopted son. For the same reason, it was a very easy matter for Rammoni to agree to the proposal. So, in 1799, Dwarakanath was a adopted as a son by Ramlochan. He was then only five years old.

In those days, there was no provisions for the teaching of English. The East India Company came to India for the purpose of trade and business, but by a fortuitous combination of circumstances acquired supreme political power in India. His defeat in the battle of Plassey, in 1757, brought about the downfall of Siraj-ud-Dolla, the Nawab of Bengal. In 1765, the East India Company was granted to act as the Dewan of Bengal, Bihar and Orissa. And the Supreme Court was established in Calcutta in 1772. With the political power of the East India Company thus firmly established, the people of this part of the country were brought in close contact with the British. The earlier dealings between the two parties were restricted to exchange of merchandise. The administration having been transferred to the hands of the British, the area of contact expanded.

These developments, however, did not lead to the growth of institutions to impart teaching of English. This was not without reason. After assuming political power, the East India Company adopted two principles for guidance. For one thing, they would not interfere with the social and religious affairs of the country. Such interference would unnecessarily add to their burden and on the other hand endanger the empire by creating disaffection among the people. The second principle was adopted to safeguard their own interest. Not long after the East India Company had established their sovereignty over Bengal, the American colonies revolted and after a long war terminating in their victory established an independent State of their own. From that time onwards, the directors of the Company did not want to propagate English education. They felt that English education would foster desire for political freedom among the Indians.

The following quotations from observations, made by the members of the Board of Directors of the East India Company, will bear this out :—

"That one of the leading and most efficient causes of the separation of the America from Great Britain, as the mother country, was the founding of colleges and establishing seminaries for education in the different provinces ...sound policy dictates that we should in the case of India avoid and steer clear of the rock we had split open in the case of America."[1]

Understandably the East India Company did not initially feel interest in providing for English education. On the contrary, they were prepared to open *tols* and *maktabr* to encourage education in the indigenous methods . Conforming to this major principle, they opened the Maddrassah in Calcutta in 1781 and Sanskrit College at Baranasi in 1791.

Consequently, no good school run by the Government was available for those who wanted to acquire knowledge of the English language. On the other hand, the need for a sound knowledge of English was being increasingly felt due to the fact that the political power had passed on to the East India Company. After the establishment of the Supreme Court in Calcutta, the need for mastery over English was keenly felt. Since the Government decided to neglect them in this respect to safeguard their own interest, the people had to remain satisfied with what inadequate facility was made available through initiative efforts. Towards the end of the eighteenth century, several schools were established, on the indicative of some English speaking individuals for imparting English education. Among them the schools of Aratoon Pidrus and Sherbowme acquired some reputation. Sherbowme's school was situated on Chitpore Road at Jorasanko.

Dwarakanath acquired knowledge of Arabic and Persian languages in conformity with the practice obtaining in those days in his childhood. He also realised the need for acquiring knowledge of English simultaneously. For that purpose, he took admission to Sherbowme's school to learn the English language. It was conveniently close to his residence also. He did not remain satisfied with taking lessons from Sherbowme's

1. Quoted in the Life of Dwarakanath Tagore by Kshitindranath Tagore.

alone. He availed himself of the assistance of several Englishmen to build up his mastery over the English language. J.G. Gordon and James Coldon were two of them. And the third person from whom he got assistance was the famous missionary, William Adams, who was an intimate friend of Rammohun. His serious efforts to acquire mastery over English language speaks of his farsightedness. He fully realized that it was essential to cultivate friendly relations with the community that had established itself on the seat of power and had more or less acquired control over foreign and international trade and commerce in the new set-up. That is why he thought mastery over the English language was essential. It was on account of this farsight that he got the opportunity of coming in close contact with the officers of the East India Company.

Dwarakanath's character displayed a rare combination of many virtues. He was endowed with all the common virtues like capacity for hard work, ambition, reliability and honesty. Additionally, he was endowed with qualities like foresight, keen business sense, interest in social reform and spread of western education. Indeed one hardly comes across such a case where a single man displays so many virtues. As a result, he established himself in life without difficulty. He earned as profusely as he spent lavishly. His character combining many virtues, personality and warmth of feelings made him equally popular both in European and Indian society. Being a man of taste, he maintained a high standard of living and loved to spend lavishly, to entertain his friends and acquaintances. He was liberal in charity for a good cause. No wonder, the European society joined the epithet "prince" with his name. Nor was there any doubt that he deserved this distinction. He was rich as the son of a king, and large-hearted as the son of an aristocratic family, and liberal like a prince in spending for charities. In the eyes of the Europeans, he was the most distinguished Indian in those days after Rammohun.

His talents and command over English drew the attention of the top officers of the East India Company when he was quite young. He was appointed the Sheristadar of the Collector of Twentyfour Parganas at the age of 24, in 1818. It was a prestigious post for an Indian. Indeed no Indian had ever occupied such a post before him except Rammohun who had competently discharged the function of the Sheristadar to the Collector of Rangpur. It was his extraordinary talents that secured for Dwarakanath such a prestigious post at such an early age.

Quick promotions are easily obtained by a gifted person. Dwarakanath's power of discrimination and administrative efficiency made such a favourable impression in the mind of his superior officers that he did not have to wait long to be rewarded. In 1823, he was appointed the Dewan of the Nimak Mahal of the Company. Five years later, he got another lift, in 1829. He was appointed the Dewan of the Custom, Salt and Opium Board. He served in this capacity efficiently till 1834. After that, he voluntarily resigned from that post with the approval and blessings of his superior officers to respond to a call for work in a bigger field.

His unlimited capacity for work enabled him to extend his activities to work outside official duties. There were no rules imposing restrictions on the activities of Government servants, in those days. The conduct rules which at present regulate and restrict the activities of Government servants had not come into being. The officers of those days enjoyed freedom of engaging themselves in business activities as well as welfare activities. The atmosphere of freedom provided Dwarakanath the opportunity for expanding the field of his activity.

At about that time, he came in close contact with a person who was instrumental in involving him in social welfare work. He was no other than Rammohun who pioneered the advent of the new age in India. It has been already stated that, during the first decade of the

Nineteenth century, Rammohun worked as the Sheristadar of John Digby Collector of Rangpur. When Digby left for England, Rammohun resigned from government service permanently and settled in Calcutta in 1814. The headquarters of the Deputy Commissioner of Police at present occupies the site on the Upper Circular Road, at present name—Acharya Profulla Chandra Road, where he built his residence. Though Dwarakanath was about 20 years junior in age to Rammohun, they came very close together as they shared common virtues. This attraction subsequently matured into intimate friendship. They used to meet frequently, either in the house of Rammohun or in the house of Dwarakanath at Jorasanko, for discussing common problems. During this time, Dwarakanath associated himself with the different social welfare activities jointly with Rammohun.

Both of them received the same kind of education. Both had mastered the English language very well. Both of them were broad minded. No wonder, both evinced a keen interest in social reform. Both favoured the promotion of western education, through the medium of English. That explains why we find that both distinguished leaders worked shoulder to shoulder for the propagation of English education as well as social reformation.

Both of them realised from their personal experience that the apathy of the Government was responsible for the absence of facilities for English education. They had both suffered for this. They had to solve their problems by their own personal efforts. So they took a leading part at their own initiative to tackle this problem. It was however a Scotsman, named David Hare, who took the most prominent part in this matter. He came to India for business in clocks and watches. He, however, fell so much in love with this country that after retirement he settled in India. He was very fond of the student community and he dedicated his life to their service.

It was through his efforts backed by public support that the Hindu College was started on 20th January, 1820, in the house of Gorachand Basak, at Garanhata. It was removed to College Square at a subsequent date. It was the first English medium educational institution, in the whole of India, a memorable day in our National life. Dwarakanath became interested in the affairs of this college. Dwarakanath was one of those who donated handsomely to this institution. It is believed that he donated ten thousand rupees. The college was expected to function as the main channel by which real knowledge may be transferred from Western sources to the Indian mind.[2] Later on, Rammohun himself established an English-medium school, at Simla in North Calcutta. Dwarakanath got, his eldest son, Debendranath admitted to this school, by way of encouragement. That is how Debendranath came in intimate contact with Rammohun at an early age.

Dwarakanath was not only enthusiastic about the propagation of English education but was very much in favour of the spread of knowledge about Western Science. That explains why he was enthusiastic about the propagation of Applied Science. The radical change introduced in the educational policy of the East India Company, under the advice of Babington, Macaulay, during the regime of Lord William Bentinck, presented him with an opportunity for releasing this wish.

It has been already mentioned that the East India Company had initially adopted the policy that Government would not encourage English education and propagation of Western Science in India. From their experience in America, they formed an impression in their mind that English education would kindle a desire for political independence among Indian's and would work against the interest of their empire. That explains why they did not give any encouragement in this regard.

---

2. 'The main channel by which real knowledge may be transferred from the European sources to the intellect of Hindustan'.

Despite that fact, desire of the people for acquiring knowledge of western science through English education intensified with the passage of time. The people could not remain satisfied with the inadequate provision of English education, at the instance of some individuals. That provided the inspiration for the establishment of the English School of David Hare and the Hindu College in 1817 through non-official enterprise. The East India Company, however, persisted in their old policy of non-cooperation, even though they failed to check the spread of English education. We find that Government established the Sanskrit College in 1825 in Calcutta, as long as eight years after the opening of the Hindu College. Thus both a Maddarssah and a Sanskrit College were established in Calcutta. A course teaching medicine according to the indigenous methods was introduced in both the institutions. The primary motive behind it was probably to stop propagation of the western method of medical treatment.

In this situation, radical changes were introduced in the educational system in 1835 Macaulay who was inspired by new ideas. In the meantime, acquaintance with western literature, through the Hindu College, had produced a new type of educated Bengalees. After coming into contact with an Anglo-Indian, Dorajio by name, they had lost respect and faith in the Hindu society worn out with age. They started a new movement styled "Young Bengal" with the object of freeing their countrymen from the superstitions cultivated in their religion and attracting them to the orientation of free thinking. Some of the participants went to the length of adopting the Christian faith. Krishna Mohan Bandyopadhyay and Madhusudan Dutta were among them. Having noted all this, Macaulay probably came to the conclusions that the spread of English education might achieve what the Missionaries failed to do. He believed that the old Hindu society worn out with age, would break up by the impact with western culture and in consequence Indians would willingly accept the Christian civilization without any mental reservation. Very probably, this prompted him to recommend that the educational policy of the Company should be radically changed, so far as English education was concerned. And the then Governor General, Lord William Bentinck, accepted his recommendation.

This is good evidence to show that a similar reason induced Macaulay to advocate this new policy. He wrote a letter to his father covering this point, the relevant part of which is quoted below :—

"Our English schools are flourishing wonderfully... The effect of this education on the Hindus is prodigious. No Hindu, who has received an English education, remains sincerely attached to his religion; some continue to profess it as a matter of policy, for a labour-saving device, but many profess themselves as a refined monotheist, and some embrace Christianity. It is my firm belief that if our plans of education are followed up, there will not be a single idolator among the respectable classes of Bengalis thirty years hence. And this will be effected without any efforts to proselytization, without the smallest interference in religious liberty, merely by the norms of knowledge and reflective thought. I heartily rejoice in the prospect." [3]

So, the Governor General adopted the new policy that, in future, provision would be made for imparting English education and through its medium propagating knowledge of Western literature and science. The relevant part of the resolution adopted in the Council runs as follows :—

"The great object of the British Government ought to be promotion of European literature and science among the natives of India, and that all the funds appropriated for the purpose of education would be best employed on English education alone. His leadership in council dictates that all the funds which these reforms will leave at the disposal of the committee be henceforth employed in imparting to this population a knowledge of English

3. G. O. Trevelyne, Life and Letters of Lord Macaulay, Vol. 1, P. 464.

literature and science, through the medium of English language."[4]

It was in conformity with this resolution, that arrangement was made to establish a Zilla school in every district. In the same connection, a decision was taken that in addition to English, education on technical subjects should also be imparted. In conformity with that decision, a medical college was established in Calcutta, to teach methods of medical treatments, in 1835. Dwarakanath was very enthusiastic on this matter and helped in different ways to propagate knowledge about the Western method of medical treatment.

After the establishment of the Medical College, he donated two thousand rupees, for encouraging the students of this college, through rewards, in 1835. The Sanskrit College had introduced a course for teaching the Ayurvedic method of treatment but it did not provide for a practical course in anatomy. Having a scientific outlook, Dwarakanath fully realised that a detailed knowledge of the anatomy of the human body was essential to qualify as a physician. So, he supported a move for the introduction of a course for the dissection of the human body. In consequence, the course was actually introduced in Sanskrit College, in January, 1840. Madhusudan Dutta took the first lesson in dissection there, under the supervision of Dr. Goodeve.

During his first visit to England, he was deeply impressed by noticing the remarkable development of the medical science in that country. After his return to home, he felt that educated young Indians should go to England to study medicine. He was able to persuade the Government to sanction two scholarships, for the study of medical science, in England. In addition to this, Dwarakanath accepted the responsibility of meeting the expenditure for medical education of two more students.

4. Resolution of the Governor-General in Council, on 2nd February, 1835.

That is how the first batch of four Bengalees got the facility for medical education there. Of them, Bholanath Bose and Gopal Chandra Shil availed themselves of the scholarships offered by the Government while Surya Kumar Chakravorty and Dwarakanath Bose availed themselves of the facilities provided for by Dwarakanath. In fact, Dwarakanath himself escorted them to England in 1845.[5]

English education produced a new class of educated young men in our country who started examining social customs with an unbiased mind. The old Hindu society worn out with age was the repository of some customs and rituals, which could not be accepted rationally and in some extreme cases violated the principles of justice. Two major examples are the burning of widows on the funeral pyre of their husbands and the custom prohibiting widow remarriage. Neither of them can claim the sanction of reason or morality. Men and women are the two classes constituting human society. It is unfair that there should be different codes applicable to men and women. It is not fair that men should enjoy certain privileges which should be denied to women. Not that the old codes supported such double-code. In fact, no law of the Hindus prescribed the burning of the widow on her husband's pyre. It grew up, long after, as special custom in localised areas of India. Nor was the remarriage of the Hindu widows banned in the Hindu Codes. On the contrary, the Parasarsamhita prescribed it as a valid rite. We need not take into account the undesirable consequences of the application of this double-code. The Hindu Society however, patronised customs which no educated man could justify logically. The practice of burning a widow on the funeral pyre of her husband evidently exposes the barbarity of an extremely perverse mind. In these circumstances, it becomes the duty of those who have been installed in the seat of sovereign power to run the Government, to eradicate such immoral customs. At

5. Kshitindranath Tagore, Biography of Dwarakanath.

that time, the East India Company had not the courage to take such steps. They apprehended that such interference would work against their interest. They had come to India, to earn money, through expansion of trade. It was not their objective, to administer the country, but this responsibility was thrust on them by some political developments. They apprehended that belonging as they do to an alien race practising a different religion, their subjects would resent their interference with social customs. In case this resentment assumed serious dimensions, it might endanger the stability of their empire. That explains why this foreign power adopted the policy of non-interference with their social customs, even on matters which appeared to them to be unjust and immoral.

In these circumstances, the demand for social reform had to come from the educated leaders of the community. As in the propagation of English education, it became necessary for the broad-minded leaders to pioneer the measures for social reformation. In fact, that is what exactly happened. It was Rammohun and Dwarakanath who drew the attention of the people as well as the rulers to the urgency of these reforms. The practice of Suttee drew their attention first as it was not only against moral principles but cruel and barbarous and a stigma to the Hindu Society. Rammohun built up opinion against this custom, through the media of writings and public speeches, for creating a favourable atmosphere, for the abolition of the same. He followed this up with a memorandum to Lord Amherst, requesting the abolition of sutteeism. But this did not produce the desired result. The mind of the administrators was so much burdened with hesitation that they did not have the courage to adopt a new policy in this regard.

Yet Rammohun left no stone unturned to make them conscious of the need for action. At first, he laid emphasis on the irrationality of the coustom and the cruelty it displayed. This will be borne out by the memorandum he submitted to the Governor-General, Lord Amherst, on August, 1818. The relevant part is quoted below :

"Your petitioners are fully obliged from their own knowledge and from the authority of credible eye-witnesses that cases have frequently occurred when women have been induced by persuasion of their heirs, interested in their destruction, to burn themselves on the funeral pyre of their husbands, that others who were induced by fear to retract a resolution rashly, expressed in the first moments of grief, of burning with their deceased husbands, have been forced upon the pyre and then tied down with ropes and pressed with green bamboos until consumed with the flames, by their relatives, and burnt to death. All these instances, your petitioners humbly submit, are murder according to every scripture, as well as to the sense of nations".

But such appeal to the emotion of the rulers did not produce any results either. They thought that interference with even such cruel practice was likely to affect their interest adversely.

Then Rammohun adopted another method. He put his case in a different form, before the rulers. He tried to convince them that it was the duty of the party holding political power to abolish this barbarous customs and that if they showed indifference to its discharge the educated community will be estranged from the rulers. Simultaneously, he pleaded that no legislation prohibiting the rite was necessary, as this custom did not enjoy the sanction of any scripture; it would be discontinued if the police actively interfered with the practice.

This fact is mentioned in the despatch sent to the Board of Directors of the East India Company by Lord Bentinck, after assuming office as the Governor-General of India. The relevant part of his despatch runs as follows :—

"It must be confessed that a similar opinion about the probable excitation of deep distrust of our future intentions was mentioned to us, in conversation by that enlightened native, Rammohun Roy, a warm advocate for the abolition of sutteeism and all other superstitions and corruptions engrafted on the Hindu religion which he considers originally to have been a pure monotheism. It was his opinion that the practice might be suppressed quietly and unobservedly, by increasing more and more difficulties and by the indirect agency of the police".[6]

This new approach admittedly softened the mind of the rulers to some extent but did not lead to the realisation of his objectives. The company could not yet pass a law abolishing the practice of sutteeism. But a new plea did achieve the objective during the administration of the same large-hearted Governor-General. It was pointed out to him that this custom neither enjoyed the sanction of morality nor of the scriptures. There was no likelihood, therefore, of any large-scale movement, if it was suppressed with a firm hand. It appears that the Governor-General in Council could summon up the courage to abolish the practice of sutteeism by the enactment of law, after receiving such assurance. The practice of sutteeism was therefore abolished by the enactment of law, on 4th December, 1829.

In this protracted movement, led by Rammohun, Dwarakanath functioned as his major supporter. His erudition, moral qualities, and broadness of mind earned for Rammohun the respect of the alien rulers. Equipped with similar qualities, Dwarakanath was also able to make his influence felt on these rulers. Noticing that, Dwarakanath corroborated the reasons put forward by Rammohun for abolition of the practice of sutteeism, they were encouraged to take positive action in this regard. In fact, during Rammohun's life, only he and Dwarakanath among Indian's enjoyed the respect of the

6. Lord Bentinck's despatch dated 8th November, 1829.

ruling community. There is evidence to show that Dwarakanath's influence was an active factor in bringing about the abolition of sutteeism. This comes in form of a letter written to him by Lady Bentinck, the relevant part of which is quoted below :—

"I have much pleasure in stating that, among the native community of Calcutta, the late Rammohun Roy and yourself were the persons who took the warmest interest and afforded the most important information tending to show that although by long established customs the awful rite has attained the effect of law, still it was not a ceremony introduced by the Hindu Scriptures".[7] The above quotation from Lady Bentinck's letter makes available to us two valuable facts. Firstly, Dwarakanath became intimately acquainted with the Governor-General and his wife, by virtue of his, personality and moral qualities, in spite of being a servant of the Government. Secondly, his advice was a factor in preparing the mind of the rulers to decide in favour of the abolition of the rule even as Rammohun's advice did.

It was trade and commerce which provides Dwarakanath the field for the application of his extra-ordinary talents. Very likely he was the only Indian, who proved his outstanding skill in running commercial firms by engaging in diverse fields of trade and commerce. Unfortunately, the well-to-do section of the Bengali society did not follow his example. They were more concerned with security than earning money through speculative enterprise. They considered it wiser to enjoy their wealth in security by avoiding the risk of investment in business. That explains why the wealthy Bengalees of those days adopted the safer course of investing their money in the purchase of estates instead of following the examples set by him. Little wonder, they failed to acquire more wealth, as the Goddess Lakshmi favours those who dare taking risk. While enjoying their landed estates, they were overtaken in due course by

7. Quoted in Dwarakanath Tagore's a biography by Khitindra Nath Tagore, p-87.

poverty as the members of their family multiplied. In this syndrome of hopelessness, and despair, Dwarakanath had shown himself as the sole exception who set a beautiful example daring to risk his fortune to establish himself in the field of commerce.

Dwarakanath belonged to the type who have an unlimited capacity for work. That explains why he was able to acquire vast wealth through independent commercial enterprise simultaneously with discharging his duties efficiently as a responsible servant of the Government. The conduct rules of the government servants of those days were liberal enough to permit this. The servants of the Company were permitted to participate in business enterprise without restriction. By taking advantage of this provision, he was able to open a bank in 1829.

At that time, there prevailed a congenial atmosphere to encourage free enterprise. The East India Company originally came to India for trade and commerce, but when they found themselves placed in the seat of power through a stroke of luck, unlimited opportunities opened out for internal trade. They took up indigo cultivation and sericulture. Cultivation of indigo by the local cultivators and export of processed indigo became in due course a major item of trade. That brought into existence of colonies of indigo planters in different parts of the country. The famous missionary of Serampore, William Carrey, found an employment in an indigo plantation, in North Bengal, after his arrival from home. Similarly, many colonies of sericulturists also sprang up. In the eighteenth century, steam engine was invented in England. This opened up the possibility of large-scale production of consumer goods which in its turn brought about a radical change in the economic set up. This is called "Industrial Revolution". Both spinning and weaving were mechanized. The cloth thus manufactured was exported to India for marketing. This boosted up the export and import trade considerably.

Banking transactions also multiplied considerably, keeping pace with the expansion of commerce. The merchants had to unload the cargo brought by ships. The importers had no capacity to make full payment of the value of goods imported and rich men were therefore needed to stand security. This function now-a-days is discharged by a reliable bank. But no banks operated in those days. So local honest moneyed men took over this function. Technically such men were known as "Banians". In those days, many families of Calcutta acquired vast wealth by operating as banians.

Dwarakanath took full advantage of this situation. While engaged as a Company's servant, he used to carry on business in this field. His talents brought such success that he was able to establish a bank with his own capital. The Bengal Bank pioneer in the field had been opened in Calcutta in 1806. As it did not function satisfactorily, the East India Company had to take it over. In this circumstance, he took full advantage of the fact that the banking business was expanding and demonstrated his acumen by opening the Union Bank on 17th August, 1829. The Bank opened with an invested capital of sixteen lac rupees. Through skilful handling its working capital increased to one crore rupees. As ill luck would have it, the Bank closed down after his death. The matter will be dealt with in detail in the next chapter. Dwarkanath provided facilities for the members of his family as well as relatives, to pick up acquaintance with the banking business. Presumably his object was to make his successors acquire enough skill through experience to be able to run the business enterprises, established by him in future. That is why he employed Debendranath, his eldest son, in his own firm, as an ordinary paid employee. He wanted that his eldest son should learn work through apprenticeship. An observation made by his grandson Rabindranath, bears relevance to this. It says:—

"My father had to work on a small allowance under the direction of my grandfather, in the Bank, where the major part of his capital was invested. My grandfather was very keen that father should gain skill in running business affairs".[8]

It appears that he appointed Debendranath a Director after he had acquired some experience. A share-script of this Union Bank has been preserved in the museum attached to the Rabindra Bharati. It records the signature of Dwarakanath Tagore, Ramanath Tagore and Debendranath Tagore, in their capacity as Directors. Ramanth was the son of Rammony's second wife, so that he was, in fact, the step-brother of Dwarakanath.

There was no sense in a person continuing in Government service who had succeeded so well in business by devoting to it only a part of his time. The prospects would indeed be bright if he resigned from the post under Government and devoted his whole energy exclusively to the work in which his skill has been demonstrated so well. Farsighted that he was, very likely such thoughts had arisen, in his mind after a few years. That explains why we find that in 1834 he was very keen to give up the post he had been holding so competently under Government. A new development forced him to take a decision, on this point quickly.

The Charter granted by the British Government, authorising the East India Company, to carry on trade in India, had been renewed every twenty years. The Charter had been renewed last time, in 1813. The East India Company used to enjoy some special rights under the provision of the Charter. The question of renewal was due to arise again in 1833. The special rights are enumerated here. Under the Charter, the East India Company enjoyed exclusive rights of trade in opium, salt, silk and other commodities. British citizens were debarred from acquiring landed property or investing in agriculture, outside Calcutta, except as a representative of the East India Company. The Company had the right to deport any British citizen at their will, without recourse to Judicial proceedings.

8. Rabindranath, Charitrapuja.

The East India Company had been enjoying special rights so long without any let or hindrance. No serious objection had been raised against that so far. But on this occasion, a strong agitation was built up against the renewal of the Charter due in 1833 long before this date. In fact, the agitation started from 1828 and gradually gave rise to serious controversies, in Calcutta as well as in England. The matter was hotly discussed in the United Kingdom in papers like "The Asiatic Journal", "The Morning Herald", "The Times" as well as papers brought out in Calcutta. The Calcutta papers that became seriously involved in this affair were "The Samachar Chandrika" and "The Sanbad Kaumudi".

There was a special reason behind this controversy. Initially, the activities of the East India Company, were restricted to export and import business. The invention of the steam engine by James Watt, however, brought about a radical change in the economic system of the United Kingdom, in the 18th century. When machine power was harnessed to industrial production, a new economic system took its birth. The consumer goods so produced were so vast in quantity that it left a huge surplus after meeting the demand of the home market. The production capacity of power operated mills increased manifold. Consequently, it became imperative to export them to foreign markets, so long the trade between United Kingdom and India had been restricted mainly to export and import of agricultural commodities. It now became necessary to import raw materials for exporting them to foreign countries and for manufacture of processed goods in power-operated factories at home. Extensive territories of India having been annexed in the meantime to the British Empire, the Indian market offered an easy solution to the indecipherable problem of marketings. It could naturally function as the market for the cloth produced in the mills of Manchester. In this situation, the new rich community which was the product of the Industrial Revolution did not tolerate the monopoly rights so long enjoyed by the East India Company under the Charter; as it went against their interest. They claimed right of free trade and agriculture in India. This could not be achieved unless they were given the right to purchase property and live anywhere they liked in the territory governed by the Company. These are the factors that contributed to the strength to the agitation. On the other hand, the East India Company would not agree to give up their vested interests. Nor did they lack power and influence. They also reacted strongly. No wonder, the agitation intensified and generated bitterness.

The Indian's did not like to remain silent spectators in the agitation that was started in India. They also joined the movement. Calcutta became the focal point of this agitation. It was the powerful rich European mercantile community who started the agitation for the withdrawal of the Charter. While, on the other hand, the supporters of the East India Company opposed the demand. Of the Indians, who took part in this agitation, some were against the renewal of the Charter and others in favour of its continuance. Those who favoured renewal of the Charter were influenced by the thought that if the Englishman was permitted to buy property and live freely, the interest of the Indians would be adversely affected. The Indians, would be ousted from their property and face competition in trade and would be subjected to large-scale oppression.

It appears that the agitation assumed its worst form in 1829. Lord William Bentinck sent a lengthy despatch this year to the Board of Directors of the Company, on this agitation, dated 30th May 1829. He tried to make out through facts and figures that if the Englishmen were granted the right of residence and trade in India, it would work more to the interest of Indians than against it.

Dwarakanath Tagore held similar views. He was holding at that time a responsible post which afforded him opportunity to mix intimately with the British community. He discovered in the character of English businessmen some qualities which commanded his respect. They were industrious, enterprising and skilled in business. They had a scientific outlook. Recently they had developed their technological skill so well that it brought about the Industrial Revolution by using mechanical power for the production of consumer goods. Secondly, from his personal experience, he had gained the impression that the Englishman of his days was prepared to work hand in glove with the Indians. He, therefore, concluded that if the Englishman was allowed more freely in India their activities will also promote the economic interest of Indians.

That explains why he whole-heartedly joined the agitation for the discontinuance of the Charter to the Company. In this connection a reference may be made to his letter published on 17th March, 1829. He recommended that the British citizen should be given the right to live and acquire property anywhere in territory under the administration of the Company.

For the same reason, we find that Dwarakanath took a leading part in the meeting held in Town Hall of Calcutta, on 15th December, 1829, to discuss the same issue. He tabled a resolution proposing the discontinuance of the East India Company's Charter. It was seconded by Rammohun, and passed in the meeting.

The agitation ended in the acceptance of the demand of the new community of the rich businessmen. The monopoly trade rights of the East India Company was withdrawn and the British citizen was conceded the right to live and acquire property in the territory under occupation of the Company. This new development was the other matter which inspired Dwarakanath to resign from the post he held under the Company and devote himself entirely to business enterprises.

This explains why he resigned from the post occupied under the Company on August, 1834. He was then occupying the post of the Dewan of the Salt Board of the Company. It was both respectable and responsible, but he realised that it did not provide him adequate scope for the application of his talents which called for a bigger field for operation. What added to his enthusiasm was the fact that under the new provisions, it would be possible for him to start business jointly with British partners and in fact, he took a British partner. But before taking up that subject, the events following his resignation should occupy any attention.

Thus he decided to use his talents in business enterprise in partnership with an Englishman, and submitted his letter of resignation from the post of the Dewan of the Salt Board, to the Board of Revenue. The Board, however, found it difficult to make up their mind on this issue. In fact they found themselves in two minds. The loss of the service of a competent and reliable men like Dwarkanath would be a misfortune. On the otherhand, having regard to the reputation he had acquired by his numerous qualities and service to the people, it was obvious that his talents could not be fully utilised in this restricted field available to a man, tied to a post. To do justice to him, therefore, the Board should accept his resignation even though it was detrimental to the interest of the Board. After deliberation, they decided for the second alternative and accepted his resignation.

A reference is necessary, in this connection, to the letter written by Henry Merredith Parker, Secretary of the Board, officially communicating to Dwarakanath the decision to accept his resignation Two facts emerge out of the contents of the letter. For one thing, the Board had felt that the restricted life as an employee was not conductive to the developments of Dwarakanath's talents. Secondly, it admitted that his qualities of characters and administrative skill had deeply impressed his superior officers. Such admission we hardly come across. The relevant part of the letter under reference is quoted below :—

"I have laid your letter before the Board and directed to communicate to you their acceptance of your resignation. I am desired to convey the expression of the regret they feel in losing the services of an officer, whose talents, zeal and experience have been so long and diligently exerted in advancing the interest of the important branch of revenue over which the Board presides. As the high sense, which the Board entertains of your qualification and integrity and of their appreciation of the advantage which public interests have derived from your connection with their office are recorded in the proceedings of the Board; it would be superfluous to say more at present than that your past services have met with the cordial approbation of the Board".[9]

Though holding a superior post, Henry Meredith Parkar entertained high respect for Dwarakanath. Consequently, a cordial relation grew up between them. Of this we have many indications. It may be mentioned in this connection that he did not remain satisfied with only an official letter. He wrote a personal letter to Dwarakanath also on the same occasion. Its contents not only prove the depth of their intimacy but also indicate how deeply he was impressed by the qualities that distinguished his character. The relevant parts of that personal letter are quoted below :—

" To say that I regret your loss in an office where your aid has been at once as valuable in itself and so cheerfully will but poorly express what I feel in losing your services,.............My dear Dwarakanath, do continue to set an example to your countrymen of honour and integrity, continue through good report and ill report, to hold fast by truth and cultivate the approbation of your own conscience, and do continue to lead in the path of true knowledge and intellectual civilization". [10]

So, In 1834, Dwarakanath resigned from the post under the Company and devoted himself whole-heartedly to independent business enterprise. What idea he entertained about the business acumen of the Englishmen has been mentioned before. His mental outlook made him look for a British partner in his

9. Letter of H. M. Parker, dt. 14.10.1834.
10. Ibid.

business. It was at about that time that Lord William Bentinck, the then Governor-General, introduced him to a British businessman named William Carr.

He established the Carr-Tagore Company in 1834 with Mr. Carr as partner. He built up this firm as a model business enterprise, in keeping with his own ideas about how it should be run. An Englishman was to be his partner and his own talents would supplement the other's business acumen and experience. That is how he wanted work to proceed. Initially, the firm had three partners:— William Carr, William Princep and Dwarakanath himself. Afterwards, some other partners were accepted including Debendranath. The firm prospered exceedingly well under the stewardship of Dwarakanath. The company extended its field of operation to all varieties of business activities practised in those days, including landed estates. It was, however, principally interested in indigo. They ran an office at Sealdah to look after transactions on indigo. That grew into such an important centre of trade in indigo that it came to be known as the "Indigo Mart".

Not content with that, the dynamic and inventive mind of Dwarakanath involved new plans for the extension of his business to other fields. Some examples can be cited, where his company achieved success in specific fields.

Under the patronage of this company a sugar mill was established at Ramnagar. There was a silk factory at Kumarkhali. The Indigo Mart at Sealdah has been already mentioned. At the initiative of Dwarakanath, the Bengal Coal Company was established for the extraction of coal from the mines of Ranigunj, very probably, it was the first coal mine to be operated in Bengal.

So long manually operated boats were the only means of river transport. The steam engine had, however, been invented a long time back. James Watt invented the steam engine. After him, Stephenson, another British engineer, invented railway engine worked by steam for transport. Subsequently the steamship was invented by the application of the same principle. Despite the availability of such technological advancement, no mechanical device had been adopted for river transport in India. Dwarakanath realised the immense potentiality behind this. He drew up a scheme for transport by boats carrying cargo with the help of tugs propelled by steam engines. Through his initiative, the scheme was put into practice in 1837, when the Steam Tugs Association was formed for river transport by steam tugs, Carr-Tagore Company was appointed agent of this company. The use of steam-operated boats created the demand for their maintenance and repair. Carr-Tagore Company opened a workshop to meet this demand at Kidderpore.

The above account will give an idea of the comprehensive character of the Company's activities. One thing to be noted in this connection is that Dwarakanath did not restrict its activities to purchase and sale of consumer goods. He was keen to undertake the production of goods: The best example in point was the scheme to extract coal from Ranigunj coal-mines. He was equally keen to utilise the new technology developed in the United Kingdom. A fine example in this regard is the use of steam tugs for river transport. He was equally interested in production, marketing and application of technology; indeed, his foresight, scientific outlook and power of organisation are worthy of administration. The example he set up by his success in free enterprise should have been followed by the Bengalees of his days. But the Bengalees of the next generation did not follow his path. They decided to invest in rent-bearing estates evidently to eliminate the risk involved in free enterprise. Had the Bengalees followed the example set by Dwarakanath, they could have acquired skill in commerce and industry like the Parsee community of Bombay.

Thus under the supervision of Dwarakanath, the Carr-Tagore Company gained recognition as one of the leading business houses of Calcutta. Having acquired a huge wealth, he was given epithet "Prince". It was by his exertions that the Tagore family of Jorasanko reached the peak of financial prosperity. A statement of his son, Debendranath, touching on the extent of his wealth may be quoted in this connection. It carries special weight as it comes from a person having personal knowledge on the subject.

"At that time he was looking after Zemindaris in the districts of Hooghli, Patna, Rajsahi, Cuttack, Midnapore, Rungpore, Tipperah as well as business in indigo, nitrate, sugar, tea and other commodities on behalf of the Carr-Tagore Company. Along with that the coal-mine industry at Ranigunj was being operated. We were then at the zenith of our prosperity". [11]

Dwarakanath had developed intimacy with Englishmen during his service life. Impressed by his noble qualities, William Meredith Parkar, Secretary of the Revenue Board, used to hold him in high respect. For the same reason, he was liked by persons holding high office in the Government. Lord William Bentinck knew him very well. Lady William Bentinck became so friendly that she exchanged letters with him. Little wonder, that intimate social relations were established between him and the European community of Calcutta. Moreover, when he gave up service and engaged himself exclusively in business, he picked up an acquaintance with a considerable number of Europeans. He consequently felt the need for frequent meetings and discussions with the members of that community. Such contact cannot be restricted to offices only in the business world.

Under the compulsion of this new situation, Dwarakanath had to undertake the responsibility of mixing intimately with the European community, respond to their invitations to parties and entertain them in return. Moreover, he belonged to the type that loves to entertain others and enjoy their company. So, this new responsibility fitted well with his inclinations. No wonder he loved to make elaborate arrangements for such entertainment. In fact, he celebrated such festivals in

11. Maharshi Debendra Nath Tagore's Autobiography.

real royal style. He spent lavishly, in these festivals and dinners in keeping with his huge earnings. That explains why the European community called him "Prince Dwarakanath."

The festivities took place in his outer house which used to be called the *Baithakkhana Bari*. That house has since disappeared altogether. The facts have been stated in a previous chapter. It stood to the contiguous west of Maharshi Bhavan and to the north of Bichitra Bhavan. It is now an open lawn where the birth anniversary of Rabindranath is celebrated, in a public meeting, on the 25th Vaisakh. This *Baithakkhana Bari* used to accommodate his office which looked after the revenue paying estates of Dwarakanath. Guests used to be entertained with lunch or dinner in this house.

But Dwarakanath could not entertain his guests in the manner he wanted within the confined space of this house. To remove this handicap, he laid out a well-planned garden at Belgachia and built a house for holding festivals. He furnished it with costly furniture imported from abroad. He used to hold parties in this spacious garden house. Apart from serving sumptuous meals, he provided for dance, music and fireworks. His parties proved very attractive to the European community and in pomp they could compare favourably with the parties given by the Governor of those days. Such parties came to be recognised as such important social events that they used to make head-line news in the papers the following morning.

All distinguished men of Calcutta used to come to these parties. The leading members of the European community joined them with enthusiasm. There is evidence that the members of the family of Lord William Bentinck also participated in them.

A report which appeared in the contemporary press on the subject may be quoted here by way of illustration. "Calcutta Courier" was one of the leading newspapers in Calcutta those days. Reporting on the party given by Dwarakanath at Belgachia on 26th February, 1841, it says:

"The assembly at Dwarakanath Tagore's last night was surpassingly brilliant. It was attended by the Honourable Miss Eden, Sir E.Ryan and a majority of other leaders of Calcutta society. The house (which had been tastefully refurbished) and the grounds were brilliantly illuminated; the fireworks were superior to any we ever before saw in India; he was as usual, courteous and sedulous for the comfort of all; and that the guests enjoyed themselves is testified by the lateness of the hour to which they lingered". [12]

Dwarakanath was thus compelled to mix intimately with the Europeans as a duty imposed by his business interest. This intercourse was not restricted to business affairs discussed in office. It extended to attending festivals and dinners. He would be invited and entertained by the members of the community in their parties. He was similarly compelled to entertain them, in his own parties in their own style as expected of a gentleman. So he would serve wine and forbidden meat in such parties. Unfortunately, this reacted sharply on his domestic life and created serious problems for him.

Dwarakanath was married to Digambari Devi about 1809. The lady was paragon of beauty. The account about her physical features confirms that she was fair-complexioned and had a charming facial expression. The family performed two *pujas* annually the *Durga puja* during the autumn festival and the *Jagaddharti puja* in winter. She was so strikingly beautiful that the people would compare her to the goddess Jagaddhatri. A story is current that the artist who moulded the image of the goddess, Jagaddharti, used Digambari's face as the model to shape the face of the image.

12. Calcutta Courier, February 26, 1841, Dwarakanath's party.

Born in the first part of the nineteenth century, this lady inherited all the ideas of the conservative Hindu society of those days. She entertained strong objection to indulging in foreign drinks and forbidden meat. When her husband indulged in such practices, she was confronted with a dilemma. On the one hand, in conformity with the Hindu ideal of womanhood, she adopted devoted service to her husband as the sole mission of her life. On the other hand, his intimacy with the foreigners gave rise to serious misgivings in her mind. Not that Dwarakanath lacked in piety. He used to perform two *pujas* annually with sincerity and pomp. The worship of the family deity used to be carried on regularly, is an intimate friend of Rammohun, he would attend the sittings of the 'Atmiya Sabha', and even encouraged the transfer of the Brahmo Samaj to the new building at Jorasanko. Even as he did not give up the practices obtaining in the family. His son Debendranath confirms in his autobiography that his father used to perform the worship of the family deity with devotion. He also mentions that occasionally it would so happen that when Rammohun called on Dwarakanath, he would find the latter engaged in worship.

Despite all this, Digambari Devi could not tolerate her husband's intimacy with the English people as it hurt her feelings. A question arose in her mind whether as an orthodox Hindu lady she would live in the same house with a husband who mixed freely with foreigners or whether she would live separately. On the other hand her deep love and respect for her husband would not allow her to severe all connection with him. She ultimately faced the situation when she had to decide between what duty dictated and what she desired. Her conduct shows that she had the capacity to decide it by herself after consulting the specialists on the subject. Evidently, she had developed a strong personality of her own. No wonder, we find her consulting a Brahmin versed in scriptures to decide her course of action. He advised that it was as much her duty to look after her husband with devotion as to protest against such conduct of her husband as did not conform to the Hindu code. On this advice, she solved her problem by adopting a middle course. As it was not possible to look after her husband, unless she lived in the same house with him, she gave up the idea of living separately. On the other hand, she would keep herself away from his touch, as her husband had become unclean by mixing intimately with foreigners. It is said that if by accident she would even touch him, she would immediately purify herself by taking a bath. This may appear as an unreasonable attitude, but looked at from her own point of view, as shaped by the tradition of the old days, she deserves our respect.

Naturally this problem must have caused Dwarakanath considerable mental discomfort. It appears, however, that he did not take any step that might embarrass his wife. His sensitive mind must have made him realise that, brought up in the orthodox style of those days; his wife would find it difficult to tolerate conduct forbidden to Hindus. To avoid further irritation, he started living in the *Baithakhana bari*. It was thus possible to provide for living close together, through mutual co-operation.

Digambari Devi died on 21st January, 1839. It is not known, how Dwarakanath faced this bereavement. There is evidence that his business activities and social life continued as before. It is, however, evident from his conduct that he was preparing himself for withdrawing from his domestic life. In 1842, he executed a will, providing for the future maintenance of his sons. In the same year, he set out for the United Kingdom. He returned home soon but could not stay long. He again sailed for the United Kingdom in 1843, and stayed on more or less permanently till death overtook him.

The noble lady must have received God's blessing in abundance. How else could her children shape into such precious gems? We have read that King Vikramaditya's court used to be adorned by nine gems. The children she gave birth to were also gems. It will be no exaggeration to say that she was the mother of gems. It is also amazing that despite the large number of children in the family, a sweet and calm atmosphere prevailed in the house. It was the deep affection mutually entertained by the brothers and sisters that made this possible. Dwijendranath discharged his role as the eldest son in a perfect manner. He showered unlimited affection on his younger brothers and sisters. He took great delight in diverse talents displayed by them. The congenial atmosphere built up in the family by the joint efforts of his brothers was a matter of pride to him. There is a poem composed by him which beautifully expresses this feeling. This may be quoted here in translation :

"Where Satya and Hem shine and Birendra shows his prowess, where Sama and Houti dispel the darkness of the mind, Where Some and Rabi add new lustre, In that abode of gods thrives this poet."

Obviously, the poem is meant to be a self-introduction but this introduction is way of listing the talents of his younger brothers. The substance of what he says is that his brothers are so gifted that they have been able to transform the house into the abode of gods. Indeed he was an appreciative eldest brother.

We may conveniently deal with the members of the family in terms of this list. Dwijendranath's second brother, Satyendranath earned the distinction of being the first Indian to compete successfully in Indian Civil Service examination. Hemendaranth, the third son of Maharshi, was very fond of wrestling, but what distinguished him was his tremendous enthusiasm for female education. In fact, he more or less compelled the women members of the family to read and write.

He not only supervised their education but also coached them. Unfortunately, he died prematurely at forty. Birendra, the fourth son of Maharshi unfortunately became a metal patient in his early youth. He was the father of Balaendranath who distinguished himself a writer. The next name listed in the poems quoted above is Gunendra. He is the younger son of Girindranath, the second brother of Maharshi. He was the father of Abanindranath the founder of the Bengal School of Painting. He was younger than Birendra but older than Maharshi, if son, Jyotirindra. His name has been inserted in between to indicate that the sons of the two brothers mere being brought up together and were treated as member of the same family. For the same reason, Gunendra, the eldest sons of Girindra, used to be called 'Mejda', (second brother) and not Satyendranath who was one year younger in age. The fact that Ganendranath's name is not listed in the poem indicate that presumably he had died before the poem was composed.

Joytinrindranath has been already mentioned. Only Some and Rabi remain to be introduced. Somendranath was older then Rabindranath by two years. They were brought up together as mentioned in Rabindranath's reminiscences. Unfortunately, he was afflicted with mental disease at an early age. The youngest brother Rabindranath needs no introduction.

It was Maharshi who created the atmosphere which helped the development of the talents of his children. Evidently, his upright conduct exercised an indirect influence but additionally the provisions he made for them were conducive to such development. For he had to discharge of the liability for the huge debt which accrued after his father's death. Maharshi was compelled to impose a life of extreme hardship on his family, for several years. No doubt, the family became affluent after the discharge of the debts and he had the capacity to provide for a life of luxury for his children usually enjoyed by the families of landed aristocrats; but he did not allow his children to adopt their style of life. They were allowed to live in comfort but not luxury. An observation of Rabindranath shows he rightly appreciated this. A translation of the same is given below. "The father never encouraged his children to indulge in a life of luxury and opulence. Like a dutiful house-holder who takes his meal after feeding his guest, he would first meet the demands of his supplicants and then look after the maintenance of his family. Thus, though brought up in affluent condition, he protected us from the allurement of a pompous life and self-indulgence. If thereby, the door of the golden cage of the goddess of wealth was only piratically opened for his children to allow them the indulgence of free movement in the spiritual world, they must be considered more fortunate than many millionaires, thanks to their father's sagacity."

Indeed, Maharshi took the right action. On the one hand, it prevented his sons from being confined in the golden cage of luxury and on the other, gave them unfettered freedom to soar in the spiritual sky. His sons enjoyed full freedom to engage themselves in literary activities, mastering music, staging plays and organising fairs of indigenous goods. This provided the proper atmosphere for the development of their latent talents. His youngest son, Rabindranath fully appreciated this as the relevant observation quoted below will show:

"Who also would more than us home much freedom he permitted us? His religious views formulated after anxious search which he stoutly defended when associated were never allowed to interfere with the freedom enjoyed by the members of the family. His example was there, nor were deprived of the benefit of his counsel; but he ever imposed on us any discipline which interfered with your freedom of thought and action."

There is independent evidence to confirm that Maharshi was in the habit of giving counsel to his sons. He used to conduct prayers every morning in an assembly attended by two children. This was followed by advice when his attention was drawn to any misconduct committed by any of them. Even grown-up children were not spared if the occasion demanded it. There is an anecdote recorded in the reminiscences of his second son, Satyendranath, which bears this out. It is worthwhile referring to it, as this will also show that Satyendranath was a worthy son of a worthy father.

Satyendranth had then returned home after being appointed a member of the Indian Civil Service. He had at that stage not only attained mentions by senriors but was holding a high post under the Government of India. By a long sojourn in the United Kingdom he had naturally imbibed some Western habits. Maharshi did not, however, like this and did not hesitate to protest against this. Let us listen to Satyendranath's account of this affair:

"Father used to counsel us occasionally after prayers. At that times, he would make special reference to our shortcomings and try to correct them when I made a parade of the English style of life I had adopted after returning home. He took up the matter in the prayer hall and scolded me severely for the blind imitation of their style and making an exhibition of the same and asked me to discard it. His advice will remain fresh in my memory permanently."

The separate treatment of each of his children may be conversantly taken up at this stage Dwarakanath returned home after that, reaching Calcutta in January, 1843. He resumed his work of supervising the management of the business concerns set up by himself. His skill and intelligent handling made them more prosperous. In fact, his activities spread to new areas. To cite an example, it was at that time that he founded the Bengal Coal Company to extract coal from the Ranigunj coal mine as mentioned before.

It became gradually apparent, however, that he was losing interest in mundane affairs. A desire to withdraw from the family and spend the last days of his life away from home was gradually gaining ascendancy in his mind. Ultimately, it became so strong and compelling that he decided to go back to the United Kingdom and stay there indefinitely. So he left again for England, on March 8, 1845, accompanied this time by his youngest son, Nagendranath. His stay was, however, cut short by untimely death which overtook him following a serious illness at his house in Surrey, near London, at the age of 52. Like Rammohun he also died abroad.

It appears that in his last years, the question of future security of his sons worried him. He had built up many a hope round his eldest son, Debendranath. He had fondly hoped that Debendranath would acquire the competence to look after his two business concerns, which he built up with considerable effort and hardwork as a worthy son. He sent Debendranath to the school founded by Rammohun for education. When he grew up, Dwarakanath made him attend the social functions he would arrange. He appointed Debendranath a probationer on a small allowance in the Union Bank to provide for his practical training. Subsequently he appointed Debendranath a Director of the same Bank. Dwarakanath made him a part-time officer of the Carr-Tagore company.

But Debendranath's own inclination pulled him another way. He became so deeply engrossed in religion in his early youth that he could not apply his mind to the affairs of business. In fact, Debendranath has mentioned this in his autobiography. The relevant part is quoted in translation below:

"One day (my father) complained about Vidyabagish that he had an impression that

Vidyabagish was a good man but to his disappointment he found that Vidyabagish was poisoning the mind of Debendranath by talking to him about Brahma; that by nature, Debendranath is averse to worldly pursuits and that distracted by preaching about Brahma he pays no attention to business affairs".[13]

The full name of the person referred to here is Ramchandra Vidyabagish. He used to give exposition of texts of the Upanishads in the Atmiya Sabha founded by Rammohun. Later he was appointed a teacher of Smriti in the Sanskrit College of Calcutta. Afterwards, when the Brahmo Samaj was founded he used to give exposition of the Upanishads at the weekly sittings of the Samaj. When Debendranath got himself initiated into the Brahmo religion, Ramchandra was appointed one of its Acharyas. Unfortunately he was struck down by paralysis soon after and died at Varanasi on 2nd March, 1845. It is natural that Debendranath should seek spiritual fulfilment according to his own inclination. It is also natural that this would disappoint Dwarakanath. The future prospect of the business concerns he had built up by his own efforts seriously worried him. He counted on his eldest son taking over the responsibility of running the huge concerns he had built up. He must have been deeply shocked, therefore, when he found that his sons was indifferent to their security.. Probably another problem also worried him seriously; the future security of his children, threatened by the uncertain prospect of his business concerns. He had amassed vast wealth. He had brought up his sons in luxury. If the business concerns failed and misfortune overtook them, they would face endless misery as they were used to a life of wealth and comfort. It appears that these apprehensions kept him seriously worried as is indicated by his subsequent conduct. He was as far-sighted as intelligent.

13. Maharshi Debendranath Tagore, Atma Tivam.

He took effective steps to protect his sons against such eventualities. They were as stated below:—

On 20th August 1840, he executed a trust deed. One and half years before, he left for the United Kingdom for the first time. This document covered both properties inherited and acquired by him. These appertained to four different estates.

(1) Sahajadpur Tahashil

(a) Dehi Sahajadpur Pargana Isapsahi Touzi No. 2 of Pabna Collectorate

(2) Birahimpur Tahashil

(b) Birahimpur, Pargana Birahimpur

Touzi No. 3430 of Nadia Collectorate

(c) Kismat Madki

Touzi No. 3437 of Nadia Collectorate

(3) Kaligram Tahashil

(d) Pargana Kaligram

No. 141 Touzi of Rajsahi Collectorate

(4) Panduya Tahashil

(e) Taluk Panduya Pargana Tiram

Touzi No. 2484 of Cuttack Collectorate

(f) Taluk Baliya Pargana Hariharpur

Touzi No. 2173 of Cuttack Collectorate

He entrusted these properties to the care of three of his close relations : Prasanna Coomar Tagore, Ramnath Tagore and Chandra Mohan Chatterjee. Prasanna Coomar Tagore was the grandson of Darpanarayan and a cousin of Dwarakanath. Ramnath Tagore was his step-brother being the son of Ramlochan's second wife. Chandra Mohan was his nephew being the son of his own sister, Rasmani. It has been already stated that this nephew accompanied Dwarakanath on his first visit to Europe. Rasmani had another son, named Madan Mohan. The road to the south of the house of the Tagores has been named after him. Their own house was situated on the other side of this road. Dwarakanath selected close relations for trusteeship in respect of this Deed as he wanted men whom he could rely on. It was another evidence of his far-sightedness.

According to the terms of the Trust Deed, so long as Dwarakanath lived, these trustees would look after those properties and enjoy the income derived from them. After his death, they would allocate equally the income of these properties among the three sons of Dwarakanath. After the death of the sons, they would distribute the income to their heirs according to the shares they would be entitled to.[14]

Two provisions of the Trust Deed call for special notice. Firstly, he separated these properties from his other properties including business concerns and entrusted them to the care of the trustees. This would keep these properties secure against demand for liquidation of debts in case his business concerns collapsed for want of proper supervision after his death.

Secondly, he did not make over these properties to his sons. He wanted that these properties are duly preserved under the management of expert close relations. Probably he could not be sure of the capacity of his sons to manage them. His ardent desire was that his sons should securely enjoy them after his death. The subsequent history of the family proved the wisdom behind these provisions. Indeed the trustees discharged their function with such efficiency and devotion that the properties were not only kept intact but more properties could be added by purchase from the surplus income which accumulated. It is necessary to deal with this matter in detail in the next chapter.

14. Dwarakanath's Deed of Trust, dated 20.8.1840.

In substance, these provisions not only bear evidence to his worry about the future security of his sons but also his far-sight and wisdom which protected them from probable misfortune. It was these steps taken by the father that made it possible for his sons to extricate themselves from the serious calamity which confronted their family after Dwarakanath's death.

4

DEBENDRANATH'S FAMILY

Dwijendranath the eldest son of Maharshi, was born in 1840. He was married to Sarbasundari Devi, Who died young. Dwijendranath was long lived like his father and died in 1926.

Dwijendranath was absentminded by nature. He felt no attraction for a life of pleasure. He lived a simple unostentatious life devoted to literary activity, in pursuit of knowledge and sundry experiments. He spent most of his time in literary activities. His articles are preserved in the different contemporary magazines. He published his articles mostly in the Tattabodhini Patrika, the Bharati, the Banga Darshan and the Sahitya.

He has enriched Bengali literature by writing outstanding books of poems. One of them is the Bengali translation of the Meghduta of Kalidas. He translated the first part in the *Payah* meter and the second part in the *Tripadi* meter. This translation was the first to distinguish itself by its quality. In this sense, he may be considered the pioneer in the field of translated literature. The Bengali version of the Meghdut a was published in 1860, a year before the birth of Rabindranath when Dwijendranath was only twenty.

'Swapna Prayan' was the second book of verse. The date of its publication was 1875. When this book of poems was composed, Rabindranath was in his teens. This book has many distinctive features. It gives an account of a person's exploration in a dream. It carries a symbolic meaning. The poems of this book have been dressed in a variety of new meters. Very likely Dwijendranath was actuated by a desire to make experiments in meters. Historically, the book carries significance from both points of view. Here is an attempt to introduce innovations in Bengali literature. There was a mark of originality in his approach. In the meantime, Madhusudan has acquired reputation by composing the epic 'Meghnath badha' and understandably his reputation had more or less influenced contemporary writers; Dwijendranath, however, kept himself strictly away from it.

Dwijendranath was the pioneer in the field of philosophies in Bengali literature. His philosophical work the 'Tatwavidya' may be mentioned in this connection. The book was published in three volumes between 1866-1868. The first volume deals with metaphysics, the second with problems of enjoyment, and the third with ethical problems. This is the first book in Bengali where philosophical problems have been discussed in a methodical manner. He is also the author of two other books dealing with philosophy. One is the book titled 'A critique of the Advaita philosophy', published in 1896. This was followed by a book with a long title, dealing with the Aryadharma, and its conflict with Buddhism published three years later.

When his younger brother, Jyotirindranath, started the magazine called 'The Bharati', Dwijendranath functioned as its first editor. It was he who suggested the name it carries. The following observation of Dwijendranath will bear this out.

"Jyoti felt a strong desire to bring out a new monthly journal; but I was not very keen. I rather desired that 'The Tattbodhini Patrika, should be improved and popularised. This did not prevent Joyti from starting his paper 'The Bharati'. His desire was to bring out a journal after the model of Bankim's 'Banga Darshan'. He asked me to take over the editorship to which I did not object. In fact, however, only but the use of my name; Jyoti took over the entire responsibility".[1]

The elite of Bengal gave due recognition to Dwijendranath for his life-long service to the cause of Bengali literature. He was elected the president of the Bangiya Sahitya Parishad for three years, from 1897-1900. He was elected as the president of the Bengali Literary Conference, held in 1916.

As regards experiments carried on by him, a reference may be made to Dwijendranath's effort to evolve a shorthand system of Bengali. The system he evolved was curiously recorded in verse. This may be treated as another example of eccentricity. The observations made by his younger brother Satyendranath are relevant. He said:-

"This book on shorthand was a unique thing. A mixture of poetic effusion and clever use of lines, its quality cannot be appreciated without examining it. This has been recently published and so if anybody is inclined he can satisfy his curiosity by referring to it. Unfortunately, no student of his has been able to show proficiency in his system of short-hand".[2]

Likewise, Dwijendranath did some experiment in the construction of boxes. He also wrote a book in English to record the result of his thought and experiments on the subject. It was published with the title 'Boxometry' in 1913. All this shows that he felt interested in diverse subjects and worked on them.

Every member of the sprawling house of the Tagores had his own area demarcated for living. Dwijendranath selected the southern verandah in the first floor of Maharshi Bhavan for spending his time.

1. Puratan Phasanga, Dwijendranath (Second series).
2. Satyendranath, Āmār Bālyakatha.

It was spacious and could be conveniently used both for receiving friends and talk to them as well as for literary activities. He functioned as the presiding deity of this area. An account recorded by Rabindranath on his life on this verandah may be conveniently quoted here :— "Eldest brother was then engaged in composing the 'Swapna-Prayan' sitting on a bedstead on the southern verandah with a table in front. Gunendra would come and sit there every morning. His unbounded enjoyment of the literary excellence of the book stimulated the poet's mind like the spring wind. Eldest brother would compose and then recite and Gunendra's loud and appreciative laughter would resound in the verandah. Like mango blossoms which fall prematurely and cover up the ground below many compositions rejected by the poet would lie scattered all round. Eldest brother's poetic faculty worked so vigorously that he was compelled to compose much more than what was necessary and so, much of his writing had to be rejected. If these could have been preserved, an entire box could have been filled with them". [3]

Dwijendranath spent his last days at Santiniketan. He used to live there in the bungalow known as the 'Nichu Bungalow'. In fact, it was a thatched cottage surrounded by flower beds. He lived their in the soothing peaceful atmosphere of the ancient hermitages, in close contact with nature and intimate friendship with animals and birds. We get an account of this in the reminiscences of a former teacher of Santiniketan. He says "He would sit in an easy-chair on the small verandah in a detached contemplative mood. His face softened by deep thoughts would look lovely adorned with a grey beard with his body reclined on easy-chair. Small birds like sparrows and Manuyas would peck at grains round him, chattering all the while and hang by his beard". [4]

3. Jivan Smriti Bari Abhawa.
4. Profulla Kumar Sarkar Gurudev's Santinikathan.

Satyendranath, second son of Maharshi, was born in 1842. He was a very meritorious student. He passed the first entrance examination conducted by the University of Calcutta, in 1857, in the First Division, from the Hindu School. Then he got his admission in the Presidency College. He then sailed for England in 1862, with a view to sitting for the competitive examination conducted for recruitment to the Indian Civil Service in London. He was promoted to do so mainly due to the encouragement of his friend, Manomohan Ghosh, who afterwards distinguished himself as a counsel. So long the recruitment of Civil Servants had been restricted to Englishmen only who would subsequently hold the top posts in the judicial and administration departments. He was the first Indian to compete with them in their own land. He was selected for the Service after successfully competiting in the examination held in 1863; and after a probation of one year he returned home in November, 1864. Appointed to the I.C.S. he was assigned to the Bombay Presidency. He spent four months in Bombay and then got his first posting at Ahmedabad.

Bombay was then the biggest province of India. It not only covered the western part of what is at present the state of Maharashtra but also Gujarat and Sind. He spent his long career as the first Indian member of the Indian Civil Service. He functioned for more or less long periods as Sub-divisional officer or District Judge in various parts of the province. He attracted many of his relatives to his place of service, who responded to his invitation and lived for sometime with him. They included not only Rabindranath but Jyotrindranath and Swarana Kumari Devi as well. Among his sisters, he was particularly fond of Swarana Kumari. Most surprisingly he was able to persuade Maharshi to come over to his place. This has been mentioned in the previous chapter.

Satyendranath resigned from the Service before completion of his term in 1899 and returned to

Calcutta. He settled permanently in a house, on the Store Road (renamed Gurusaday Dutta Road) situated to the north of the Ballygunge Cricket Club ground. It was a house with a spacious compound. The site is now occupied by the Birla Science Museum. He died in mature age after a long spell of retired life.

Satyendranath distinguished himself most by leading a movement for the emancipation of women from bondage. In those days, women were given away in marriage in very early age and were brought to their husbands, house in tender age. Women of respectable classes were not allowed to move outside their houses. They were compelled to live in confinement in the inner apartments of their houses. They enjoyed no freedom of action, speech or thought. Economic freedom was out of question. They had to live under the protection of their fathers in childhood and of their husbands in youth and their sons in old age. Endowed with a sensitive mind, he could not tolerate the confined life they were subjected to.

This injustice to women produced an impact on the mind of Satyendranath even in his boyhood. No wonder, he started protesting against the imposition of this constricted way of life on women from his boyhood. It is mentioned in his boyhood reminiscences that he would enter into controversy with his mother on this subject, when he was a mere boy. His relevant remark may be quoted here in translation:

"From the very childhood, I advocated free life for women. Mother would scold me for this, saying: Do you want to take our women to the Maidan for a walk after the fashion of European ladies. I did not like the life of confinement of women in the inner apartment following the tradition of illustrious aristocracy. I felt that the *purdah* system was not an indigenous practice but was cultivated to initate the muslim practice.[5] After his marriage, he never hesitated to

5. Satyendranath Tagore Åmār Bālyakatha.

oppose his mother when she would want to impose her wish on his wife Jnanadanandini Devi. It appears that he took upon himself the role of a fighter for the freedom of the women of his family. A small incident in the family will bear out how strongly he felt on the subject.

Jnanadanandini's father lived in Jessore district and owned no house in Calcutta. Her parents happened to live in Calcutta for a short while on one occasion. Her mother expressed a desire to bring Jnanadanandini to the rented house they were living in, and spent a few days with her. Satyendranath's mother, however, did not consent to this. What stood in the way was the sense of exaggerated dignity of her husband's house which she entertained in her mind. She reasoned that if a daughter-in-law of the famous family of the Tagores went to meet a relative in a rented house, it will be derogatory to the prestige of the family. This rule should apply to the case of parents also. When his mother's decision on the issue was communicated to Satyendranath, he thought that this should not be submitted to his mind though it came from his mother it was tantamount to an act of oppression inflicted on his wife and would cause a pain and shock to the relatives. He reported the matter to his father. What his mother failed to appreciate was easily brought home to his father. He immediately want to Sarada Devi. Let us hear what he told her from the mouth of Satyendranath's wife. She has recorded as follows in her reminiscences:—

"He came to mother-in-law and said, 'Is it a fact that you did not permit Satyendranath's wife to go to her mother who sent a palanquin for her transport? Why a rented house? If a mother lives under a tree, it is the duty of the daughter to meet her there. Send her to her mother immediately".

The desire that sprouted in Satyendranath in his boyhood gathered strength from his experience during his stay in the United Kingdom. He lived there in a society where unrestricted free movement of women was fully encouraged; women enjoyed equal social rights with men. He noted that it was the members of this same society who had distinguished themselves most in prowess, bravery and power, in the whole world. He, therefore, concluded that their prosperity stemmed from the fact that their women enjoyed freedom. His ideas is not logically unsound. The body of the society stands on two legs, one of which is the male and the other the female. It is a fact that in our country the restrictive code of conduct imposed on our women hampered their development and brought on themselves the misfortune that falls in the lot of a lame man. The letters he wrote to Jnanadanandini Devi during his sojourn in Europe clearly reflect these thoughts. One of the letters is quoted below:

"Despite the difference with our country in many respects, all the prosperity and progress, all that is good and beautiful in this country stems from the freedom enjoyed by its women. When will our country attain the same condition of excellence? Where women do not enjoy freedom in any field and are strictly controlled the traditional customs, directions of their husbands and advice by others, women's freedom is a far cry".

This awareness made him entertain a strong desire to bring his wife Jnanadanadini Devi to the United Kingdom during his sojourn in that country. The idea behind was that she should acquire a first hand knowledge about the extent of freedom enjoyed by the women of Western society, so that a desire may be roused in her to work for creating a similar condition in her own society. He did not hesitate to communicate his desire to his father; but Maharshi did not consent to this. He felt hurt in consequence and tried to lighten his sorrow by expressing his disappointment in his letter to his wife, the relevant part of which is quoted below:-

"I thought that if you could come once to England and live for sometime in this advanced society, you could share the knowledge and progress achieved by these people. So I wrote to father requesting him to arrange for this. But my efforts failed. Father desires that I should not make proposals which work against the honour and prestige of the women of the family".[6]

When he returned to Calcutta in 1864, before joining his post as a covenanted civil servant, Satyendranath had formed the firm decision that he would fight the system which keeps women confined to the inner apartment like birds confined in cages. He has recorded this fact in his reminiscences as follows :

"Our women live a constricted life in the gloomy confinement of their houses; lacking freedom of movement, their minds do not develop, their natural capacity to learn to acquire strength and capacity for work withers away. On return from England, my desire to do away with the *purdah* system was intensified".[7]

This campaign for the abolition of the *purdah* system was initiated by his wife, Jnanadanandini Devi who behaved fittingly as the worthy wife of a worthy husband. She defied the rules imposed by the *prudish* system when she accompanied her husband to Bombay to which province he had been allotted. She was the first to set the example as a daughter-in-law of the family to appear in the public in full view of men. Afterwards during the service life of her husband in Bombay Presidency she, adopted the style of life lived by the wives of the European civilians.

When the couple returned to Calcutta to spend their earned leave for the first time, they create by their conduct a sensation of the first order in the Hindu community. According to the custom obtaining at the time the couple were invited to a reception at

6. Puratani, edited by Indira Devi, a letter written by Satyendranath on 2.7.1864.

7. Satyenderanath Åmār Bālyakarthā.

Government House. They attended the party and thereby dealt a deadly blow to the *purdah* system practised by the family. The story as narrated by Satyendranath himself is quoted below:

"After my first return, from Bombay I took my house wife to the Government House. What a sensation it created! My wife was the only Bengali lady in this assembly of hundreds of English ladies. Prasanna Kumar Tagore was then alive. On seeing the daughter-in-law of the house in this public gathering he ran away in shame".[8] Prasanna Kumar belonged to the Pathuriaghata branch of the Tagore family and was related to Satyendranath's father as an uncle.

It has been already mentioned that during his sojourn Satyendranath felt a strong desire to bring his wife Jnanadanandini Devi over to England to enable her to pick up an acquaintance with the local society. He entertained a firm conviction that if she came in contact with English ladies who enjoyed freedom of movement, his wife would be in a position to spearhead the freedom movement for women in India. This wish had remained unfulfilled on account of his father's opposition.

Satyendranath, however did not give it up when he started living independently as a member of the Indian Civil Service in the Bombay Presidency, he decided that Jnanadanandini Devi would go over to England with her children in advance and he would join the latter and stay with them as long as possible by taking long leave. Accordingly Jnanadanandini Devi sailed for England accomplished by an English couple probably in 1877.[19] Jnanendranath Tagore, a son of Prasanna Kumar Tagore and related to Maharishi, as a cousin, was then living there. Jnanadanandini Devi spent a few days with him along with her children after disembaration. Subsequently she settled in

8. Satyendranath, Âmār Bayakartha.

9. Vid Puratain, Edited by Indira.

Brighton. Unfortunately, her younger son died there. Satyendranath joined the family on earned leave. He took with him his youngest brother, Rabindranath. He has recorded an account of the days spent in Brighton with his nephew and nice under the affection, care of his sister-in-law in his 'Jivan Smriti'. After the expiry of Satyendranath's leave, they returned to India in May, 1880. By long sojourn in England in a society where women enjoy freedom of movement Janandanandini Devi acquired the necessary strength of mind to live as a woman. The spirit of self-reliance she displayed in handling the situation created by the premature death of her younger son during her sojourn without any adult member to help her.

When he joined his family at Brighton on earned leave, Satyendranath took Rabindranath with his. That was Rabindranath's first visit to England. As has been already stated, he has narrated in detail in his book of reminiscences, the story of his stay at Brighton in company with his nephew and niece and enjoying the hospitality of his sister-in-law.

Her long sojourn in England imparted to Jnandanandini Devi the right outlook to pay the role of a wife expected to participate in the movement to be initiated by her husband for freedom of women, on their return home. On coming in close touch with English women, she imbibed their fine qualities thereby fulfilling the hope entertained by her husband in this respect. As expected by her husband, she helped him to abolish the *purdah* system practised by her family, both by example and conduct. In the process, she discharged their role of a pioneer by initiating the first phase of the movement for freedom of women in the country. As a worthy wife, she thus fulfilled the desire fervently entertained by her husband.

We get an idea of the radical change brought about in the style of living of the women of the Tagore family of Jorasanko from an observation made by the eldest daughter of Maharshi, Saudamini Devi. It is quoted in translation below:

"It was second brother who radically changed the style of our life. When we appeared before the public dressed in chemise, blouse and shoes in our horse-drawn coaches, people denounced us in a manner unthinkable in the present age".[10]

Drawn by respect for his follower Satyendranath felt deeply interested in the Brahmo religion founded by his father. He composed many hymns for his religion. As a student reading in England, he did not limit his activities to the prosecution of his studies. He took deep interest in the publicity work of the new religion. He carried on a discussion with the famous Indologist, Maxmuller on the subject.

At a subsequent stage when he joined his new post at Ahmedabad on return from England, he wrote a brief but comprehensive account of the Brahmo religion, for despatch to Maxmuller. This account has found a place in the appendix of the biography of Maxmuller, written by his wife, by virtue of its own merit.[11]

Satyendranath entertained deep patriotic feelings. The fact that he was the first Indian to become a Civilian could not modify this attitude the least, consistently with the ideals cherished by his family. His association with the Hindu mela indicates the depth of his patriotic feelings. The institution of the Hindu mela took its birth during the phase of transition, when the feelings of nationalism had just started germinating among the educated people of the society. The activities of Nabagopal Mitra, a prominent organiser of the Hindu mela, will bear this out. He started the 'National Paper' in 1868, to initiate the people of his country into nationalism. At

10. Saudamini Devi Pitri Smiriti.

11. Life and Letters of Maxmuller Appendix.

a subsequent stage, he organised the Hindu mela with the help of Dwijendranath, the eldest son of Maharshi and his nephew Ganandranath who gave liberal financial assistance to the cause.

The first 'Hindu Fair' was opened on 12th April, 1867 (1273, Bengali era, on Chaitra Shangkranti). The major object behind it was to infuse patriotic feelings among the people. Holding musical performances, staging dreams and exhibition of indigenously produced goods formed parts of the programme.

Ganendranath explained its objectives in the inaugural session as follows :

"We assemble here not in pursuit of religion nor of pleasure nor of amusement but for the uplift of our country, our dear motherland". During the next session of the Hindu mela held in Chaitra the following year, Satyendranath was enjoying long leave in his paternal home at Jorasanko in Calcutta. This enabled him to participate in the organisational work of the mela. Ganendranath gave a recitation of a patriotic song, composed by himself on this occasion. This was also the occasion for Satyendranath, to compose the patriotic song, which begins with the lines 'Let all Indians sing together in Union'. His deep interest in this swadeshi mela has found expression in his recorded reminiscences. The relevant passage is quoted below :

"A short time after, I joined my post in Bombay Presidency; the institution of swadeshi mela was founded in Calcutta. My eldest brother started it with the help of Nabagopal Mitra. "It started flourishing when my first cousin-brother interested himself in it. This mela would sit for three or four days every year in a park in the suburb of Calcutta. Efforts were made to awaken patriotic feelings among our people by exhibiting home-made goods, singing of patriotic songs and delivering public speeches. My elder cousin composed several patriotic songs for this mela and it also provided me the inspiration for the song titled 'Bharat Sangeet'.[12]

The cousin referred to in this quotation is Ganendranath the eldest son of Girindranath. He was younger in age than Dwijendranath but older than Satyendranath. So he became the Mejda of the family. The children of the two brothers Debendranath and Girindranath, used to be treated in those days as members of the same family.

That the way of life of the women of the Tagore family had undergone radical change is clearly indicated in the observation of Saudamini Devi referred to before. The lady who brought this about was Jnandanandini Devi, wife of Satyendranath. She introduced these changes by boldly adopting them herself in the face of strong opposition. In the process, she introduced some changes in the style of dress for women to equip them better for appearance in public.

In those days, women belonging to a respectable family were kept confined within the inner apartments of their house. The more respectable a family, the stricter was the rule of enforced confinement. The women of the Tagore family were not allowed to go out except in a palanquin. It is said that when they would take a bath in the Bhagirathi, they were forced to do it, sitting inside the palanquin. Women had no dress suitable for appearance outdoor. It was Jnandanandini Devi who intoduced the use of underwear for women. The style of wearing saries among fashionable women practised in our days traces its origin from her own innovation.

A certain innovations were introduced by her to add a touch of sweetness to domestic life, in particular to brighten the life of children. One such measure is the institution of celebrating the birth

12. Satyendranath, Balyasmriti.

anniversary of children, introduced for the first time, by her with a view to giving children a taste of literature she started a children's magazine, titled 'The Balak' in 1885. Probably it is the first children's magazine in Bengali literature. It was subsequently merged with the Bharati.

After retirement, Satyendranath lived for sometime in a rented house in Park Street. Then he shifted to his own house at Ballygunge. Thanks to the hospitality of his wife, Jnandanandini Devi, their home became a centre of attraction in the society. It attracted not only the members of the Tagore family but also many distinguished persons belonging to the educated class. They included Tarak Palit, Satyendra Prasanna Sinha, Umesh Chandra Banerjee, Krishna Gobinda Gupta and Bihari Lal Gupta.

Maharshi's third son, Hemendranath, died young at the age of forty, in 1884. He was survived by three sons and five daughters. The responsibility of looking after this big family devolved on Maharshi in his old age.

Like other sons of Maharshi, he was also endowed with many virtues. He studied the medical science in the Medical College for a short period. He became interested in physical culture, particularly in wrestling, in his youth. Their was a vacant space to the north of the Thakurdalan which used to be known as Golabari. The boys of the family used to do physical exercise there. A Punjabi wrestler named Hira Singh was Hemendranath's instructor. Hemendranath was equally interested in the exercise of the mind. In fact, he developed a keen interest in western literature and science.

The virtue that merited appreciation was his desire to help the women members of the family to pick acquantaince with Bengali literature. He even compelled the young girls who came to the family as daughters-in-law to learn to read Bengali. Jyotirindranath says in his biography that

Hemendranath took full charge of teaching him in his boyhood. Rabindranath also gratefully remembers that Hemedranath's coaching in Bengali stood him in good state. Hemendranath devotion to the Bengali literature helped to create a favourable atmosphere in the family congenial to teaching Bengali. An observation of Rabindranath, having a bearing on the subject, is quoted below:

"The coaching I received in Bengali in boyhood enabled me to use my mind properly. Teaching should be a process as far as possible like taking food. If the mind is not given the scope for exercise from the beginning, it loses its capacity to work. I offer my grateful respect to my deceased third elder brother who had the courage of undertaking teaching us Bengali over a long period, when English education became highly fashionable." [13]

Birendranath, the fourth son of Maharshi, was younger than Hemendranath, by only one year. Two sisters were married to these two brothers. Hemendranath was married to Nipamayi Devi, and Birendranath to Profullamayee. The two sisters were the daughters of Haradev Chattopadhya of Santaraganchi. As bad luck would have it, Birendranath was stricken with insanity, a few years after marriage, which continued till his death in 1915. Maharshi provided for his maintenance, till death, in his testament.

Jyotirindranath, the fifth son of Maharshi, was gifted with extraordinary talents. The dazzling glow of Rabindranath's achievements prevents us to appreciate properly his merits. Had he been born in another family, it would have proved easy to assess him. Thank god that it did not happen like that. The birth of so many talented persons, in the same family, one after another, carried great significance. Jyotirindranath was as much as twelve years. Older than Rabindranath, having been born in May 1849.

13. Rabindranath, Jivan Smriti Shikshan Abasān.

The difference of age between the two brothers proved to be an advantage. It appears that Jyotirindranath was destined to be born in the family of the Tagore, to help Rabindranth develop his intellectual powers, by the example of his own achievement, words of encouragement and companionship. He not only created an atmosphere which was conducive to the blooming of Rabindranath's sensitive mind, but also assigned to him the position of a disciple of promise, by accepting him without reservation as a fellow-worker, in his creative activities. It does not matter, if the glow of the genius of Rabindranath overshadowed the achievements of Jyotirindranath.

Jyotirindranath took his first lesson from a private tuitor, according to the tradition obtaining in the family and afterwards Hemendranath coached him. Then he got his admission to a school. After reading in St. Paul's School and then Montagu's School he got his admission to Hindu School. He passed the Entrance Examination in 1864. Ramesh Chandra Dutta, a renowned historian and literature, was his class-mate there. He then got his admission to the Presidency College. After attending classes for a short period, he discontinued his academic studies.

Jyotirindranath took keen interest in writing and staging dramas, from a student. The atmosphere at home encouraged such pursuits. Ganendranath, the eldest son of Girindranath, the younger brother of Maharshi, took particular interest in staging dramas. As he was older in age than Satyendranath, the younger boys of the family called him 'Mejda' an appellation for the second brother of the family. He lived in the premises No. 5 of Dwarakanath Tagore Lane, which used to be called the 'Baithakana bari', during the days of Dwarakanath. He founded a dramatic club, in 1865, at Jorasanko. He staged 'Krishna Kumari', a drama written by Madhusudan Dutta, under its auspices the same year. Jyotirindranath appeared in the role of 'Ahalya', in that performance. The encouragement he received in his early years may have provided him the inspiration to shape himself as one of the best dramatists at that time.

Then we see Jyotirindranath in the role of one of the organisers of the Hindu mela. It has been previously mentioned that his cousin, Ganendranath, was one of the founder of the fair. In fact, he was the General Secretary of the organisation. The Hindu mela was opened for the first time in 1867, when Jyotirindranath was only eighteen years of age. It was Ganendranath who persuaded him to participate in its activities. Nabagopal Mitra asked Jyotirindranath to compose patriotic poems and read them in the mela. This request was complied with by Jyotirindranath the next year. That is how he was initiated into patriotic as well as literary activities.

The impact of these two events, at this early age, prompted Jyotirindranath to write dramas, calculated to rouse patriotic feelings. But writing of a drama is only half of the work; it has to be staged also. It was with this end in view that a cultural organisation was set up in the family house, principally through the initiative of Jyotirindranath. It was founded on 18th April, 1874 and named 'Bidyadjan Samagam'. It was under the auspices of this institution that Jyotirindranath engaged himself in writing dramas, depicting acts of heroism which excite patriotic feelings. His first drama 'Puru Vikram' (The heroism of Puru) was based on the story of Alexander and Puru, the hero of the Punjab. Mention may be made in this connection of similar dramas, written by Dwijendra Lal Roy', in a later period. 'Chandra Gupta' is comparable to 'Puru Vikram'. The historical dramas written by Dwijendranath, based on the different stories of Rajasthan, are also comparable to the dramas based on the stories of Rajasthan, written by Jyotirindranath. Very likely the example set by Jyotirindranath inspired Roy to write these dramas.

In the first sitting of the 'Intellectuals' get-together Jyotirindranath gave a reading of the drama, 'The heroism of Puru' (Puru Vikram). The drama was staged subsequently. It was under the auspices of the same organisation that a few dramas written by Rabindranath, in his early age, were also staged. He staged the drama 'Valmiki Pratibha', a lyrical drama, composed immediately after his return from the United Kingdom, in 1881. His drama 'Kalamrigaya' was staged next year. Jyotirindarnath appeared in the role of king 'Dasaratha' in this play.

Jyotirindranath also staged two satirical dramas, written by himself under its patronage. He composed the drama, Eman Karma and Karbarna (I shall never do this again) in 1881. The other satire was written in 1884 and originally named 'Hathat Nabab' (Sudden elevation to the position of a Nawab. It was staged the same year under the patronage of the Bidyad Jana Samagam'. The drama was subsequently named 'Alik Babu' (The Imposter). It still continues to be a popular drama.

As a dramatist with originality Jyotirindranath's dramatic talents found expression in two distinct lines. One line led to the production of comical dramas and the other to historical dramas depicting patriotic and heroic acts. Jyotirindranath's dramas enjoyed tremendous popularity in those days; and many of them were played on public stages, by professional actors. His first drama was a comic sketch, written even before 'Puru Vikram'. It was named 'Kinchit Jaloyog' (A light meal). It was staged by the National Theatre, on 20th April, 1873. And 'Puru Vikram' was staged by the Bengal Theatre, on 22nd August, 1874.

Jyotirindarnath wrote the drama 'Sarojini' in 1875. Sarojini, daughter of Lakshman Singh, the Rana of Mewar, was the heroine of this drama. It was a tragedy. At the end, there is a scene, depicting the performance of the Jaharbrata (self-immolation by fire), prompted by the sack of Chittore, by Alauddin Khilji. It was while composing this drama that Jyotirindranath got positive evidence of the poetic talents of his younger brother, Rabindranath and his aptitude for literary pursuits. Rabindranath was then a boy of fourteen. It so happened that Rabindranath was taking his lessons from his teacher of Sanskrit, in a room contiguous to the room used by Jyotirindranath, for his literary pursuits. His teacher, Ramsarveswar Pundit, used to help correcting the proof of this drama, at that stage. No wonder, Rabindranath felt interested in this drama. At one stage, Rabindranath suggested that a particular prose passage in the drama, should be substituted by a song and on getting the approval of his elder brother, composed the song to replace it. His offer was readily accepted. Jyotirindranath gave his account of this offer as follows:

"I had composed a speech in prose to be placed in the beginning of a scene, where the Rajput ladies were expected to jump to a pyre for self-immolation. When the proof of this passage was being examined Rabindranath was listening to it from the adjoining room while learning his lessons. Young Rabi rushed into my room as he felt that the prose composition did not fit in with the scene. He insisted that a poetical composition was the only suitable thing for the occasion. I had to take the suggestion seriously as I myself was disappointed with the speech from the inception. When I raised the question of time, whereupon Rabindranath undertook to compose a song immediately and within a short time presented me with the song the first line of which is 'Burst into flame at pyre with double fury".[14]

Jyotirindranath followed this up with the drama 'Ashrumati' in 1877, written on a historical background. The play is based on an imaginary story on a historical background but somewhat bold.

---

14. Jyotirindarnath Smirti.

Evidently, it was a pioneering effort in romantic drama, but incidentaly it led to some hostile demonstration against Jyotirindranath. In the play 'Ashrumati' the daughter of Rana Pratap has been depicted as the lover of Muslim youth. It involved a clash between romantic love and filial affection which undesirably is a fine subject for literary treatment. Naturally it earned a lot of popularity and translation in Hindi and Marathi were brought out. When however, the information that a daughter of the Rana's family had been painted as the lover of a Muslim was transmitted to the Rana, he felt outraged. Things came to such a pass that Jyotirindranath had to write to him a letter of apology to mollify him.

After that, Jyotirindranath composed another drama and a comic sketch. After that, however, he devoted his time to the translation of outstanding book into Bengali. Here again, he showed his preference for drama. Though other kinds of literary works also drew his attention of the books in English selected by him for translation 'thoughts on soul' by Marcus Aurelius and the Counsel of Epietates' deserve mention. The book that deserves special mention in this connection, is the translation of Shakespeare's 'Julius Caesar' in Bengali. He also translated several French classics. Of them Piere Lotis 'India without the Englishman' and the two novels of Gautier entitled 'Militona' and 'The Incarnation' deserve mention.

Jyotirindranath achieved his greatest success as a translator through his translation of Sanskrit classics. Between 1899 and 1905, he translated as many as seventeen Sanskrit dramas. They included 'Abhignasakuntalam' and two other dramas of Kalidas and the other top classics the 'Uttara Ram Charita', the 'Malati Madhaba', the 'Mrichhakatika'. The dramas of Bhasa were left out probably because they had not yet been discovered.

Jyotirindranath's talents found expression in diverse ways. He took delight in applying them to different fields. He even worked enthusiastically on a subject for some days which is far removed from literature. He once engaged himself in commercial enterprise. Probably the outstanding achievements of his grandfather, Dwarakanath, in this field worked as an incentive when a suitable opportunity presented itself.

In those days, indigo plantation was a lucrative enterprise. Jyotirindranath stated an indigo farm on the right bank of the Padma. He started earnings profit in due course. Unfortunately, however, the formulation of a chemical process for the synthetic production of indigo dealt a death blow to indigo plantation in India. His indigo farm however lift him with a sizable capital which encouraged him to venture on a commercial enterprise. The need for a river transport service between Khulna and Barisal was then keenly felt. Jyotirindranath decided to finance a river transport service with that money. For this purpose, he bought the shell of a steamer which had been put to auction for Rs. 7000/-. He then fitted an engine to it and named it. 'The Sarojini'. Evidently, this was a favourite name of his. Previously, he had also named a drama 'Sarojini'. He opened a steamer service with this ship between Khulna and Barisal, on May, 1884.

In the meantime, an English company named the Flotilla Company had appeared in theatre. So a keen competition ensued between the two companies. To successfully contest the competition with his rival, Jyotirindranath bought four more ships. He named them 'the Swadeshi', 'the Bharat' 'the Bhagya Lakshmi' and 'the Lord Ripon' At one stage, he reduced the fare so much as a part of the strategy that his Company suffered loss. This did not dampen Jyotirindranath's spirit at all. But a cruel stroke of fate, forced him to withdraw from contest. The steamship 'Swadeshi' collided with a jetty near the

Howarh Bridge while plying on the Hooghli and sank. The Flotilla company sent a proposal for compromise just after this disaster. Jyotirindranath took advantage of this and withdrew from the competition after selling the remaining four ships to the Company.

Jyotirindranath also evinced keen interest in music. Thanks to his efforts, an atmosphere congenial to practice of music was built up in the family. Akshay Kumar Chaudhury, a solicitor of the Calcutta High Court, holding M.A. and B.L. degrees proved a competent assistant in this matter. Both shared common interest in music and literature. In fact, they were driven to each other for their common interest. Jyotirindranath's interest in music was so deep that he not only took lessons in music but in singing also and he worked hard to be a composer. He used to compose tunes played on the piano. Akshay Kumar Chaudhury was one of his collaborators.

Jyotirindranath found a second collaborator, in his younger brother, Rabindranath. Though still a boy, Jyotirindranath raised him to this position after being acquainted with his uncommon talents. How he made this discovery while writing his play 'Sarojini' has been narrated earlier. Jyotirindranath also mentions this in his reminiscences. This is what he says, "Just after the publication of Sarojini we raised Rabi to the status of our collaborator. Then onwards I myself carried our musical and literary activities together". [15]

Jyotirindranath would play the new tune on the piano, while both Akshay Chaudhury and Rabindranath would adapt them to suitable words in form of a song. Rabindranath described the process as follows:

"There was a stage when Jyotida was wholly occupied in composing new tune on the piano. Every day the dance of his fingers would produce a shower of music. It became the duty of Akhay Babu and myself to preserved them by linking them with words.

15. Rabindranath, Jivan Smriti.

It was this intensive practice of music which enabled Jyotirindranath to enrich Bengali music. He was the man who invented a system of notation for Bengali music. Admittedly, his elder brother Dwijendranath had carried on some pioneering work, but it is Jyotirindranath's system of notation which has gained wide acceptance. The gains of Dwijendranath's research in the field were embodied in an article bearing the title 'Sangeet Lipibaddha Karibar Pranali' (the Bengali system of notation) published in 1869 in the Tattabodini Patrika. By way of demonstration, five hymns of the Brahmo Samaj were shown in the notation proposed by him. Continuing his research on the same line Jyotirindranath at first introduced a system of notation based on number. His thesis on the subject named 'Ganer Swaralipi' (The Bengali system of notation) was published in the Bharati in 1295 B.S. (1889 A.D.) Sometime after this, he formulated the system of Notation based on vertical symbols. He gave complete shape to the new systems at the end of 1905 by introducing a complete set of symbols for this new system which has found general acceptance.

Jyotirindranath did not stop with inventing the new system of notation. He took special measures to give it publicity and popularise it. He compiled a book of 168 songs of distinguished composers together with their notation. It was published in 1897 under the title 'Swaralipi Geetimala' (Songs with their Notation) by Dwarkin & Company, famous dealers in musical instruments. The firm brought out a journal of music named 'Vinabadini'. The same year under the editorship of Jyotirindranath. According to Dr. Sushil Roy, the biographer of Jyotirindranath, that was the first journal on music in Bengali. Gopeswar Banerjee, a famous musician, however, says that claim should go to 'Alapani' a music journal, brought out by Manmathanath De before it.

Jyotirindranath's talents also found expression in some artistic works the value of which is being deeply appreciated. He was very fond of drawing. He used this skill in sketching portraits in lines of the different members of the Tagore family. He left numerous sketches of Rabindranath's face in different poses. In fact, his sketches covered almost every member of the family. In consequence, when no photography is available of a particular member of the family his sketch provides a fairly reliable substitute. These sketches, preserved in the museum attached to the Rabindranath Bharati University, are being extensively used for this purpose.

As works of art, these drawings had considerable merit. His linear drawings were highly appreciated by Western artists. Some of the portraits drawn by him were published in the Falgun issue of the Bharati in 1318. When these reached the hands of Rothenstein, the British artists, he expressed a desire to see more such drawings. In compliance with this wish, Rabindranath took with him more such portraits when he visited the United Kingdom for the third time in 1912. Rothenstein was deeply impressed. He communicated to Jyotirindranath by letter how much he liked them. The relevant part of the letter is quoted below:

"Let me thank you for your kindness in sending over the three books containing your drawings. As I expected from the reproductions, I saw in an article of your brother they are admirable. I know of few drawings which show at the same time so much sensitiveness of lines and sincerity in characterisation and there is a beauty and nobility in the expression you give to your portraits, which it will be difficult to match".[16]

Twentyfive collotypes from the original drawings of Jyotirindranath Tagore were published in England with the help of Rothenstein.[17]

---

16. Letter written by Rothenstein on 14th September 1912.

17. Twenty five collotypes from the original drawings of Jyotirindranath Tagore.

The most significant achievement of Jyotirindranath was his contribution towards the development of Rabindranath's talents. In age Jyotirindranath was older by twelve years, a gap which hardly permits any intimacy to grow between the two brothers. Even so, such intimacy did grow, thanks to two major factors. For one thing, Jyotirindranath was not only an artist but had the broadness of mind to appreciate talents of others. He would consequently, accept readily as partner anybody in whom he discovered talents.

Secondly, Rabindranath was himself so highly talented that his elder brother had no difficulty in discovering his talents at an early age. As already stated, the discovery was made through a dramatic situation. Jyotirindranath had, therefore, no hesitation in accepting this younger brother as a partner in artistic and literary pursuits on equal terms. It was proper that this should have happened. Otherwise, Rabindranath's talents would not have blossomed as they did. It appears that Rabindranath was aware of this. That is what inspired him to dedicate his play bearing the title 'Rudra Chanda' composed in his early age to Jyotirindranath as a token of gratitude. The contents of the dedicatory note gives a clear indications of his feelings as will be evident from the following quotation in translation:

"From childhood brother, you have led me by the hand.

And never allowed me to part company.

How carefully under the shade of your affection

You have protected me from hostile forces.

Today, I have to leave your protection to proceed abroad.

So I have come to you to bid you good-bye.

I have nothing to give worthy of your great love;

Still I have brought a gift which is within my capacity".

It will not, however, be correct to say that Jyotirindranath was the only person who helded in developing the talents of Rabindranath. The contribution made by another member of the family towards this objective is too valuable to be overlooked. She was Kadambari Devi, wife of Jyotirindranath. She came to this house as a newly-married bride on 5th July, 1868. She was endowed with qualities which attracted Rabindranth towards her spontaneously. She met some essential needs of the developing mind of Rabindranath by giving him her companionship, affection and unflinching service. The boy who had been denied looking after by a mother burdened with numerous children and had been brought up under the supervision of negligent servants, was overwhelmed with the affection and care showered by a new-comer made possible by a sudden stroke of luck. Indeed, to love-starved Rabindranath the advent of this young bride appeared to usher in his life a new chapter of happiness. His feelings find expression in the following poetical passage reminiscent of his boyhood days:

"In my early days when a daughter-in-law came to the family

From another house,

My mind which was like a boat in anchor

was tossed about by a tide.

The nationed pleasures of my routine life

were replaced by bounty".[18]

A sweet relationship grow up between the brother-in-law and the sister-in-law in due course. In diverse way did Rabindranath try to draw the affectionate attraction of his sister-in-law. There is a poem of Rabindranath dealing with the subject. He had acquired on one occasion some coloured glass beads and had hoped to spring a pleasant surprise by

18. Ākash Pradip, Kānch Āam.

presenting them to his sister-in-law. He hardly realised that though she was older by only two years she had attained enough maturity to descard them. So the present provoked her to remark disdainfully that she had no interest in things which can appeal to the fancy of children only. The poet describes the incident as follows in his reminiscences:

"One day this luckless one acquired
    Some coloured beads of glass
And thought he would spring a surprise
    She only laughed and said
'What shall I do with them?' [19]

The brother-in-law failed again and again in his efforts to please the sister-in-law. So he drew the conclusion that they had been made up different ingredients.

This unpleasant experience however, did not go altogether in vain. He made the discovery that there was a small door which gave access to the mind of his sister-in-law. The fact was that she was very fond of green mangoes which treated with chilly and an aromatic herb proved a delicacy to her taste. So this intelligent brother-in-law would collect green mangoes from the garden and supply them and in return be rewarded by kindly looks from her.

Not that this produced result every time. An instance of such failure finds mention at the end of the same poem. Many mangoes were dislodged from the trees on one occasion under the fury of a hailstorm. The young brother-in-law brought a basketful of them to the lady. Unfortunately, instead of rewarding, with a word of appreciation she took him to task for bringing them to her. This is how he describes in the poem how he felt and what he said in reply and followed it up by what action.

'One day I picked up a basketful of mangoes during a hailstorm.

19. Ākash Pradip, Kãncha Aãm

She said "Who asked you for them?"

I replied 'Nobody'.

I threw away the basket and left the place.[20]

During his boyhood he would pester his sister-in-law in many ways. He has left some record of them in his writings which may be conveniently recalled here. There was a time when the evening sittings on the roof of the family residence conducted by Jyotirindranath acquired considerable prestige. Jyotirindranath used to occupy in those days the suite of rooms in the western part of the second floor of the house. To its contiguous south was the garden of Kadambari Devi on the spacious roof. She had reared many flowering plants in coloured pots to decorate it. Music was served there in those evening sittings. Rabindranath was then too young to qualify for admission. One of the jokes played by him was to leave his study to steal a visit to the place and take away the ring of keys tied to the end of his sister-in-law's sari and hide it under a pot while she remained occupied with looking after the comfort of the guests. The poet records it as follows:

"On the roof, elder brother would play the violin placed on the shoulder"

And would play a tune matching with the serenity of the evening star.

I would approach sister-in-law discontinuing my evening lessons, to find

Her face reddened with the red border of her sari.

I would take her ring of keys and hide it under a pot-plant.

This is an example of the many ways in which

I gave expression of my love by playing Jokes".[21]

---

20. Ākash Pradip, Kāncha Āam

21. Chharāh chabi Balākā.

This is how this lady completely transformed the life of her brother-in-law by smothering him with affection and love. Nor did she fail to administer to his comforts with care and attention. Rabindranath's reminiscences bear clear evidence of the same. Rabindranath had not completed fourteen years of age when his mother died. Of the many daughters-in-law of the family, it was this lady who came forward to lighten his burden of grief in those dismal days by words of comfort and personal attention. Rabindranath acknowledges this debt to her as follows:

"It was the youngest daughter-in-law of the family who took charge of these orphaned boys. It was she who tried night and day to make us forget our loss by looking after us and keeping us close to her". [22]

At a later stage, when Rabindranath's poetical talent made its existence felt, it was again this lady who provided him the umbrage of affection to help him develop as a poet. She would not only encourage him to compose poems but never failed to make herself available to listen to their first recital. This is how this budding poet passed his period of probation under her sympathetic patronage. Fortunately, the lady had not only acquired the necessary skill to create the atmosphere for the development of the power of the uncommon boy-poet, but also to direct him along right lines. Her early marriage imposed by social custom prevailing in those days, failed to kill her natural interest in literary works. Her keen interest in the subject enabled her to create the atmosphere necessary to sustain her literally interests in the house of her father-in-law. Reading was not a mere pastime to her, but a subject which drew her serious attention. Even as Jyotirindranath had accepted Rabindranath as a collaborator in his musical studies, Kadambari Devi made him a partner in her literary pursuits. The following observation of Rabindranath becomes relevant in this connection deeply:

22. Jiban Smriti Mityo Sokha.

"She did not read Bengali books just to while away the time but she enjoyed reading with her entire mental faculty. I joined her in her literary pursuits".[23]

During this period Beharilal Chakravorty had found recognition as one of the leading poets of this time. In fact, he played a significant role in the history of the Bengali poetical literature of the nineteenth century. Ishwar Chandra Gupta who flourished in the first half of the century, was the only poet left completely untouched by Western culture. After him, contact with English literature made its influence felt on Bengali poetry. Michael Madhusudan Dutta was the leader who initiated the change. It was he who introduced the blank verse in Bengali literature and introduced a new diction in his epic poem, 'Meghnadbadh'. It was again he who introduced the sonnet in Bengali literature. No wonder, he was a dominating force in Bengali literature towards the end of the century. Hemchandra Banerjee and Nabing Chandra Sen followed his example by producing more epics in blank verse.

But Bengali poetry did not evolve on the line adopted by Michael. It showed its preference for the lyrical style instead and it was Beharilal Chakravorti, who set the example. He avoided the style introduced by Michael in his own epic 'Sarada Mangal' also. He used the rhymed verse instead which displayed considerable lyrical quality.

Beharilal was the friend of Dwijendranath, the eldest brother of Rabindranath, and used to visit the residence of the Tagores off and on. After reading his 'Sarada Mangal' Kadambari Devi became one of his staunchest admirers. Her admiration found expression in entertaining Beharilal, when he would visit their house. No wonder, a sweet relationship developed between the poet and his admirer with poetry serving as the link.

23. Jiban Smriti, Sahity Sangi.

Kadambari Devi's profound interest for this poet did not find full satisfaction by entertaining him only, but also compelled her to give him a present as well. The present she decided on not only speaks of her originality, but also deep interest in poetry. She weaved for him a small carpet to sit on in the centre of which she quoted a stanza from the poet's 'Sarada Mangal'. A translation of the same is given below:

"Oh supreme Mediator sitting on the
Seat of meditation with
Two unseeing eyes
Whom do you meditate on,
in utter unconcern?"

She named the carpet 'Sadher Asan'. Rabindranath makes the following observation about this.

"At about this time, Beharilal Chakravorty's 'Sarada Mangal' and songs were appearing in the journal 'Aryadarshan'. Sister-in-law was overwhelmed with the lyrical excellence of the poetical composition. She even committed to memory a considerable part of it. She used to invite him to dinner frequently and on one occasion presented him a carpet seat woven by herself".

The concluding part of the story about this present may be conveniently narrated here. The sudden death of Kadambari Devi hurt the poet deeply and he felt that he should answer the question quoted in the carpet. So his pen produced another book of poem which also he named 'Sadher Asan'. An attempt was made her to surmise what the creator meditates on. The story of the birth of this book is as fascinating, as the subject matter is extraordinary. So Kadambari Devi continued to enrich Bengali literature even after her death in different ways.

We may now return to the main topic. It appears that there was need for such an affectionate sister-in-law deeply interested in literature to guide along the right course this budding poet of promise, as he crossed his state of adolescence into youth. Rabindranath has himself labelled this stage of his poetical life as the stage of copy book that is probation. The term is apt, for this is the stage when on the one hand, the poet should be encouraged to compose poem, it was also necessary to prevent him develop any feeling of egotism by becoming conscious of his extraordinary talents. At this stage of immaturity excess of confidence in his power was likely to hamper attainment of greater excellence.

It may be presumed that his sister-in-law was awake to the need for such a rigorous prescription. On the one hand, we find her a sympathetic listener, who encouraged the poet to compose poems and publish them in the form of books. On the other hand, she would not hesitate to discourage him by belittling his poetical power to save him from the contagion of egotism induced by a feeling of satisfaction.

This lady provided Rabindranath constant companionship during this formative stage. When they stayed at the family residence at Jorasanko they would naturally be together. When she would live with her husband away from home, she would also take Rabindranath with her. Thus when this couple lived in a hired house at Chandra Nagar, Rabindranath stayed with them. That was the time when he composed the collection of poems bearing the title 'Sandhya Sangit'. At a subsequent stage, when they lived in a rented house at Sudder Street in Calcutta. Rabindranath was with them. It was here that the scenic beauty of sunrise experienced by him provided him the inspiration that produced the famous poem 'Nirjharer Swapnabhanga' (the Awakening of the Cataract).

Rabindranath gratefully acknowledges his debt in the year of Kadamabari Devi's death that during his boyhood, she had listened to his poem with sympathy and encouraged him to write. The lady committed suicide on 11th April 1884 for a reason which is still a mystery. Tagore. published two books of poems composed in his boyhood days immediately after 'Bhanu Singh Thakur's Padabali' is one of them. Rabindranath made the discovery that Thomas Chatterton created considerable sensation in his boyhood by successfully imitating the style of earlier poets. Spurred by a desire to follow his example, Rabindranath also composed some poems, after the style of the Vaisnava poets. These were published in different issues of the family magazine 'Bharati' between 1877 and 1881. This period covered the age from sixteen to twenty years of the poet. The dedicatory remarks of the poet clearly indicate that it was Kadambari Devi who had encouraged him to write these poems. This book of poems was first published in 1884 immediately after the death of Kadambari Devi and was dedicated to her. The dedication is worded as follows:

"You had requested me repeatedly to publish the poems of 'Bhanu Singh's Padabali'. But it did not comply with your request. Today I have published it; but you are not here to see them".

The second book bears the title 'The Saishab Sangeet'. It was very probably published immediately after the other book in the same year 1884. Previous to that several other books of his like 'Valmiki Pratibha', 'Sandhya Sangit and 'Prabhat Sangit' had been already published. The poems which found place in the Saishab Sangit' had been composed before them. The author himself states that they had been composed between the ages of thirteen to eighteen years. Presumably, he did not publish them earlier as they were immature in character. But we find that he published them immediately after the death of his sister-in-law. Probably, the shock of her death induced him to publish them. Presumably he desired to dedicate them to the lady whose affectionate encouragement made them blossom. This will be borne out by the dedicatory remarks of the 'Saishab Sangit' which run as follows:

"I give these poems to you. It is a long time ago that I used to compose them in your presence and recite them to you. They embody the memory of your affection. So I am led to believe that your eyes will not fail to see them".

This is one side of the picture. The sister-in-law had equal skill to encourage the poet to write and to restrain him when necessary. There was the possibility that continuous praise of a person who had showed his poetic powers from early age might feed his egotism and lead to the slackening of efforts for self-improvement. Kadambari Devi took necessary steps to prevent that possibility, through her own conduct. She would never allow this young poet to realise how well he wrote; on the contrary, she took care to make him believe that his poetic talents were moderate. The following observations of Rabindranath will bear this out:

"My ambition in those days made me aspire to write poems like Beharilal at most. There might have been days when I might have indulged in the thought that my poems are so good as his; but this admirer of poet, Beharilal, prevented me from indulging in such vain thoughts. She would always remind me that being endowed with scanty skill, ran the risk of making myself ridiculous by entertaining such ideas. She must have realised that once my egotism was allowed to raise its head; it would be difficult to keep it under control". [24]

Swarna Kumari Devi, fourth daughter of Maharshi, distinguished herself most among his daughters. She was five years older than Rabindranath and was married to Janakinath Ghoshal. The atmosphere that fostered literary activity among the men of the family appeared to have penetrated into the inner apartments of the women. She was equally at ease in producing short stories, novels and dramas. Her first novel bearing the title 'The Dipnirvan' was published

24. Jiban Samriti, Sahityer Sangi.

in 1870. She was also a competent composer of poems. Her numerous literary works include two songs with musical notations. She edited the family magazine named, 'Bharati' for serval years. Admittedly, she was the first Bengali lady who distinguished herself as a writer.

Jyotirindranath has recorded some observations about the literary talents of this lady in his reminiscences. It has been already stated that he had mentioned there that Akshay Chaudhury was his principal collaborator in his literary pursuits and that he accepted Rabindranath also, as collaborator, in spite of the difference of age between them, in consideration of his literary skill. In the same context, he observes that he also accepted his sister, Swarana Kumari as a co-worker of competence. The relevant passage is quoted below in translation:

"When Janaki (her husband) proceeded to the United Kingdom for higher education, Swaran Kumari came to live with us. This enabled us to have her as another worthy fellow-worker in our literary pursuits". [25]

25. Jyotirindranath's Smriti.

5

RABINDRANATH-I

It is proposed to treat Rabindranath as the youngest son of Maharshi. It is true that another son was born after him; but he died a baby in the very first year of his life. Rabindranath was born in his paternal house at Jorasanko, on 25th Vaisakh, 1265, of the Bengali calendar. This day is, at present, observed as a day of great rejoicing in Bengali society. It corresponded to 7th May 1861, of the English calendar. At present, the link is not being maintained as 25th Baiskah tends to correspond with 8th May.

The curiosity of the fellow countrymen of such an outstanding personality cannot be satisfied by the mere acquaintance of the house where he was born. They would additionally expect to know in which room of the house at Jorasanko the happy event of his birth took place. Extensive investigation on the point appears to have yielded some result. The matter may be conveniently disposed of before taking up the life story of Rabindranath.

Of all the numerous books dealing with Rabindranath, Asit Halder's book 'The Rabitirths' alone touches on this subject. Evidently, he was competent to speak on it as he happened to be the grandson of Maharshi's daughter Swarna Kumari and had by virtue of this kinship had occasion to visit the house and live there in many occasions. It was during one such visit that Saudamini Devi, eldest daughter of Maharshi showed him the room in which Rabindranath was born. Asit Halder writes as follows on the subject in his book:

"I had the good fortune of being showed the room in which the distinguished father and son (Debendranath and Rabindranath respectively) were born when I was a boy of about nine to ten. My eldest great-aunt (Saudamini Devi) took me one day for some reason I cannot explain, up the badly lighted staircase of the inner apartment of the Jorasanko house. The room was assessible both half-way from the staircase and from the higher level of the second storey. It initiates the condition of Harish Chandra of the Purana in that it appears to hang between the ground floor and the first floor. It is fitted with only two doors at the two ends and consequently did not admit much light. Pointing to this room, great aunt said 'look Asit, this is the room in which father was born and all his children including your mother were born. You were also born in this same room". [1]

Luckily for us, I got Asit Halder one day at the Maharshi Bhavan. I took this opportunity of drawing his attention to the observation in his book referred to above and requested him to find out for us the room described by him. There are many staircases in this sprawling house. The room in question must be linked with one of them. He tried but to our misfortune failed to identify it. He was, however, positive that this staircase was located in the middle of the southern part of the house. I had also heard from other members of the family that the room of the confinement was located in the southern part of the house as stated by Asit Halder. Nobody who had direct knowledge, however, was living at the time. Incidentally, I had an occasion to discuss the matter with Amita Devi, wife of Ajinendranath, grandson of Dwijendranath Tagore. She confirmed Asit Halder's

1. Aist Halder, Rabi Tirtha.

claim in substance. She also showed me a room which she thought was the room pointed out to Asit Halder by his great-aunt. It was indeed linked with a staircase. It is situated between the big courtyard adjoining the 'Thakurdalan' in the western part of the house and the small courtyard to its east in the southern part of the house. It was linked with the staircase at the middle part but no link existed with the stair at the time though there was indication that there had been a link in the past. It was apparent that the exit had been walled up at a subsequent stage. I got access to it from the first floor and was satisfied that it had only two doors.

For confirmation that this was the room which had been shown to Asit Halder by Saudamini Devi, we asked Hemlata Devi, the eldest daughter-in-law of Dwijendranath, the oldest member of the family then living, whether she kept any information about the matter. Her opinion on the question has been recorded for preservation and is quoted below:

"You have asked me to identify the room of the Jorasanko where uncle Rabindranath was born. There was a bathroom in the east on the second storey of that part of the building of the courtyard in the south. It fell to our share and Ajin used to live there at a later stage. The room contiguous to the bathroom was used for confinement for delivery. The members of the family including uncle Rabindranath were born there. Unfortunately, we could not preserve the room. When the family expanded that room along with the bathroom was demolished and new rooms were constructed".[2]

Evidently, she does not corroborate Asit Halder's version. He meant a room to the west of the same courtyard. It is difficult, therefore, to come to a positive finding on the issue. According to Hemlata Devi, the room in question has disappeared; but the room referred to by Asit Halder still exists. What makes his version more reliable is the fact that he

2. This comment is taken from a tape record of Hemlata Devi.

had been shown the room by nobody other than Rabindranath's eldest sister who attended the birth. On the other hand, Hemlata Devi's version is based on hearsay. Saudamini Devi's version appears to be more reliable.

A person born as the youngest child of a numerous family has to face many inconveniences. This holds good of poor families; nor are affluent families immune. Rabindranath's childhood is a fine example in point. Mother of numerous children, Sarada Devi had lost the capacity to look after him. So he was entrusted to the care of servants. Very aptly, Rabindranath has labelled this period of his life as the period of 'citizenship in the kingdom of servants.' After shutting him up in a room situated in a corner of the southern part of the house, the servants used to attend to their chores. Luckily for him, a window to the south admitted access to a view of a stretch of a garden with a pond in the centre. But for this, his days of confinement would have been unbearable. He records the memory of these days in a poem as follows:

"I remained confined in a room
In the corner of a very old house;
I was forbidden to move out.
The servants prepared betel leaf—for chewing and
Stained the walls by rubbing their hands on them,
And hummed the tune of Madhukan's songs.
The floor of the room was of cement concrete
And the windows were fitted with Venetion shutters.
Down below was a pond with masonry stairs
And a line of coconut palms along the boundary wall.
Clinging to its east bank
With stout roots stood a banyan tree with aerial roots".[3]

3. Punacha, Bālak.

The presiding deity of this Kingdom of servants was a man named Iswar. Having functioned as a primary school teacher in his early life he had acquired some education. Unfortunately, he was addicted to opium, an addiction which demands nutritous food. He felt no brick of conscience to take advantage of the fact that he had been entrusted with the duty of feeding the children of the family, to deprive them of their due share of food for providing himself with nutritous food. Consequently, Rabindranath was deprived of nourishing food in his boyhood. Not that this servant left no pleasant memories at all. He used to give readings from the Ramayana and the Mahabharata to entertain the children in the evening. This must have been a pleasant experience to this imaginative boy. It appears that as he grew up he was allowed some freedom of movement. Otherwise, how could he steal visits to the bathroom fitted with taps in the third storey reserved for his father? As his father then spent most of the time away from home in the Himalayas; it was not difficult for him to enjoy the thrill of a shower bath in that bathroom.

It is lucky that during Rabindranath's boyhood, then compound of the house of the Tagores had not been denuded of trees and shrubs as at present. In those days the compound enclosed two gardens, one situated to the east of Maharshi Bhavan and the other to its south. The southern garden contained a tank fitted with masonry stairs. On its south-east bank stood a banyan tree of the Chinese variety putting into shade a considerable area. Along the eastern fringe of both the gardens was a row of coconut palms. The space at present occupied by the Vichitra Bhavan lay vacant at the time. It was used for exercising the horses maintained for pulling carriage. To its north-west stood a gigantic tamarind tree. The shrubs and trees situated all about the compound offered some contact with nature to young Rabindranath, though born in an urban setting.

It was this pond, these trees and these gardens which were the major objects of interest to Rabindranath in his boyhood. The rays of the morning sun playing on the rows of coconut palms charmed him. No wonder, he would leave his bed every day before sunrise to visit the garden. He hated to miss this lovely sight even for a day. The aesthetic sense of one who was destined to be the greatest poet of his country thus asserted itself at this tender age of his life. He recalls this pleasant experience in his old age as follows:

"I used to get up to pay a visit to the garden

Long before the crow called

Lest I was denied

Presence in the ritual of sunrise

Through the undulating leaves of the coconut palms.[4]

In his childhood days the entire world appeared to him to be packed with wonder. The endless flow of life all round him moved him deeply. The plants produced flowers, flowers produced fruits, furits produced seeds and from seeds sprang other trees. This chain of events filled his mind with a sense of mystery and wonder. To satisfy his curiosity he collected in the corner of his study some dust and sand and planted in it the seed of custard apple on one.

Occasion and eagerly awaited the day when he would see a plant sprout from it. The memory of such events would revive in old age. He recalls his experience in a poem as follows:

"I had a great expectation in my mind

That I shall get custard apple from

(the plant that will germinate from)

the seed I shall sow.

---

4. Shesh Sahtak-46.

I was then only ten years old.

How some thing comes out of something

was a mystery to me.

In a corner of the spacious verandah of the first floor

I gathered rubbish for his purpose".[5]

No efforts were showed in this family to educate the children. There was also provision for physical culture and music lessons. There was an open space to the north of the house known as the storage yard. Wrestling used to take place in plot contiguous to that. The place subsequently housed of a factory for the production of perfumes; but it is now vacant. The land lies to the contiguous north of the prayer hall. A Punjabi wrestler used to teach wrestling there. The services of distinguished musicians were engaged to give lessons in music. Bishnu Chakravarty was one of them. Having a natural aptitude for music, Rabindranath used to pick up his lessons quickly. At that time, there were three boys of more or less the same age in the family; Rabindranath, immediate elder brother, Somendra and Satyo, the son of their eldest sister and Rabindranath. The other two were only two years older than Rabindranath. They used to take lessons together, go to school together, play together and sleep together in the same room.

Lessons in the alphabet bored young Rabindranath very much. He had not the patience to learn the shape of the letters of the alphbet and the transformation they undergo, when joined with other letters and then master a whole sentence constituted by several words. No wonder, reading was a painful process to him. Luckily in course of taking lessons in the first part of Iswar Chandra Vidyasagar's alphabet book, he came across the rhymed sentences, 'Rain is falling, leaves are dancing'. The passage thrilled him.

5. Chharāh Chhabi, Āfār Bichi.

The beauty of nature thus captured in rhymed words held him spell-bound. He realised that the painful process of mastering the alphabet does bring compensation; it gives access to the world of poetry. This discovery induced him to take his Bengali lessons seriously. Rabindranath has put on record the thrill he felt on discovering that letters can combine to produce rhymed words. A quotation of the same is given below in translation :

"The rhymed words 'Rain is falling, leaves are dancing' come back to memory again and again. I had then just weathered the storm of lessons of spelling. And then I came across words in verse like this. To me that appeared to be the first poem written by the first poet when. I recall the joy I felt that day, I realise why rhyme is such an essential part of poetry".[6]

These three boys got admitted to the Oriental Seminary. They did not, however, stay there long. Be that as it may, the first lessons at school must have deeply impressed Rabindranath. That explains why he desired at this stage to play the role of a teacher. That desire used to be fulfilled by treating the railings of the verandahs of his house as his pupils and maintaining discipline with the help of a stick.

After a short stay at the Oriental Seminary, they get themselves admitted to the Normal School. Rabindranath passed very miserable days there. He used to avoid the company of fellow-students and while away his time alone. The vulgar conduct of the class-fellows repelled him. He stood first in Bengali in the annual examination here. Presumably, his introduction to poetry in course of taking lessons in the alphabet developed his interest in Bengali literature and made this possible. He was not a boy to take examinations seriously.

It was at this stage that he got his first lessons in the art of writing poems. It was a nephew of his

6. Jiban Smriti, Shiksharambh.

name Jyotiprakash who encouraged him in these efforts. He was the daughter of Girindranath, second brother of Debendranath and was seven to eight years older. He even taught Rabindranath how to compose verse in the 'payer' metre with fourteen letters in a line rhyming at the end. A fertile soil yields quick harvest. The pupil soon developed an itch to write poems. He started writing poems on a book with blue covers, supplied by a member of the staff of the family estates. His elder brother Somendranath not only listened to these poems, but became proud of his younger brother's achievement. To give publicity to his brother's performance, he even showed these poems to Nabagopal Mitra. It is a pity that one who felt so much proud of the poetical talent of his younger brother in his boyhood was denied the delight he would have felt to see his brothers achieve world-wide fame afterwards through subsequent loss of sanity.

In no time the news spread that this boy could write poems. It reached even the ears of a teacher of his school who questioned him for confirmation and then listened to his poems. But the westener whom he appreciated most was Srikanta Sinha. He was the uncle of Lord Satyendra Prasanna Sinha and as old as his grandfather. He had the wonderful capacity of being at ease in company of people of all ages. Incidentally, he turned into an intimate friend of these boys. It was through his good offices that a group photo of these three boys is available today. He had the inspiration of taking these boys one day to a British photographer and get a group photo taken inclusive of himself. Incidentally, this happens to be the first photograph ever taken of Rabindranath.

The boys were withdrawn from the Normal School on account of an unforeseen development. The matter was simple; but their nephew Satya's mishandling turned it into a disaster. A teacher of this school wanted to read the biography of Dwarkanath written by Kishori Chand Mitra. This could be had only by directly approaching Debendranath himself. Satya was entrusted with the task. He thought that a senior member of the family should not be spoken to in colloquial language and so asked for the book in chaste language. Debendranath mistook this to be a speciman of the style of Bengali taught in their school. So he forbade them to take lessons in Bengali there. In consequence, they were withdrawn from the school.

After that, they were admitted to a school named Bengal Academy run by an Anglo-Indian. They were not burdened there with heavy tasks, nor were they denied freedom of movement. But young Rabindranath did not like the atmosphere there and so he through of all possible tricks to play truant successfully. In the process, he discovered an easy way. At that time, his elder brothers had engaged the services of a scholar to teach them Persian. This training would generously comply with young Rabindranath's request to address a letter to the Headmaster asking him to permit the boy to absent himself from school. Needless to add, frequently used of this trick.

Then came the sacred thread ceremony of these three boys simultaneously. So Maharshi had to come down from the tells to perform the ceremony. After this, he decided to take his youngest son with him on his next trip. On the way, he halted at Bolpur for a few days. That was incidentally the first occasion Rabindranath travelled by railway train. A few months later Rabindranath returned home. After testing a life of freedom the idea of attending school repelled him. He was then admitted to the St. Xavier's School for a change; but his attitude did not change, Unfortunately, he discontinued attending school of his own accord. His father was an absentee from home. His elder brothers failed to persuade him to attend school. So they gave up in despair in desperation. His eldest sister expressed her regret. Rabindranath recollects these unpleasant memories thus:

"My elder brothers gave up all hope for me after some futile efforts. They even discontinued scolding me. One day eldest sister remarked, 'we had all hoped that Rabi will distinguish himself in life; but it was his prospects which were blighted most'. One, however, feels curious to know what reaction was produced in his eldest sister's mind when, confounding everybody who had entertained no hope for his future, Rabindranath captured the heart of the people of the world by winning the position of a poet with international fame. This affectionate sister must have felt infinite joy to find that her hope had been realised in a different way".

Young Rabindranath's stay in the Himalayas in company of his father for a few months carried special significance, in that it influenced his future career. His father used to travel alone and had never taken any of his sons to keep him company. He had come to Calcutta to supervise the sacred thread ceremony of his two sons and grandson. Ordinarily, he should have left alone after the completion of the ceremony. It was a good stroke of luck that he decided to take Rabindranath with him. There is no reason to explain why he chose thus particular boy in a group of three, when all of them were being brought up together, questions like this expect an answer. Probably, he found some promise of future greatness in Rabindranath which roused in his a desire that his own personality should produce an impact on the boy. Needless to say that the result of the impact proved wholly satisfactory. This small episode carried considerable significance in preparing this boy for his future career.

It was decided that on the way to the Himalayas, Maharshi would spend a few days in the Ashram of Santiniketan. This small affair exercised profound influence on the life of Rabindranath. He was stepping into adolescence, but had little experience of life outside his home at Jorasanko. Only once during his early life the members of the family spent a few days in the garden house of Ashutosh Deb at Panihati, when a dengue epidemic raged over Calcutta. That was the first occasion he lived outside Calcutta. But he could not enjoy his stay as his guardian denied him the liberty of free movement. He had to remain confined within the house. On this background, the prospect of living for a few days at Bolpur became an attractive proposition to Rabindranath. The experience of his recent journey by railway to Bolpur as narrated by his nephew Satya who used to be his constant companion, added to his excitement. But this was partly mixed up with apprehension, as Satya had expressed an apprehension on the basis of his own experience that journey by railway was unsafe, unless one had special skill to avoid danger there was considerable risk of being thrown down when the train is in motion. So he got into the train with much trepidation, but was relieved to find that his own experience did not confirm his nephew's version. Evidently, the nephew had given a fanciful description to boost his own egotism.

His first stay at Santiniketan proved to be the first experience of romance in Rabindranath's life. This is not to be accounted for by the scenic beauty of the boundless expanse of fields touching the horizon of the rush of rainwater on the undulated terrain of the place. The major factor was his father, who gave him the freedom to have unrestricted access to the terrain of Bolpur. He felt he was playing the role of Living stone in this unexplored area. Far from discouraging his son, Maharshi gave him all possible incentives. When he would present pebbles collected in course of his rambles, his father would thrill him with words of appreciation of the beauty of his collection. The following extract from a poem shows that he retained vividly in his old age the memory of the pleasant days he passed at Santiniketan.

"I had come there in my boyhood;

I had imagined fanciful mysteries,

Round tiny caves on mounds

And the gushing rain waters;

I had played with pebbles;

In lovely noons all by myself.[7]

It is perhaps the fact that the first days passed at Santiniketan, which proved such a romantic experience sweetened by pleasant memories, that a strong bond was forged between Rabindranath and Bolpur. That perhaps explains why. Bolpur inexorably induced him to select it as the place of his activities in the latter part of his life. This association with Maharshi appears to have profoundly influenced his future life.

His life at Brakrutan in the Dalhousie area with his father exercised an equally profound influence on him. The father and the son paid a visit to Amritsar on the way and then started living in a bungalow on the top of a hill. The scenic beauty of this region enscoved in the Himalaya must have overwhelmed this boy, brought up on the plains of Bengal. His father also provided him the full opportunity to enjoy his stay. He gave him the permission to move about freely in the fine forest. Moreover, the profound respect he felt for his father for his saintly character, piety unruffled conduct and outstanding personality sweetened their relationship by enhancing his affection for his father. It must have indirectly exercised tremendous influence on his character. How could he otherwise acquire the competence to compose the poems published in the 'Naivedya' and 'Gitanjali'.

It is very likely that his father kept Rabindranath near him for some time, deliberately for the purpose of infusing a desire in him to acquire knowledge. This

7. Punarcha Khoyai.

is suggested by Maharshi's conduct. He brought with him a large number of text books which included 'Parley's Tales' the Biography of Benjamin Franklin', 'Riju Path (second part), Astronomy of Proctor. A rigorous course of teaching was enforced in course of the day. The first sitting took place in the morning, followed by a second sitting after morning walk. The last sitting followed the midday meal. The method of teaching was distinctly original. When a lesson of the Sanskrit primer the 'Raju Path' were finished, he encouraged his son to make sentences with the new words learned by him. He would teach some facts of astronomy and then asked the boy to put in writing what he had been taught. The method distinguished itself scope for freedom in pursuit of knowledge.[8]

It appears that despite its short duration, this coaching left lesting influence on his youngest son. There is no doubt that this coaching increased Rabindranath's interest in Sanskrit literature. Immediately after return from the Himalayas, he sprang a surprise on his mother by giving a reading of a passage from the Ramayana of Valmiki. This story, reported previously, shows that such contact with Sanskrit classical literature deeply impressed him. There is a long dissertation bearing the title 'Tapovan' in the collection of essays named 'Santiniketan'. We find in it an interesting and detailed account of the ancient forest settlement given in Sanskrit poetical works, dramas and epics. That shows that Rabindranath had read Sanskrit literature seriously. In fact, he was deeply impressed by the impact produced by hermitages on the educational system of those ancient days. This is what led him to build up his school at Santiniketan after the model of these forest settlements. Similarly, the lessons given in astronomy must have attracted him to the study of science. His poetical aptitude did not stifle his interest in science. An example in point in the fact that he employed scientific methods in his rural

8. Jiban Smirit a Journey to Himalaya.

development scheme at Sriniketan for improving agricultural methods. In fact, his poetry never ignored established scientific theories; on the contrary, his power of imagination spun out fascinating poems based on scientific facts. A reference may be made in this connection to the philosophy of creation as described in the poem bearing the title 'Nataraj'. In it, astronomical facts have been transformed by the magic touch of his poetic powers into a work of art. There is an account recorded by the poet himself of the deep interest his father took in teaching him astronomy. He says : "I accompanied father to Dalhousie when I was twelve years of age. After a day-long journey carried on the shoulders of porters we reached our destination in the evening. He would sit in the courtyard on a stool. Presently the stars appeared to descend into the transparent blackness of the night filling the deep blue sky framed among the encircling mountain ranges. He would identify to me the different stars and planets. He also told me the distance of the orbits of the different planets from the sun, the time they took to go round the sun, and other related facts". [9]

After return from the Himalyas Rabindranath's aversion to formal education intensified. When he gave up attending school the senior members of his family despaired about his future. His subsequent conduct will, however, show that he was different from boys who play truant. There is no doubt that he developed an aversion for school but his earning for acquisition of knowledge continued. Small wonder, we find him initiate a process of self-education. This allowed him the freedom to select his own subject of study and in consequence, the process of self-education was conducted to his own satisfaction, in keeping with his own taste and inclination. Some relevant materials may be referred to in this connection.

9. Viswaparichaya.

The boy felt a special attraction for books which were kept beyond the reach of young boys educated in schools, far being considered unsuitable for them. 'Jamai Barik' a comic by Dinabandhu Mitra had just been published. It had been kept in a box by a lady of the family. He had no hesitation to steal the ring of keys tied to the corner of her sari to get access to it. He mentions about this thrilling experience in his reminiscences.

There was a bound book containing a collection of several issues of the journal 'Bibidhartha Sangraha' edited by Rajendralal Mitra in an almirah belonging to his third brother Hemendranath. He found a lot of interest in the contents of this journal. There was another monthly journal named 'Abodh Bandhu'. The issues of this journal were felt unbound in an almirah belonging to his eldest brother Dwijendranath. He read them also. The Tagores regularly subscribed for the compilation called 'Prachin Kavya Sangraha' (collection of old poetry) edited by Sarada Charan Mitra and Akshayay Sarkar. It used to publish poems of Vidyapati, Chandidas, Govindadas and other poets. Vaisnava which proved very interesting to him. It was thus possible for him to acquire intimate knowledge about Vaisnava literature at such early stage enabled him to spring a surpirise on the literary world by producing a book like the 'Bhanusingher Padavali'. Thomas Chatterton's example prompted him to compose the poems contained in it after the style of the Vaisnava poets. The adoption of a pseudonym caused a lot of confusion. The invitation of the style adopted in Vaisnava poetry was executed with such skill that scholars mistook Bnanusinha Thakur to be an old Vaisnava poet and serious research work was undertaken an this fictitious writer. There is no second example of such curious development in the history of the literature of the world.

Afterwards when he was seventeen, it was decided that Rabindranath should go to the United Kingdom for education at the suggestion of his second brother Satyendranath Tagore. His father consented to this when Satyendranath pressed hand for this. It was decided that Rabindranath should be trained for being called to the Bar. Satyendranath's wife was then staying at Brighton with her children, while he himself was stationed at Ahmedabad as the District Judge. At the behest of his second brother, Rabindranath joined him at his place of work, preparatory to their departure for England. Satyendranath's residential house was located at Shahibag in the outskirts of the city, on the bank of the Sabarmati river. It was in fact an old place built during the time of the Mughal emperors. When his brother would work in his court, Rabindranath had to stay alone in that ancient house. That is what provided him the inspiration for his famous story named 'Kshudhita Pashan' (Hungry Stones). The unusual atmsphere of this palace not only activated his imagination, but also provided him the opportunity for self-education. He was shortly to leave for England but his command over English was not satisfactory. Facing this challenge, the young man felt that he should utilise the quiet atmosphere of the house to brush up his knowledge of English. For this he depended entirely on his own resources. He started reading books of English literature selected from his elder brother's collection and read them assiduously with the aid of a dictionary.

Rabindranath embarked with his brother for the United Kingdom on 20th September 1878. After arrival he joined his sister-in-law's establishment at Brighton, and got admitted to a local school. After sometime he moved to a house in London near Regent Park. London wearing its winter garment of snow did not please him at all. He then left that place to live as a paying guest of a gentleman named Scott. He liked the place. He then took admission to the University College where he picked up acquaintance with Loken Palit who was preparing for the I.C.S. competitive examination. Despite some difference in age a friendship bound them together for long years. In after-life Loken Palit exchanged views on different aspects of literature with Rabindranath and took a lively interest in his literacy activities.

In the meantime, his elder brother's long leave was about to expire. Their father directed that Rabindranath should come back along with his brother. So the desire to come back as a barrister remained unrealised. The eighteen months' stay in the United Kingdom, however, enriched his student life in diverse ways. For one thing, intimate contact with a powerful, vigorous and lively race is itself a great reward. Secondly, it offered him an opportunity for study of English literature. Incidentally, his sojourn enabled him to pick up an acquaintance with Western music. Such experience was indispensable for one who had to distinguish himself as one of the leading composers of his country in after-life. He returned home in February 1880.

Ordinarily, it is the lot of the youngest child of a family to face many inconveniences. Parents cannot pay the necessary attention to them simply because they have hardly the capacity to do so. Moreover, the attention paid to him by the numerous elder brothers and sisters subject him to such extreme pressure that his talents are stifled. Between absence of attention from one party and overdose of the same from another the child's mind is ground to pieces.

Rabindranath's case was, however, an exception. Admittedly, his mother could not look after him at all. On the other hand, his father was an absentee from home as he spent most of his days in contemplation and devotional practices in the Himalayas. But that was more than compensated for by the congenial atmosphere created in the family by his elder brother, sister and sister-in-law. The members of the families of the two sons of Dwarkanath lived together in the residential houses of Jorasanko. The family of the first occupied the older building at present called the Maharshi Bhavan. The family of Girindra, the second brother lived in the contiguous building to the south-west. They were so closely linked together that they behaved like a single family. Gunendra, the eldest son of Girindra, enjoyed the status of the Mejda (Second brother) in the two families as he was born just after Dwijendranath, the eldest son of Debenaranath.

The members of both the families were inspired by a sense of high idealism. They were all imbued with intense patriotic feelings. They adhered strictly to a national style of living and dressing. They developed an intense desire to enrich their language, literature and cultural heritage. This inspired the different members of the family to build up an atmosphere in the family hardly met with elsewhere. It is this atmosphere which was a major factor in shaping Rabindranath's character in his early life.

It appears that Rabindranath himself was fully aware of this. His reminiscences which recall the contribution of his elder brothers towards building up the atmosphere in the house will bear this out.

"My elder brothers were very enthusiastic about literature and fine arts. They tried their best to foster the renaissance movement of Bengal. An all-round patriotic idealism asserted itself through their style or dressing, their compositions, their paintings and dramas, and their religious and patriotic activities".[10]

It is this rare atmosphere obtaining in the family which contributed mainly to the development of Rabindranath's diverse talents. It functioned like the congenial conditions which help a flower-plant to blossom. The attention of florist is, of course, desirable, but good soil, open surroundings and sunlight are essential conditions. This analogy aptly applies to the case of Rabindranath. Admittedly, he was endowed with extraordinary talents; but he should be considered fortunate that he was given an atmosphere which seldom falls in the lot of the others. Few have the luck of being blessed with such sympathetic and talented elder members of the family.

10. Jivan Smirit Barir Ãhāwā.

There is no doubt at all that the congenial atmosphere they built up in their home through their diverse activities facilitated the development of Rabindranath's talents. The different members of the family assiduously applied their talents to diverse fields like literature, music promotion of nationalistic feelings, staging of dramas and similar subjects. In fact, the house of the Tagores at Jorasanko functioned as a centre of all progressive and cultural movements of those days. Some account has already been given of this in the previous chapter. Our attention is proposed to be restricted here to the question how such activities helped to develop the mind of young Rabindranath.

Literary activities may be taken up first. Rabindranath's aptitude for poetical composition was in evidence in his boyhood. The beauty of rhymed words in the alphabet book thrilled him in his childhood. He got his first lesson in writing poems from his nephew Jyotiprakash. In due course, the news of his poetical talents reached the ears of his school-teacher. At this stage, the atmosphere of the house not only acted as an incentive but also put him in contact with poetry of high quality and poets of distinction. His immediate elder brother, Somendra, used to take delight in proclaiming his poetical powers. Moreover, there were capable poets in the very family. His eldest brother, Dwijendranath, was a distinguished poet; second brother, Satyendranath, also wrote poems, fifth brother Jyotirindranath was also skilled in versification. All this provided all the encouragement necessary for the youngest brother to try his hand as well in poetry. The eldest brother in particular had distinguished himself as an outstanding poet. Having original ideas he invented many new metres. It is natural for a budding poet brought up with such accomplished poets to entertain an ambition to be a great poet. There was also much to learn from the fifth brother, Joytirindranath. The cultural atmosphere he built up in cooperation with his wife, Kadmabari Devi, drew Rabindranath close to them. He was permitted by them to participate in the cultural sittings on the roof of the third story of the house in the evening. When Jyotirindranath was engaged in writing the drama named 'Sarojini', Rabindranath was only thirteen. It has been already mentioned that he composed a song for insertion in this drama. For this, Jyotirindranath rewarded him by making him a partner in his literary pursuits, their difference in age proving no bar. Presumably, such congenial atmosphere must have acted as a spur to Rabindranath's literary efforts.

But the credit for this should mainly go to Kadambari Devi, wife of Jyotirindranath. This uncommon lady not only made Rabindranath forget the loss of his mother by smothering him with affection and care, but took all the care to nurture his poetic talent. Herself a connoisseur of literature, she must have read in him the promise of a glorious future. She, therefore, took care to see to his advancement through a cautious approach of encouraging him on the one hand and preventing him, on the other, from being conscious of his poetical powers prematurely. This point has also been dealt with in the previous chapter, but will have to be reopened partially with reference to the present context.

There is good evidence to show that Kadambari Devi exercised beneficent influence on Rabindranath in his early youth. During his sojourn in the United Kingdom. Rabindranath composed a book of poems which he named 'Bhagno Hriday' (The Broken Heart). It was published in 1881 after his return home. The person to whom it was dedicated was not referred to by name; but the wording of the dedication leaves us no doubt that it was no other than his loving sister-in-law, Kadambari Devi. One point to be noted here is that all the other books that had been dedicated to her were published immediately after her death in 1884; but this was dedicated much earlier when the poet was studying in the United Kingdom.

It appears that even when he was deprived of the affectionate umbrage of his sister-in-law, her benevolent influence continued to persist even during her physical absence. The dedication bears this out. The relevant part is quoted in translation :

Bathed in the sunlight of your affection

My heart opened up

And composed this latest book away from home.

It eagerly awaits your words of appreciation.

Do shed a tear for it.

Farewell for the present. Shall we meet again?

Will the light of your affection make my heart sing again?

Small wonder, when the cruel hand of death snatched her away in 1884, the poet felt a shock of grief more intense than the grief caused by the death of his mother, as he admits. Death never dealt a more cruel blow to him. He records this experience as follows :

'My confrontation with death at the age of twenty-four left a permanent impression. Subsequent shocks of grief linked up with it to weave a garland of tears. Childhood's light mood can easily stand the shock of death of close relations; but in mature age there is no way facilitating easy escape from the shock of death. So I had to face the unberable shock of that tragic day".[11]

That explains why the memory of the lady who used to be his constant companion in his literary pursuits in early age haunted Rabindranath throughout his life. His philosophical attitude would not advise him to carry the burden of old sorrow. He was also by nature averse to embarrass others by giving public expression of personal sorrow. Despite however, these restrictive forces this old sorrow

11. Jivan smirit, Mrityushok.

could revive in a moment of weakness and would find expression in exquisite doleful songs. Some examples may be cited :

The book of poems bearing the title "Chaitali" was composed in young age in the last decade of the last century, when the poet was staying in North Bengal to look after the family estates. The book made its first appearance in 1890. It includes a poem named "Smriti" which recalls the memory of Kadambari Devi.

The relevant stanza of the same is quoted below in translation:

The exuberance of her affection like a dancing cataract,

Would overwhelm me in diverse ways.

Where can she be today in this immense universe?

A thought that brings tears to my eyes.

The book of poems called 'Chitra' was composed nearabout the same time and published in 1896. It recalls an insignificant event which is reminiscent of the sweet days passed with his affectionate sister-in-law. She used to present him champak and bel. (jasmine) flowers in his early days, On the day the poem as composed, some admirer of his had presented him the same champak and bel flowers. This revived the memory of similar presents from his sister-in-law in days long gone by and the thought that the would never meet her again brought tears to his eyes. So the poet says :

The same champak, the same bel flowers—

Who is he that placed them in my hand?

My eyes are suffused with tears, my heart is overwhelmed.

Why do tears flow? This is because they remind him that a long time ago an affectionate lady would give him the same present.

Many an evening have I put round my neck

A garland woven with boxul blossoms.

by a lòving hand.

It pleased me immensely when I used to receive as present

The same champak and the same bel.

The 'Balaka' was published in 1916. The poem 'Chhabi' included in this collection is addressed to Kadambari Devi. The poet's biographer, Prabhat Kumar Mukherjee, has recorded the following information in this connection. Rabindranath paid a visit to his nephew Satyaprasad's son-in-law Pyarimohan Banerjee at Allahabad in 1914. During his stay here, unexpectedly he saw a portrait of Kadambari Devi, the reaction to which was recorded in this poem.[12] It proved to be one of the best poems written by Rabindranath and the inspiration came from the same gracious lady.

Tagore was a poet with uncommon grounding in music. A composer of his excellence is a rarity. He composed over two thousand songs and what is most remarkable is that he set each of them to music himself, an achievement which is not known to have been repeated. It was his uncommon command over music which made this possible. He had a natural aptitude for both poetry and music. He acquired mastery over music at a very early age. Evidently, the atmosphere in the family helped to develop this natural aptitude. There was a tradition in the family to engaged distinguished musicians to learn music. The famous musician Jadu Bhatta was one of such teachers with whom Rabindranath came in contact. Nor was there any dearth of gifted musicians among the members of the family. His elder brother, Jyotirindranath, distinguished himself as a composer whose friend, Akshay Chaudhuri, was also a competent collaborator; Jyotirindranath; encouraged Rabindranath in joining him both in literary and musical activities.

---

12. Prabhat Kumar Mukherjee Rabindra Jian Katha .

Evidently, that provided him with the first lessons in composing songs. When Jyotirindranath composed new tunes on the piano he entrusted the work of recording them to Akshay Chaudhuri and Rabindranath. Jyotirindranath has recorded in his reminiscences how this used to be done thus :

"During these days I used to give shape to new tunes on the piano. On my two sides would sit Akshay Chandra and Rabindranath, with paper and pencil in hand. No sooner did I compose a tune than they would compose a song to fit in with it".[13]

The tradition of patriotism built up in the family through generations exercised a profound influence on the young mind of Rabindranath. At that time of our history, nationalistic feelings did not dominate the thought and action of our people. The religious movements dominated the scene in the nineteenth century. The major issue was whether the worship of images of God should be discontinued. The movement was still continuing when Rabindranath was a boy. It was, however, Bengali literature which drew most of the attention of the Bengali elite during his early youth. It was well on the way to attaining the status of a viable aesthetically rich modern literature, thanks to the case bestowed on it by Bankim Chandra. National literature thus became the major object of attraction. The political movement for self-government was yet to be born. On the contrary, the trend was towards imitating the Englishman in dress, style of living and talking in English among affluent families in general and particularly those who had been educated in the United Kingdom. The family of the Tagores was a notable exception.

The patriotism of the Tagore family had a long history behind. Though Dwarakanath maintained intimate contact with the Europeans in his commercial transactions, he dressed and lived in the

13. Jyotirindra Smriti.

Indian style. He used the dress fashionable among Indians of high society in those days. He used to smoke in the Indian fashion with a hubble-bubble. During his long stay in England, he continued to live exclusively in the Indian style. During his second visit to the United Kingdom, his youngest son Nagendranath accompanied him. When his father died there after a long stay Nagendranath returned home. When he disembarked at the port in Calcutta, he sprang a pleasant surprise on his countrymen by appearing in Indian dress. Debendranath maintained his correspondence exclusively in Bengali and hated writing letters in English.

The tradition thus established by the earlier generation was not only scrupulously maintained by the subsequent generation, but enforced with greater vigour. Debendranath's eldest son, Dwijendranath, engaged himself in enriching Bengali literature. His second son who was the first Indian to be selected as a member of the Indian Civil Service should have been thoroughly westernised; but he never gave up Bengali as the medium of expression of his thoughts. His close friend, Monmohan Ghosh, went to the length of making his wife use gowns instead of saris; but his wife Jnandanandini Devi continued to dress in saris. When he first came to Calcutta to spend his long leave, he busied himself in the affairs of the Swadeshi Mela introduced by Nabagopal Mitra. It was in this connection that he wrote a patriotic song which was the first of its kind in Bengali literature. Maharshi's third son, Hemendranath, entertained great love for his mother tongue. He introduced the practice of using Bengali as the medium of instruction for the members of the family. His fifth son, Joytirindranath, distinguished himself by his contributions towards the enrichment of Bengali literature and song.

Debendranath's nephew Ganendranath's activities in the field also deserve mention. He took keen interest in the production of Bengali plays and their staging. He was also one of the prominent organizers of the Hindu Mela. In collaboration with Nabagopal Mitra, he initiated the first efforts to revive indigenous industries and organised the annual fair for inculcating patriotic feelings among his countrymen. Small wonder, such favourable circumstances would sow the seed of patriotic feelings in young Rabindranath's mind. They gave clear indication of their presence when he actively participated in the affairs of the Hindu Mela. There is clear evidence that he gave recital of poems composed by himself in two sittings of the Hindu Mela, organised annually. The first sitting of the mela took place in 1867 when he was a boy of six only. As soon as he grew up a little, he started actively participating in its annual sittings enthusiastically. He recited a poem for the first time in the Mela of 1875 in a gathering presided over by Rajnarayan Bose. The Indian Daily News, a leading English daily in those days, published the news in its issue dated February 15, 1875 as follows:

"Baboo Rabindranath Tagore, the youngest son of Baboo Debendranath Tagore, a handsome lad of some 15, had composed a Bengali poem on Bharat (India) which he delivered from memory. The suavity of his tone much pleased the audience". [14]

The contents of the poem recited by him on this occasion deserve a little scrutiny. The poet imagines that the sage Vyas was calling back to memory the glory of ancient India sitting in the Himalayas and was wondering whether those days would ever return and if they do not, let there be an end of it. Its contents give an idea of the depth of his patriotic feeling with which it is surcharged. The following quotation will show how keenly this budding poet of India yearned for the return of those glorious days at such early age:

Will the skeleton of ancient India
Again be resusciatated to life?
Will not fire flare up from the ashes
of ancient India.
To illuminate the world?

14. Indian Daily News, Februray 15, 1875.

He composed another poem in the sitting of 1877 and recited it standing in the shade of a tree. He named it 'Delhi Durbar'. This event finds mention in his book of reminiscences. The poem could not, however, be traced out. Poet Nabin Chandra Sen happened to be present at the function. He was deeply impressed by the recital given by Abanindranath and recorded it in his autobiography as one of the treasured experiences of his life. The relevant entry may be conveniently quoted below:—

"I remember that in 1876 while spending my leave in Calcutta, I paid a visit to a national fair in some park in the outskirts of Calcutta. A new acquaintance of mine got hold of me in the crowded fair and reported that a certain person wanted to be introduced to me. He took me by the hand to a corner of the park under the shade of a huge tree. I noticed the presence of a handsome young man dressed in loose pyjama and chapkan. Clam and composed, he looked to be eighteen to nineteen years of age and could be mistaken for an image in gold. My friend said: 'He is the youngest son of Maharshi Debendranath Tagore....'

He took out a notebook from his pocket and sung a few songs and recited a few poems in his musical voice. I was overwhelmed with the sweet vioce which put to shame a woman's voice and the excellent quality of the poem of that budding genius.[15]

It is a rare fortune for a young writer to be admitted to the patronage of literary journals. It helps the development of literary power in diverse ways. For one thing, publication of a composition works as an incentive. Secondly by making such literary work accessible to the reading public a writer gets introduced to them. Thirdly, pressure from the editor does not allow the writer to slacken his efforts. Continuous practice thus helps to develop a writer's

15. Nabindra Chandra Sen, Amar Jivan, p. 264.

capacity. Even a young writer lacking intrinisc merit can establish himslef, if such patronage is available to him. On the other hand, such advantages speed up the process of the developments of the talents of a writer who is extraordinarily gifted. Thanks to the atomsphere prevailing in his family, Rabindranath enjoyed a surfeit of such facilities.

The family journal called the 'Tatvabodhini Patrika' had been started by his father long before Rabindranath's birth. It established itself as the leading literary journal of those days. It was in this journal that one of his early poems was first published. It bore the title 'Abhilas' (Desire) and was published in the Agrahayana issue of 1796 saka era corresponding to December 1874 of the 'Tatvabodhini Patrika'. The name of the author did not find mention but the authorship was ascribed to a boy of the age of twelve. Circumstantial evidence supports the inference that the author was Rabindranath. For the composition of a boy of twelve to be published in the leading journal of the day was rare luck indeed. Such experience is as rare as it is thrilling and must have filled the heart of this young poet with joy. It must have inevitably worked as a powerful incentive.

The contents of the poem deserve some reference as they carry some significance. From a boy of twelve one would naturally expect a poem on a simple theme like flowers, rivers or scenic beauty. But this boy proved to be different. He chose a subject which does not naturally suggest itself to a young mind. The subject selected was ambition which is basically reflective. The last stanza may be quoted with advantage in translation :

If every body remained satisfied

With the condition he found himself in his own wisdom,

Would progress have ever

Showered its rays in the world?

Indeed without ambition nobody can establish himself in life. This shows what serious thoughts engaged the attention of this young boy at such tender age. Presumably, he entertained the ambition of shaping himself as an outstanding poet from that early age.

Maharshi started the Tatvabodhini Patrika primarily for carrying one publicity for the Brahmo Samaj. When his sons grew up, they became more interested in cultural affairs. No wonder, they felt the need for starting a literary magazine. It was Jyotirindranath, backed by his friend, Akshay Chandra Chaudhuri, who took the initiative. They persuaded Dwijendranath to accept the editorship of the proposed journal. That is how the new magazine 'Bharati' started its life as the second magazine run by the family. Its first issue was published in Sravan 1284 Bengali era corresponding to July-August, 1877.

Rabindranath was then only sixteen years of age, but already qualified by merit for participation in the literary activities of the family along with his elder brothers. The editor himself and other members of the family regularly contributed to this journal. Satyendranath would contribute articles from his place of work in Bombay Presidency. Both Jyotirindranath and Swarna Kumari Devi also wrote for this journal. The acceptance of young Rabindranath also as a contributor opened for him immense possibilities. By becoming a regular contributor to a literary journal at such an early age he was encouraged to write under pressure which undoubtedly helped to attain maturity quickly.

Information about the extent to which he used the 'Bharati' for the publication of his literary works becomes relevant in this context. His short story 'Bhikharini' appeared in the very first issue of the 'Bharati'. After that, his long story 'Karma' appeared in instalments in the issues of Aswin 1284 Bengali era to Bhadra 1285 Bengali era. The same journal published his review of the Meghnadbadh Kavya of Michal Madhusudhan Dutta in 1284. This account will show how enthusiastically he started contributing to the 'Bharati'. When he left for the United Kingdom for higher studies next year, he started sending letters recording his experience there for publication in the 'Bharati'. These letters were subsequently compiled together in the form of a book and published under the title 'Europe Prabasir Patra'. His first novel named 'Bow Thakuranir Hat' was also published serially in the same journal.

Rabindranath's second sister-in-law Jnandanandini Devi started a children's magazine named 'Balak' for the entertainment of the children of the family in 1885. It maintained separate existence for three years and their was merged with the 'Bharati'. The new children's magazine encouraged Rabindranath to write poems enjoyable by children. Several such poems were published in different issues of the 'Balak' in 1885. He resumed writing children's poems a long time after, when his wife died. His book of children's verses named 'Shishu' is a collection of the poems written during both the periods.

It has been mentioned in a previous chapter that the members of the Tagore family took keen interest in staging dramas. The interest was sustained through generations. Ganendranath was the first member to interest himself in this affair. It is not possible, however, for Rabindranath to come in direct contact with this cousin as he died young in 1869. Rabindranath was then only eight years old, too young to be interested in dramas. It was under the patronage of Jyotirindranath that dramas received vigorous attention of the members of the family. He was not only a playwright but was very much interested in staging dramas. In 1874 he founded a cultural organisation in the family which he named the 'Bidwajana Samagāma'. This institution first interested itself in literary compositions. At a later stage it also took to staging of plays. When

Rabindranath returned from the United Kingdom he found it functioning vigorously. This new atmosphere in the family encouraged him to write plays and participate in staging them.

He used this opportunity, to make some experiments in the field. During his sojourn in the United Kingdom, he picked up some acquaintance with Western music. He had also an opportunity to make himself familiar with the opera which combines acting and music in drama. Music, however, is the dominant element. In our country, music had not so far been used as a medium, of acting. The prevailing tradition of those days restricted its use to drawing room sittings in form of musical soirees. Rabindranath wanted to see whether such restrictions could be removed and music can be put to wider practice. In other words, he wanted to see whether music could function as medium, for the histrionic art.

It was with this end in view that he composed the play named 'Valmiki Pratibha'. We are all familiar with the story it tells. It shows how a robber, named Ratnakar became transformed into the poet, Valmiki. The drama was composed wholly in the form of poetry. He set it to music by the application of principles borrowed for three different schools. He adopted the Tilana tunes of the Indian classical school, the tunes formulated by Jyotirindranath and thirdly, tunes borrowed from Western schools of music. The Western style is in evidence in the chorus sung by the robbers and the mourning of the deity of the forest. A quotation of the relevant part of Rabindranath's own comments on the subject as given below:

"The Valmiki Pratibha" was the child born out of the wedding of Eastern music with Western music. Most of the tunes applied to it have been borrowed from the Indian classical style which had been kept exclusively restricted to musical soirees. What is used to soaring in the sky has been made to run of firm ground".[16]

He further observes:

"Valmiki Pratibha' is not meant to be read as a poem; it is a new experiment in music. It is not possible to savour its taste unless it is accompanied with action on the stage. 'Valmiki Pratibha' is not an opera, in the sense the term is used in the West; it is a musical playlet, that is to say, music has not been allowed to dominate here; only its verbal element is to be expressed in musical form".[17]

In the first staging of the playlet, Rabindranath himself appeared in the role of Valmiki and his niece Pratibha Devi played the part of the goddess Saraswati in the guise of a girl. This staging thus acquired some distinctive features of its own. Staged by the 'Bidyajjana Samagam' it claimed for its audience many distinguished men of society. They included Bankim Chandra Chaterjee, Gurudas Benerjee and Haraprasad Sastri. It succeeded in impressing favourable these guests. It can, therefore, be said that the experiment using music as the medium of expression did prove successful.

Gurudas Banerjee in particular was overwhelmed with the excellence of both the acting and the literary quality of the show. He composed a poem in appreciation of the performance, which shows how deeply he had been moved. The relevant extract is placed below in translation :

Wake up Mother Bengal, do not sleep any more;
The darkness of ignorance has been
dispelled by the morning light.
A new sun has appeared on the horizon
    to bring into view a new world,
To usher the blossoming of a new Valmiki.

---

16. Jiban Smriti, Valmiki Pratibha.
17. Jiban Smriti, Valmiki Pratibha.

Few young poets has ever had the luck to be greeted with such appreciation. Evidently, Gurudas Banerjee in his wisdom, discovered in this musical playlet, the promise of a glorious future, that he foresaw, that Rabindranath would shape like another Valimki, an idea which must have thrilled him.

Rabindranath wrote and staged another play under the auspices of the 'Biddyajjana Samāgama' entitled 'Kāla Mrigayā'. It tells the story of the blind sage recorded in the 'Ramayana'. Its first staging also took place in the house of the Tagores on a temporary stage erected on the roof of the third storey. Rabindranath played the part of the blind sage, while Jyotirindranath took over the role of king Dasratha. Ritendranath, the son of their third brother Hemendranath, appeared in the role of the son of the blind sage while his sister Abhijna Devi played the part of the daughter of the sage. Here also Western and Eastern tunes were used and the show was enjoyed by the audience which included many distinguished men.

Rabindranath was very happy to find that the experiment made through these two playlets had proved successful. The first point of departure was taking music out of its customary setting of a soiree and using it as medium for a play. The reaction of the audience was favourable to it. The second point of departure was the simultaneous application of Western and Eastern music to the play. That this was received favourably is indicated by the warm appreciation that followed. The favourable reception accorded to both the musical dramas gave Rabindranath much satisfaction.

His observations on the point may be conveniently quoted here: "These two playlets brought about a radical revolution upsetting old tradition. In keeping with this spirit, the playlets include dance of rowdy element and English and Bengali tunes have been indiscriminately used. Many a time have I given offence to my readers by inflicting on them my non-conformist views and stylistic innovations. What surprised me, however, was the fact that the departure dared in these two playlets was not received unfavourably; on the contrary the audience departed in a happy mood". [18]

The above observation indicates that Rabindranath cause for apprehension that his experimental efforts on this line might not be accorded a favourable reception. No wonder, he was immensely pleased to find that instead of facing hostile criticism, they received warm appreciation.

It has been already noted that Rabindranath composed a poem at the early age of twelve which had ambition for its theme. He wanted to establish that without ambition human society cannot prosper. Evidently, he appreciated that ambition is a quality which matters. Then again he recited another poem in the Hindu Mela at the age of seventeen which was surcharged with patriotic feelings. He imagined that the sage Vyas was recalling the past glory of India seated on a peak of the Himalayas and deploring that it had been buried under ashes. He was worried whether fire would flare up out of the dead ambers with a new glow at all. The poet was thus inspired with the twin feelings of ambition and patriotism. Presumably, he had been deeply moved by the memory of past glory as contrasted with the then low state of his country. This must have generated in his mind a yearning to revive the glory of India's past. There are several observations of his to indicate that this yearning became the dominant ambition of his life.

It pained him to see that while other people of the world were attaining new heights of glory, India's past glory is covered with ashes. This poor state of affairs roused in his mind a strong desire to present something of value to the world on behalf of India in general, and Bengal in particular. He entertained the

18. Jiban Smriti Valmiki Pratibha.

hope of charming the world with the magic power of his pen. The following observation of his will bear this out:

"We have been receiving calls from the different people of the world for ages past; shall we return their greeting by publishing a few small newspapers in English? Other countries are carving their name on the edicts of history. Should the Bengali rest content with putting his signature on the second page of an application? The spirit of man has taken up the challange of inert matter; it has sounded it clarion-call in all directions to assemble together its soldiers; shall we keep ourselves occupied with litigation over the ownership of gourds and pumpkins grown in our courtyards?

"Having maintained silence for long years, Bengal wants to speak at last. Let her give expressions to her feelings in her own language. That will contribute to the sweetness of the orchestra of the world".[19]

---

19. Rabindranath Rachanavali (Viswabharati Edition) Vol. V Bibidha Prabandha page 440.

6

RABINDRANATH-II

It appears that Rabindranath took over the duty of contributing to the world culture on behalf of the Bengali from boyhood. No wonder, he subjected himself from an early age to a rigorous training for discharging the role of an extraordinary poet. The atmosphere in the family was favourable. What is more fortunate is that he got in the family an affectionate sympathetic well-wisher who gave him the necessary guidance to put him on the right track in the person of his sister-in-law, Kadambari Davi. Luck was thus doubly kind to him. While patriotic feelings inspired him with the ambition of being an outstanding poet, the congenial atmosphere in the people backed by the patronage of a sympathetic lady went a long way to help him to achieve it. He also got a model to follow in the person of his eldest brother Dwijendranath. The latter's friend Beharilal Chakravarti also paid frequent visits to the house. Small wonder, his poetic talents matured quickly.

Rabindranath's first book of poems culled 'The Kabikahini' was published in 1878, when he was only seventeen years of age, the next outstanding book, 'Valmiki Pratibha' came out in 1881 followed by 'Sandhya Sangeet' in 1882. 'Valmiki Pratiba' is a musical play while 'Sandhya Sangeet' is a collection of lyrical poems. The book which published his earliest compositions is the 'Saisab Sangeet'. It is a collection of poems written by the poet while he was between thirteen and eighteen years of age. It was, however, published after the books mentioned above in 1884.

According to the poet's own classification, the poems composed upto the time of the completion of 'Sandhya Sangeet' represent the first stage of his poetry. He has called it the 'copy book stage'. Just as a child has to imitate the copy book to acquire skill in handwriting, Rabindranath also engaged himself in this period of his literary career in acquiring skill in composing verses. A poet has to pass through these stages of immaturity in the first phase before he can acquire some confidence in his powers after passing through it. That is why he remarks that the 'Sandhaya Sangeet' made its appearance when he had just crossed the threshold of 'the copy book stages'. This was the first book that gave some indications of his originality and what is more important, it carried positive promise of future greatness.

Bankim Chandra was then the undisputed leader of the literary world. He had the discerning eye to discover this quality of 'Sandhya Sangeet'. No wonder, he communicated his apperciation to this budding poet at the very first opportunity. The story has been recorded by Rabindranath himself and may be conveniently quoted her :

"The birth of 'Sandhaya Sangeet' was heralded by the loud blowing conch shells; it was not, however, denied a gesture of affection. I have mentoned in one of my essays that I found Bankim Chandra standing at the entrance of the reception hall on the occasion of the marriage of Ramesh Chandra's eldest daughter. Ramesh Chandra was about to put a garland on the neck of Bankim Chandra. Just at that point of time I put in my appearance. Immediately, Bankim Chandra santched away the garland and put it on my neck and said' This is the person who deserves it. Ramesh, have you read 'Sandhya Sangeet'? The latter replied he had not. Thereupon Bankim Chandra made an appreciative remark about a poem contained in the book which made me feel that I had been highly rewarded".[1]

These words of appreciation from Bankim Chandra must have deeply impressed him.

But he did not quite discover his true poetic self in the poems of 'Sandhya Sangeet'. From a boy, he was deeply interested in nature. When he wrote 'Sandhya Sangeet' he had acquired some skill in versification, but unfortunately, lost contact with nature. Consequently, he lacked inspiration. He started composing on themes which had no link with reality. This explains why these poems are pervaded by a pessimistic tone. Was it named 'Sandhya Sangeet' to signify this ? It was a vision which brought release to him from this feeling of despair and confinement. He was then staying with Jyotirindranath in a rented house at Sudder Street in central Calcutta. Free School Street is situated to its east. It was ten lined with trees. One morning the sun rose before his eyes, as he stood on an open verandah which opened on Sudder Street. Its rays penetrated the veil of fog to uncover its glory. This made him feel that a screen had been removed from before his eyes and the environment became filled with sublime grandery. That feeling provided him the inspiration for his poem entitled 'Nirjharer Swapnabhanga' (Awakening of the cataract). The feeling of confinement built up round him during the phase when the 'Sandhya Sangeet' was composed, thus dispelled and his link with the outside world was reestablished and he got back nature. Then onwards his poetry chalked out its own course towards fulfilment. He got back his lost self.

This is how the poet records his own feelings at this stage of his life:

---

1. Jiban Smriti, Gangatir.

"At last one day the closed door appeared to yield suddenly to hard knocking and I got back what I had lost. I not only got that back but through the barrier of separation I became more intimate with it. A sense of fulfilment accompanies access to an object which has been rendered difficult. Thus, when I got back the world of my boyhood days in the 'Prabhat Sangeet' I got something more. Thus was completed the first chapter of my poetical life through the three phases of easy access to nature, followed by separation and then by reunion".[2]

From the very beginning, Rabindranath's literary activities were directed to many channels. The 'Rudra Chanda' was his first drama, having been published in 1881. The musical drama 'Valmiki Pratibha' was also published in the same year. That was followed by 'Raja-O-Rani' and 'Visarjan'. 'Visarjan' was composed in blank verse, the story having been suggested by a dream. Rabindranath's dramatic talents attained maturity in this book. A short time after, the poetical drama 'Chitrangada' was written. It is distinguished by its exquisite lyrical quality.

'The Bau Thakuranir Hat' is the first novel written by Rabindranath, its date of publication being 1883. When he was twenty three years of age, too young to acquire adequate experience. Consequently, this work is patently immature. The next novel 'Rajarshi' was published in 1887. It embodies the same story as the drama 'Visarjan'. It is mature, but does not reflect adequately Rabindranath's skill as a fiction writer. The first book that bore the stamp of maturity is the 'Chokher bali' published in 1903. This was the book that established his fame as a novelist.

The early literary works of Rabindranath faced no adverse criticism. On the contrary, they won high appreciation on two occasions. 'Valmiki Pratibha' deeply impressed Gooroodas Banerjee. Bankim Chandra himself made appreciative remarks about

2. Jivan Smriti, Prabhat Sangeet.

'Sandhya Sangeet'. When however, his reputation as a poet was firmly established, his books were greeted with severe criticism. Presumably, his growing popularity attracted such hostility. It was about the time that 'Kari-O-Komal' a book of poems was published (1886). Three books were subjected to hostile criticism. 'Kari-O-Komal' the lyrical drama 'Chitrangada' and the novel 'Chokher bali' Strangely though, all three of them made the marks as excellent literary works.

This hostile criticism was mainly carried on by three prominent writers. Kaliprasanna Kavya Visarad, poet and editor of a journal was one of them. In adopting the role of a critic of Rabindranath, he described himself as Rahu. His special target was the book of poems 'Kari-O-Komal'. The second critic was Suresh Chandra Samajpati, editor of the literary journal 'Sahitya'. Suresh Chandra Samajpati subjected 'Chokher bali' to severe criticism.

The critic who distinguished himself, however, as the most cruel and vituperative in his attack was Dwijendra Lal Roy, himself a writer of distinction. He does not appear to have assumed a pseudonym as Rabindranath's critic; but the distinguished literary critic. Lalit Chandra Banerjee described him as the 'Kala Megha'. (abscuring cloud) of the literary works of Rabindranath, evidently an apt epithet. It appears that Dwijindra Lal Roy took over the role of Rabindranath's critic with the determination that he would shift the other's literary efforts by attacking him mercilessly. That probably explains why his attacks were extensive and wide ranging. He carried on his campaign of vilification in diverse ways. He would make parodies or his poems of Tagore which he disliked to ridicule him. In some cases he would make the characters of his drama denounce Rabindranath's poems. In other cases, he would openly attack him in his critical essays.

A man destined to be a writer of distinction naturally attracts criticism. Some notable example can be cited from the history of world literature. In ancient times, poet Kalidas had to face the hostile criticism of two persons named Nichula and Duiganga. His lamentation over the hostile reception of his works clearly establish that poet Bhababhuti had to face severe criticism. He asserted that those who showed him contempt knew little and he had not written for them; he was prepared to wait patiently for long years for properly qualified readers to be born to appreciate him. Time being limitless, and the earth extensive, this possibility can be expected to materialise. The history of English literature can also supply some instances. Even a stalwart like Shakespeare had to face criticism by a contemporary in the person of Robert Green. He accused Shakespeare of being highly egotistic though lacking in literary excellence. Poet Wordsworth was also subjected to criticism in the beginning of the nineteenth century. To shield himself against such hostile attacks he taught himself to treat them with indifference.

Rabindranath's reaction to such criticism, however, was of a different kind. He did not denounce his critics as lacking in learning, nor did seek refuge indifference. Indeed such criticism did hurt him; but that did not provoke him to hit back; he used very polite language to say that if his poems lacked quality his readers would forget about them soon and so there is hardly any need for hurting the writer by using barbed expressions.

What he said, in addition speaks, highly of his magnanimity. Instead of hitting back or despising them he gave them his best wishes that their literary talents might find fulfilment in success. He said:

May you acquire fame,

May your pen find fulfilments,

May your talents prosper

To overwhelm all readers. [3]

No wonder, Rabindranath's qualities of character not only conquers our heart but also excites our admiration.

Adverse criticism can never stifle the efforts of a person who is intrinsically endowed with talent. No wonder, in the not too distant future when Rabindranath's poetic talents matured and shone with the brightness of the midday sun, neither Rahu nor Kalmegh could dim its glow. While Dwijendra Lal was spreading calumny against him through the mouth of a character in his drama 'Ananda Vidya'; people across the seas turned his admirers on reading his English 'Gitanjali'. Soon after, followed the award of the Nobel Prize marking him out as one of the greatest writers of his age. His own people realised through the eyes of the people of the world that he was an extra-ordinary poet of whom they could be proved.

Rabindranath was married to Bhabatarini Devi on 9th December 1883. She was not allowed to retain the name given by her parents and was renamed Mrinalini Devi. The conjugal life built up between them became enriched in diverse ways. There are positive indications that they enjoyed a happy life together. A minor example will suffice. When Rabindranath left for the United Kingdom in 1890 for a short stay for three months he regularly wrote letters to his wife and expected to get replies. If the expected letters were delayed he would feel very much upset. The manner in which he addressed his wife in his letters was a departure from the ordinary practice. Ordinarily, he would address her as 'Bhai Choto Bau' (Dear youngest daughter-in-law). At one stage, it was shortened into 'Bhai Chhuti' (Dear Holiday). This is as charming as it is significant. It is easy to conjecture how dear the wife must have been to him whom he looked upon as holiday personified.

3. Marasi, Ninduker Prati.

The suite of rooms in the west of the third storey of the residential house at Jorasanko used to remain vacant after the death of Kadambari Devi. Rabindranath started occupying these rooms after his marriage. It was here that his family grew up. All his children were born here. As in the days of Kadambari Davi, Rabindranath would hold his evening sittings on the contiguous roof to the south and the duty of looking after guests would be discharged by Mrinalini Devi. Rathindranath has recorded a fine account of such sittings in his reminiscence which can be conveniently reproduced here:

"In the third storey of the house of the Tagores in Jorasanko there is a flat roof, spacious enough to accommodate two tennis courts. Children used it as their playground. Women of the house used to assemble there in the evening. The central part of the roof was at a higher level. They would spread carpets on it and place pillows to sit there comfortably. The custom of serving tea had not yet taken root; but Rathindranath's mother used to entertain the guests with sweets and light drinks. When night set in male members of the family would join. Songs were sung to entertain the assembly . [4]

It was at about that time that Maharshi entrusted the care of the landed properties of the family to Rabindranath. He looked after the administration initially from the Calcutta, office of the estate and would occasionally go out on tours of inspection. Except the properties situated in the Cuttack district, the rest of the Zamindari estates were located in North Bengal. Some belonged to the Rajsahi district, some to Pabna district and others to Nadia district. All of them were accessible by river transport. There was a bungalow on the left bank of the Padma at Shiladah in the north of Nadia district. That functioned as the central office of the estates.

It appears that Rabindranath took over the charge of the administration of these estates in 1889. This is

4. Rabindranath Tagore, On the Edges of Time.

borne out by the fact that he wrote the drama 'Visarjan', while staying in a guest house attached to the office of the Sahajadpur circle of the estates. His family used to live in the residential house of Jorasanko. He would live in Calcutta and go out on tours of inspection of the local offices. At that stage, he had to contribute regularly to the two family journals 'Bharati' and 'Sadhana'. His days away from home were spent either in the bungalows attached to the outlying offices or on house boats in close contact with nature. He used to carry on his literary activities there undisturbed by company. When the writings would be ready for the press he would return home to arrange for their publication. His time would thus be distributed between looking after his family, pursuit of literary interests and administration of the Zamindari estates.

It was during this period that the cultural institution named 'Kham Kheyāli Sabhā', was started in the family. This was also a family institution modelled after the 'Biddyajjana Samāgam' founded by Jyotirindranath at an earlier stage. The elite of Calcutta society used to assemble in the sittings organised by this institution. Rabindranath and his nephew Balendranath were the main organisers of such sittings. The institution maintained no rules of business. The members used to entertain the assembled guests by rotation limiting their number to twenty. They included, poets, singers, actors and instrument players. When the burden of entertainment fell on Rabindranath, it would turn into an impressive affair. The services of artists from Krishnagar would be requisitioned to decorate the place of sitting. Food would be served in white marble plates and the task of preparing the meals would devolve on Mrinalini Devi. She had to invent new recipes for the purpose as desired by her husband.

The guests would assemble in the drawing room after dinner to be entertained with a cultural feast.

Different writers and artists would recite poems, read short stories and sing. Occasionally, single act plays were also staged. The gusets who attended these sittings included Maharaja Jagadindranath Roy of Natore, Jagadish Chandra Bose, Akshoy Kumar Chaudhuri, Priyanath Sen, Chittaranjan Das, Pramajhanath Roy Choudhuri, Raja of Santosh and Dwijendra Lal Roy. It appears that all distinguished persons interested in literature would be attracted to these sittings. Rabindranath would ordinarily give the first reading of his latest writings in the sittings of the 'Kham-Kheyali Sabha'. His two books 'Bani Kanthen Katha' and 'Bini Payasar Bhoj' (A feast without cost) were specifically written for the entertainment of guests attending its sittings. [5]

The 'Kham-Kheyali Sabha', ceased to functions from 1897 when Rabindranath removed his family to Shiladaha for residence on a permanent footing. With Rabindranath who was the life of the institution staying away from Calcutta, it died out for want of a dependable person to look after it. It was the problem of education of his growing children which induced Rabindranath to transfer his family to Shiladaha. The couple had been in the meantime blessed with five children. The eldest child, a daughter had completed eleven years of age. The second child, a son, was ten years old. The second daughter, Renuka, was eight, the youngest daughter Meera was six and the youngest son Samindra was four. All of them were old enough to be taught. On the other hand, the house at Jorasanko was too overcrowded to provide a suitable atmosphere for teaching.

At Shiladaha, the style of living of the family was radically changed. The urban setting of Calcutta was conspicuous by its absence. The family lived on a lovely bungalow situated on the bank of the Padma, in a quiet village. Having no society there, they had to live completely alone. But there were compensations.

5. Rabindranath Tagore, on the Edges of the Time p. 17.

the crowd of the huge joint family, this family had lost its identity. After removal to Shiladaha, they became completely separated from both the family and society and consequently, the members moved closer to one another. In fact, during the few years he stayed there, the full joy of conjugal life became accessible to Rabindranath. It was the education of the children which first engaged his attention. Arrangements were made for coaching them at home, as no school was available in this rural area. Another reason was that Rabindranath had developed a prejudice against school education of the basis of his own personal experience. He engaged an English, man named Lawrence for teaching English and put him up in an adjoining house. Jagadananda Roy was taken over from the office of the estate and assigned the task of teaching Mathematics, as his grounding in the subject had impressed Rabindranath. A Sanskrit Scholar named Sibdhan Vidyaratna was appointed to teach Sanskrit. [6] He himself took over the charge of teaching Bengali.

Rabindranath was very keen to get his children acquainted with the contents of the Ramayana and the Mahabharata because these two epics give the best introduction to the national ethos. He has compared them to the Ganges and the Jamuna which provide food for the people. As both the Bengali versions of the two epics by Kritibas and Kasiramdas are big in size, he felt the need for smaller versions. That is why he encouraged his nephew Surendranath to produce a condensed form of the Mahabharata and entrusted Mrinalini Devi with the task of writing a short version of the Ramayana. He desired that the condensed form of the Ramayana should be based on the original Ramayana of Valmiki. Mrinalini Devi tried her best to fulfil the wish of her husband by carrying

6. Prabhat Kumar Mukherjee, Rabindra Jiban Katha, p. 80

out the difficult task assigned to her, with the help of Sanskrit scholars. Unfortunately, death overtook her before she could complete the task. It appears that the incomplete manuscript of the book has been lost.[7]

While the father took over the charge of the education of the children, the mother took over the complementary task of initiating them in the discharge of household chores. Every Sunday, she would give leave of absence to the domestic assistants. The eldest daughter Madhurilata and the eldest son Rathindranath were asked to discharge the functions assigned to the domestic assistants. The younger children were too young for work. There is perhaps no second example of a mistress of a household adopting such measures.

Like the scented flowers that attract bees in the wilderness, a gifted writer attracts lovers of literature wherever he may happen to be. No wonder, Rabindranath was not spared the attention of persons interested in literature even when he was passing his days in self-exilement in the rural setting of Shiladaha. Round him grew up a literary circle in this remote village.

Dwijendra Lal Roy was then the Sub-Divisional Officer of Kushtia which was a short distance from Shiladaha across a river. This enabled him to came over to Shiladaha whenever he could make time, in between his official duties. He took great interest in assisting Rabindranath in running his vegetable garden by applying his technical knowledge acquired as an agronomist.

Jagdish Chandra would occasionally visit the place from his Calcutta home. He loved to spend his days in winter in a house boat. When the low water level of the Padma would throw up numerous islets on its bossom, the guests would crowd on them

7. Rathindranath Tagore, On the Edges of Time.

during the holidays. Rabindranath would entertain Jagadish Chandra by reading out his short stories to him. It may be mentioned that it was during these days that Rabindranath was engaged in writing the short stories which have found place in the compilation named the 'Galpaguchha', and those were the stories which he read to Jagadish Chandra.

Akshay Kumar Maitreya who practised in the Judge's Court at Rajsahi found more interest in historical research than in his profession, for which purpose he founded the Barendra Research Society. He was also a regular visitor. He enjoyed the days spent here by discussing sundry subjects with Rabindranath.

Other two distinguished visitors were Loken Palit with whom he picked up acquaintance during his sojourn in the United Kingdom and Raja Jagadindranath of Natore. The contributions of Jagadindranath who was equally gifted as a writer and musician, enlivened these cultural sittings which enjoyed the service of another musician in the person of Amala Das, sister of Chittaranjan, Das Rabindranath was very fond of listening to her sweet voice. When Jagadindranath and Amala Das happened to be together at Shilaidaha, the musical soirees became as enjoyable as the meals that were served to the guests. With Amala Das helping Mrinalini Devi in cooking many tasteful courses were produced. On the other hand, Rabindranath and Amala Das entertained the guests with their songs by them.

Rabindranath spent three years with his family in the idyllic sitting of Shilaidaha. But after that his mind was disturbed by a feeling of discontentment. It stemmed from two facts. For one thing, Rathindranath had attained the age when he should get admitted to an educational institution; he had outlived the stage of private coaching at home. Secondly, he developed a yearning for taking up some activity which would promote the welfare of the community. In no time this yearning developed into a compulsive urge. That is how he formulated a new object, namely founding a school, at Santiniketan, which would provide facilities for the education of his own son along with other boys.

In the scheme he drew up for the proposed educational institution he was profoundly influenced by the model adopted in ancient India. According to this model, the student would leave his parental home to stay with his teacher during the first phase of his life for his education, the student used to be called Antibasi (one who lives in close proximity of the teacher) as he used to live as a member of his teacher's family in close contact with the teacher. This provision appealed to him strongly. The description as given in the different books in Sanskrit also captured his imagination. After reading the accounts given in the forest settlement of Vasistha appearing in the 'Raghuvansam' and Kanva in the 'Abhijana Sakuntalam', he came to the positive conclusion that education should be imparted in close proximity of nature, in the environment characteristic of such settlements. He has given elaborate reasons to substantiate this provision in his long essay bearing the title the 'Tapovana'.[8]

Accordingly, he proposed to open an educational institution at the settlement called Santiniketan founded by Debendranath. His father, had executed a trust deed for the maintenance of the Asram, providing a grant of Rs. 1800/- for the purpose and earmarked landed property to meet this demand. The trust deed provides for the opening of a school for Brahmos among other things. The proposal, therefore, filled in nicely and consequently, was blessed with the approval of his father.

It was decided that the institution would be named Brahmacharya Asram. It was opened on 7th Paus, 1308, Bengalee era, corresponding to 22nd

8. Shantiniketan, part-I

December, 1901, with five students on the roll, including Rathindranath whose 'Upanayana' ceremony had just been gone through. On the opening day, the students were initiated into their new life dressed in silk dhoti and wrapper. Satyendranath conducted the prayers as the Acharya. The silk dress was subsequently replaced by saffron cloth.

Sibdhan Vidyaratna, a former tuitor of Rathindranath, was appointed one of the teachers and a Sindhi named Rai Chand was recruited to teach English. Subodh Chandra Majumder was appointed to teach Bengali. At a subsequent stage, Brahmabandhab Upadhayay joined as a member of the staff. But he could not stay longer there four months as the pull of politics proved stronger.

The problem of financing the institution had to be tackled. The provision of Rs. 150/- a month in the trust deed was too meagre to meet the expenses. So Rabindranath had to supplement it with contributions from his personal allowance of Rs. 200/- per month sanctioned by his father. To meet the deficit, he sold a house he had built at Puri. When the fund thus raised was exhausted he had to sell his wife Mrinalini Devi's ornaments. She gladly agreed to part with them to fulfill her husband's wish.

Mrinalini Devi was keen to marry off her first two daughters before shifting to Santiniketan. So the marriage of both of them was performed in the month of Sraban of the same year. The eldest daughter, Madhurilata, was married to Sarat Chandra Chakravorty, a son of poet Beharilal Chakravarty. He was a practising lawyer at Mujaffarpur in Bihar.

The second daughter, Renuka, then aged only twelve years was married to a medical student named Satyendranath Bhattacharjee. As the bride was too young, the 'Fulasja' ceremony did not take place. The bridegroom left for the United States of America immediately after marriage for higher education.

Rabindranath's family life at Shantiniketan did not, however, last long. His wife, Mrinalini Devi, fell ill during the monsoon of the following year. Treatment by local doctors, produced no results. So she was brought to the family residence at Jorasanko for treatment. It is reported that the manner in which Rabindranath nursed her during her long illness rarely falls in the lot of a woman. The disease showed no sign of yielding to treatment. Mrinalini Devi realised that her death was imminent. She expressed a desire to see the 'Fulsajja' ceremony of her second daughter Renuka, performed before her death. So Satyendranath was called back from the United States and she had the satisfaction of witnessing the ceremony of her dear daughter performed. She did not survive long after, this death overtaking her at the family residence at Jorasanko on 23rd November 1902 in a room in the first floor of the house named 'Vichitra'.

It is reported that Rabindranath spent the entire night following her death by walking on the roof all by himself. After that there was no outward expression of his grief. This is consistent with the principle he had adopted; he disliked embarrassing people by giving expression to them of his personal sorrow. This is reflected in a poem written by him in mature age, the relevant part of which is quoted below in translation:

In a day of grief I tell my pen

    Do not put me to shame;

Do not place before the public eye,

    The grief that is not shared by others.

Do not cover your face with a dark veil,

    Do not belt your door.

It appears that he avoided giving expression to his grief following the death of his wife through his conduct successfully; but he could not restrain his pen. It refused to keep silent over the fact that his married life built up round Mrinalini Devi spreading over only nineteen years had been saturated with happiness. No wonder, we find that soon after her death, he composed a number of poems within a span of only two months entirely inspired by the shock of her death. They show how unbearable was the sorrow the poet suffered. He published them in a compilation which he named 'Smaran' (Memory). He did not dedicate it to his wife by name but only printed the date of her death, 13th Agrayan, 1307, in the page earmarked for dedication. Presumably, it was dedicated to that black date of sorrow. One of the poems in the compilation contains the following lines:

> Love came, but has gone away by
>
> opening the door,
>
> Never to return.
>
> I await the arrival of only another guest,
>
> Which will be the last event of my life.

Evidently, the other guest is death. But these are words of despondency stemming from the impact of his sorrow, which might have made the pilot of his life smile. He had yet to traverse alone the long path of glory earmarked for him. Many an honour was yet to be bestowed on him. Indeed, the lord of his life wanted him to transcend the dark world of sorrow to find access to the world of utter bliss.

7

RABINDRANATH-III

Rabindranath passed the next few years of his life in extreme sorrow and distress. It is said that misfortunes were come alone. The events of this period of his life fully bear this out. Death of close relatives political upheaval, difference of views among political leaders and similar developments caused him extreme distress.

Soon after his return to Santiniketan following the death of his wife, Rabindranath's second daughter fell seriously ill. She pthysis was found to be suffering from phthisis and so it became necessary to remove her to a pthysis climate. Rabindranath first took her to Hajaribagh. As this change of climate did not produce any favourable reaction, Rabindranath removed her to Almorah.

While nursing his sick child at Almorah he started writing children's verses to amuse her. He had produced such verses a long time ago to feed the family magazine called 'Balak'. The proximity of the sick child revived the theme and allowed it to reassert itself. The poems composed during this stage were published in form of a collection named. 'The Shishu' (The Child). The hero of the poems is 'Khoka' who represents his younger son 'Samindra'. Both Samindra and his youngest daughter Meera were then living away from him. To be able to give undivided attention to his sick daughter, he had left them in charge of his sister-in-law, Jnandanandini Devi. In this situation, how is it that the absent son became the leading figure of these poems ? Rabindranath himself explains the apparent anomaly thus: Samindra happened to be the youngest child of his wife and consequently, his departed wife appeared in his memory closely linked with Samindra who came uppermost in his thoughts at that stage. The explanation is given in a letter written by the poet to his friend, Mohit Chandra Sen, the relevant part of which is quoted below:-

"All the poems of this collection are associated with Khoka...............Khoka and his sweet and intimate relation with his mother constituted the latest memory of the joys of my family life. The youngest daughter was not allowed to be near her ailing mother at that stage. Khoka reigned supreme in the bed of his sick mother. Consequently, whenever I would sit to compose poems the memory of Khoka and his mother would tinge my memory like purple clouds at sunset. The tears brought to my eyes by the splendour of the sweet parting made me adopt such a course and I could not resist that".

A touching exposition! So these verses for children were incidentally a homage to the mother-image of his departed wife.

Renuka showed same improvement after a stay of about three months at Almorah, permitting him to remove her to Jorasanko. Unfortunately, there was a relapse soon after in a vigorous form. Inexorably, her death followed in September 1903. Rabindranath thus suffered a second bereavement by the death of his daughter within ten months of the death of his wife.

There were more shocks to follow in deadlier form. His youngest son had developed an intimacy with his class fellow, Sarojendra, son of Suresh Chandra Majumder. The two went to the Monghyer to spend their holidays in the maternal uncle's house of Sarojindra. Samindra was attacked with cholera during his stay there. The information was communicated by telegram to Rabindranath. He hurried to Munghyer, but could not save his son. Thus the hero of the poems of his Shishu' followed the footsteps of his mother into the other world. In this period of his life packed with tragedies, however, he never neglected his duties nor did he give any outward expression of his grief. He conformed to his principle that the sorrow that was exclusively his own should not embarrass those who do not share it and should be suffered alone.

The shock of his youngest son's death was however, too strong to permit him to keep his mental poise. After return to Shantiniketan, he made a temporary arrangement for running the affairs of his school and went straight to Shilaidaha. He even absented himself from the annual 'Pous Mela', at Santiniketan. To regain his composure he had to spend as long as five months alone at Shilaidaha.

More misfortune came his way. Before the death of his youngest son, his father died at the ancestral house at Jorasanko in 1905 in ripe old age. When his father fell critically ill, Rabindranath had to hurry to Jorasanko and had to stay on for a long time there, after his father's death. First came the funeral ceremony. Then came the question of settling family affairs including partition of properties, necessitated by the death of the head of the family, which was a time consuming process. After that, the brothers set up separate establishments, according to the provisions of the will left by the father.

Simultaneously a political upheaval took place in the country. Calcutta, the then the capital of India, happened to be situated in Bengal. So the Bengali community was the first cultural group to come in close contact with Western culture in the nineteenth century; the impact of which brought about what is called the renaissance movement of Bengal, under the leadership of some distinguished Bengali intellectuals. Initially, this movement interested itself in the reformative measures, calculated to resuscitate the society which had suffered decay under the burden of age. Under the leadership of Rammohun Roy and Iswar Chandra Vidyasagar, some major evils were attended to. The practice of burning widows on the funeral pyre of their husband was abolished by law. A law was passed validating the remarriage of Hindu widows. Female education received its due share of attention. Then came Bankim Chandra who raised Bengali literature to a position of eminence by enriching it. Then the community started interesting itself in the political rights of the people under the leadership of Surendranath Banerjee. His own English daily, the Bengali and the newly established newspaper, the Amrita Bazar Patrika engaged in a campaign to inculcate patriotic feelings among the masses.

No wonder, the imperial power felt worried. The Bengali community had so longer limited its attention to affairs which did not directly threaten the interest of British power. When, however, they launched a political movement they felt that their imperial interest was being imperilled. The then Viceroy of India, Lord Curzon, advised that the remedy lay in neutralising the influence of the Bengali on other communities of India. That could be achieved by splitting the community into two, so that it is rendered weak. It was decreed, therefore, that Bengali should be partitioned. The province of Bengal as constituted at that time covered extensive territories. It comprised Bengal as it stood before independence as well as Bihar and Orissa.

Evidently, the partition was motivated and not dictated purely by administrative interest. The imperial power had noticed that it was the Bengali Hindu who led all progressive movements of those days. What is called for, therefore, is that this community should be so divided up that its cohesive strength is destroyed. So a new province was created by joining the eastern part of the Bengali speaking area with the province of Assam to form a Muslim majority area. Simultaneously the western part of the Bengali speaking area was joined with Bihar and Orissa so that though it formed a Hindu majority area, the Bangali Hindu was reduced to a minority community. These facts clearly establish that the motive that worked behind was to split up the Bengali Hindu community by putting them under two different administrative system, so that it loses its identity and is weakened by being, reduced to a minority community in both the newly created provinces. When this decision was announced, the Bengalis reacted sharply. The leaders had no difficulty in discovering the motive that worked behind it. They decided to register their protest by launching a powerful political movement. When the threat of this danger to the nation roused his countrymen to such patriotic upsurge, Rabindranath could not keep himself aloof, A poet to the core of his heart, he felt strongly the indignation of this unfair act of the rulers. Small wonder, he enthusiastically joined the fray.

There was a second reason for this. Rabindranath had imbibed patriotic ideas in his boyhood, thanks to the atmosphere prevailing in the family in which he had been brought up. He had on two occasions actively participated in the movement launched by his elder brother for the spread of patriotic ideas through the institution of the Hindu Mela. The seed thus sown in boyhood acquired strength as he grew up to provide additional inspiration. National dress and national language were dearer to him than life.

There is a fine anecdote to show how strongly patriotic feelings worked in his mind. It was the year of the great earthquake of 1897. A sitting of the Bengal Provincial Conference was organised that year at Natore with the Maharaja of Natore as the chairman of the reception committee. In those days, the medium of communication of such political assemblies used to be English exclusively. This system was absolutely repugnant to Rabindranath. No wonder, he tabled a resolution that Bengali should be the medium of discussion. The leaders of the assembly led by Lal Mohan Ghosh strongly objected to this and some of them even insinuated that Rabindranath had been actuated to move the resolution for his weak command over English. Luckily, he got the support of the younger delegates who included his nephew, Abanindranath. The strong opposition could not dissuade Rabindranath from reiterating his motion. An account of what followed has been given by Abanindranath which is quoted below in translation:

"We took our seats in the pandal and as soon as any body stood up to address the assembly we shouted in one voice. 'Speak in Bengali', please. We allowed nobody to open his mouth. Whenever anybody starts in English we shouted 'Talk in Bengali'. After sometime, many of the leaders submitted to our wish. Even Lal Mohan Ghosh who had been thoroughly westernised and had ceased altogether to talk in Bengali addressed the meeting in Bengali to the surprise of everybody."[1]

How could a man who had developed such a mental attitude and was endowed with a highly sensitive heart remain a silent spectator of the movement started during this political

1. Abanindranath, Gharoa (Recorded by Rani Chanda).

crisis ? Rabindranath got deeply involved in the movement and even happened to lead it. The leaders decided to launch a movement for the boycott of British goods as a protest against the proposed partition. This decision was announced formally on 7th August, 1905. This was the occasion when the poet, Rajani Kanto Sen, composed the popular song which starts with the lines 'Graciously accept, my brother, the coarse cloth given by mother'.

Rabindranath employed his pen vigorously in denouncing the decision about partition. It produced songs with a new flavour. The patriotic songs he composed at this stage were surcharged with a strong emotional appeal and have enriched the quality of Bengali patriotic songs. An extract from a song addressed to the British power which ruled India is reproduced below by way of illustration :

You consider yourself powerful enough
to destroy what God had ordained;
But are you really so powerful?
You have the conceit to think
that you can treat us anyway you like;
such indeed is your conceit.

It was notified by Government that order about partition would come into force with effect from 16th October, 1905. Rabindranath drew up an elaborate programme for observing the date as a days of protest and mourning. It was decided that no food would be cooked that day in any home and that Bengalis would take a bath in the Hughlee first thing in the morning and then tie *Rakhis* (a band symbolising friendship) on the wrist of other Bengalis. This ceremony of tying *Rakhis* symbolised the idea that persons who had grown up in close intimacy as children of the same soil under decree of God cannot be separated by the directive of the political authority.

Rabindranath decided to lead the procession timed for that date himself. He was accompanied by his two nephews, Abanindranath and Surendranath. Led by Rabindranath, the procession started from the house of the Tagores at Jorasanko and proceeded to the river bank for a bath. The ceremony roused tremendous enthusiasm among the local people. People line up on both sides of the route in large numbers to see the precisionists who sang peridoic songs as they marched on. Let us hear what followed from Abanindranath who gives an eye witeness account of the same:

"We proceeded towards the river for a bath. Both sides of the road through which the procession was due to pass were crowded with spectators, who had also filled the roofs of housing lining the route. Women were scattering fried rice and blowing conch-shell with great enthusiasm to add dignity to the procession. Led by Dinendranath, the processionists sang as follows as they proceeded along the route:

Let Bengal's soil and Bengal's water,

Bengal's air and Bengal's fruits

Be associated with sanctity

This song had been composed for use on this occasion. A huge crowd had assembled in the bathing place to have a look at uncle Rabi. Bath over, we started tying Rakhis on one another's wrist, a huge stock of which, we carried with us".[2]

In course of the procession, Rabindranath interested himself vigorously in tying Rakhis on everybody he came across, regardless of age, race or community. He happened to see some syces engaged in massaging their horses. He tied Rakhis on their wrists. A man of caution by nature, Abanindranath apprehended that the reaction of the syces who were Muslims, might take a violent form. Thank God, they did not protest at all. In the meantime the procession reached the crossing of Chitpore Road. Rabindranath

2. Abanindranath, Gharoa (Recorded by Rani Chanda).

expressed his intention to proceed to the big mosque to the south and tie Rakhis on the wrist of the Maulavis assembled there. Abanindranath smelt danger. He apprehended that such action would end in violence leading to blood-shed. Lacking the courage to dissuade his uncle, he decided on a course to save himself. We may listen to his own account of how he executed his decision:

"What I did was this. As soon as the procession reached the point where the lame leading to our house branches out, I slipped into its security. Uncle never noticed it. He proceeded without concern to the mosque accompanied by Dinu, Suren and other dare-devils" [3]

It was, however, found that there was no need for such precaution. The men at the mosque submitted to the gesture peacefully.

That is how the Swadeshi movement was initiated. As a measure against the movement for the boycott of British goods, the government issued a directive to the authorities of all schools and colleges that the students should not be allowed to participate in the movement. The leaders of the movement reacted by calling a meeting, which passed a resolution to release education from the control of the government. The National Council of Education was established on 15th August, 1906 to give effect to this decision with Sri Aurobindo as its Director. The seed thus sown has now sprouted into the magnificent tree which is the Jadavpur University today. It is a strange coincidence that on exactly the same day fortyone years after India became independent. Be that as it may, Rabindranath joined the institution enthusiastically. He took an active part in drawing up the constitution and syllabus of this institution.

Soon, however, the movement took a very different turn. The leaders directed it to a course which was not to Rabindranath's liking. He favoured constructive

3 . Abanindranath, Gharoa, (Recorded by Rani Chanda).

work; but the movement tended to feed the emotion through meetings, processions and boycotts of British goods. Rabindranath had personal views on this issue which has been eladorated in the essay bearing the title 'Swadeshi Samaj'. In short he held the view that movements at best generate a short lived emotional upheaval, but cannot prepare the mind for a long programme of sacrifice. On the other hand, political independence can be achieved only through a long period of patient constructive activity. A programme of reconstruction should be initiated at the first instance at the level of the villages. Village societies should be set up to unite the rural people and to teach them to be self-sufficient through cooperative endeavour. If these villages can thus be taught to be self-sufficient in agriculture and industry, this bondage imposed from outside will disappear automatically.

These are the reasons why Rabindranath did not like the method initiated by the political leaders, which discards a constructive approach and encourages emotional excitement limiting action to movement alone. So he gave it up and resumed his work at Santiniketan. One of the poems contained in collection bearing the title 'Kheya' which was published at the time, gives a realistic picture of the anguish suffered by the poet on this occasion. It can be quoted with advantage here. What interested him as an abiding passion was the Brahmacharya Ashram established by him at Santiniketan after the model of the ancient forest settlements. His protest against the partition of Bengal by the fiat of a foreign power was only a temporary diversion. As his interest in this second affair cooled off his true object of loved pulled her again towards it. This finds expression themeof the poem referred to above. It says :

Farewell, my brothers, forgive my offence;

I shall no more participate in your work.

Go ahead in large numbers;

Win as many laurels as you can.

I want to go away unnoticed
    To the shade of my woods. [4]

Towards the end of the poem, he makes it clear that he had lost interest in the movement on account of the form it eventually assumed.

The things that attract you to day
Hold no charm for me.
Seeking out treasures, demolishing states,
Fighting at home and abroad
    for a view-point
Are as good as pouring water
    At the root
Of a tall champak tree.

It appears that the real reason behind this parting was that political movements did not suit his taste. On the other hand, being endowed with acute sensitivity, he could not resist his patriotic feelings getting the better of him and involving him in politics to protest against unjust measures adopted by the ruling power . Neither the atmosphere created by the political movements that followed, nor the programme adopted by it were, however, liked by him. That is why politics could not hold his attention for long. This proposition is confirmed by the observations made by him in a letter written to his friend C.F. Andrews, the relevant extract of which is quoted below:

"Swadeshi swarajism ordinarily produced intense excitement in the minds of my countrymen because they carry in them some fervour of a passion, generated by the exclusiveness of their rage. It cannot be said that I am untouched by this heat and movement. But somehow by my temperament as a poet, I am incapable of accepting these objects as final". [5]

---

4. Kheya, Biday.
5. Rathindranath Tagore, on the Edges of Time, the Swadeshi Movement.

The above observation throws considerable light on his attitude to political movements. In substance, he could not help reacting sharply against any outrage committed by the rulers. He would not find peace of mind until he lodged his protest in his own way to such acts. On the other hand, he would not feel himself in his elements in politics and so he could not seriously get involved in it. No wonder, he responded to the call for protest against the passing of the Rowlatt Act under similar circumstance when a powerful movement started.

The tragedy which started it occurred on 13th April 1919. At the terminations of the First World War the British government introduced the Rowlatt Act in the Legislative Council, to equip themselves with a law authorising detention of any person without trial. That was intended as a measure to suppress the increasing political unrest in the country. A powerful movement was, however, launched against it under the leadership of Mahatma Gandhi. The protest ended in a major tragedy in the Punjab. A few thousand men had assembled in an open space at Jalianwalabag General Dyer was deputed with a contingent of troops to disperse the people assembled there. The people had assembled in a field enclosed on three sides with walls. The soldiers took their position on the open side thereby effectively blocking their exit and opened fire under the order of Gerenal Dyer on the unarmed crowd. Denied the means of escape the majority of the people perished under gun fire 379 persons died and a larger number was wounded.

When the news of this tragedy reached Rabindranath at Santiniketan, he was overwhelmed with shock. He felt that his ribs were on fire. Unable to decide what to do, he went to Calcutta. After a good deal of deliberational, he decided to lodge a personal protest with the British government. He sent a letter to the Viceroy of India on 29th April, renouncing his knighthood.

How grievously this act of butchery pained his heart, is indicated by the contents of this letter. A relevant extract is quoted below:

"The enormity of the measures taking by the Government of the Punjab for quelling some local disturbances has with a rude shock, revealed to our minds the helplessness of our position as British subjects in India. The disproportionate severity of the punishment inflicted upon the unfortunate people and the methods of carrying them out we are confident without parallel in the history of civilised governments barring some conspicuous exceptions. Considering that such treatment has been meted out to a population disarmed and resourcless by a power which had the most terribly efficient organisation for destrucetion of human lives, we must strongly assert that it can claim no political expediency, far less moral justification."

The above quotation which formed the introductory part of the letter was followed by the renunciation of the Knighthood. The language used in this connection is as sober as it is indignant and runs as follows:

"The time has come when badges of honour make our shame glaring in the incongruous context of humiliation and I, for my part, of wish to stand shown of all special distinctions by the side of those of my countrymen who, for their so called insignificance, are liable to suffer degradation not fit for human beings."

At this stage of his life he had to attend to certain duties in respect of his children, in the absence of his deceased wife. His eldest son Rathindranath had since passed the Entrance Examination of the Calcutta University. He had to arrange for the higher education of Rathindranath outside India. Luckily, an American institution had in the meantime experssed its willingness to impart higher education to Indians. Rathindranath was selected as a member of the first batch of students and was asked to proceed to his destination via Japan. He was to undergo training in agronomy. Accordingly, he sailed for the United States in April, 1906. After completing a three year course at Illinois University he returned home in 1909 with a Bachelors Degree in Science. Thereafter Rabindranath sent him to Shiladaha to look after the family estates. It was also arranged that he would start an agricultural farm there to try out his newly acquired agricultural farm there to try out his newly acquired technical skill. Next year, he married Rathindranath to Pratima Devi who was the daughter of his cousin's family. In fact, she was the widowed daughter of Benayani Devi grand-daughter of Girindranath, second brother of Debendranath.So it was a case of a daughter of the family returning to the home as a daughter-in-law.

There was another duty for him to discharge. He married his youngest daughter Meera to Nagendranath Ganguly in Jyaistah, 1314, Bengali era corresponding to 1907 A.D. Rabindranath sent him also to the United States for training in agronomy. Presumably, the idea of rural reconstruction through improved agricultural practices loomed large in his mind at that stage and prompted him to train both his son and son-in-law as experts in agriculture. Evidently, any programme for community development in rural areas has to be based on improved agricultural practices, where agriculture forms the economic base of a country.

8

RABINDRANATH-IV

The period that followed the death of his wife in Rabindranath's life may be called the period of travail. He was put to severe test in two different ways. On the one hand, he had to face bereavement after bereavement, death striking down most cruelly one after another his close relatives, whose absence makes life miserable. First to go was Mrinalini Devi followed by his second daughter, Renuka. Then he lost his father and last to go was his youngest son, Samindra. All these bereavements were packed into a span of only five years. On the other hand, a strong political movement swept the country. It attracted him so strongly that he could not help joining the movement heart and soul. Eventually, he came to the turning point of his life. Teaching and literary activity were the things he dearly loved. Political leadership provided a new attraction. His strong patriotic feelings pulled him strongly to it. His powerful pen supplied to his countrymen a number of patriotic songs at the initial stage which proved to be a tremendous source of inspiration. If he so desired, he could have committed himself to a life of politics; but he did not. The main reason was that the complexity of political life did not suit his taste; it did not conform to his style of life. So he returned to his old life.

When, however, he returned he had been transformed into new man. The ordeal by fire he faced brought to him a sense of balance. The unpleasant experience of his political life released him from the sense of unbalance engendered by the two opposite pulls. He accepted the path of his choice with his whole heart unreservedly.

The two pulls made their presence felt for the first time in his book of poems entitled 'the Chitra'.

Two poems of this collection are relevant to the present topic. One of them bears the title 'Ebar Firao Moro' (Take Me Back This Time). It gives expression to a feeling that versification had ceased to hold his interest and he feels a strong yearning to give relief to the poor, neglected and underprivileged section of his countrymen and rescue them from the life of misery they live. He has been commanded to answer the call from this new quarter. The relevant quotation from the poem referred to above will bear this out:

> There is misery, there is pain, there is a hard life in front,
>
> There is poverty abounding-empty, mean, constricted and filled with darkness.
>
> What is wanted is food, life, light and free air,
>
> And a capacious heart full of courage.
>
> Into this gloom of poverty
>
> oh poet, bring
>
> Down from heaven the spirit of confidence. [1]

There was a second yearning raising its head at the corner. It was a yearning to be with God all by himself to be close to Him as a pious devotee. The other poem gives experssion to this in symbolic language and bears the title 'Ābedan'. He asks in it the favour of being appointed the garland-maker of the flower garden of the object of his love.

It appears that he joined the anti-partition movement under the inspiration of the first yearning. Evidently, it was one of the opposite pulls that got the better of him here. As this did not fit in with his inclination, he had to withdraw from the movement subsequently. It was time for the other pull to assert itself. He responded to its call and in the process he discovered his God whom he calls 'Jivandevata' (The Lord of My Heart) and built round Him his own personal religion.

1. Ebar Firao moro, Chitra.

Consequently, this proved to be the period when he attained spiritual self-realisation. It was during this time that he attained maturity in his poetical power as well as spiritual thought simultaneously. This is explained by the fact that his view on religion did not conform to the traditional religion accepted in society. Both his poetry and his religion attained fulfilment by pursuing the same comman path. They reached their destination together like two pilgrims joining in companionship in their journey. The story of that interesting journey will presently engage our attention. That it was a common journey shared together will be borne out by the following observation made by the poet himself:

"My religious life has followed the same mysterious line of growth as has my poetic life. Somehow thev are wedded to each other and though their betrothal had a long period of ceremony, it was kept a secret to me ".[2]

It appears that death perpared the way for it by dealing repeated blows to open the door to self-realisation. A song composed by him begins thus :

> If the dark night of sorrow can make
> thy benign light glow
> Let it be so.
> If death can bring near thy kingdom
> of bliss,
> Let it be so.

This is what took place in his life. The repeated shocks of death in the family brought nearer to him the kingdom of heaven. Through meditation and poetical pursuits he discovered his Jivan Devata (The Lord of Life) and at the end of his spiritual quest rediscovered him again in humanity. Thus during this chapter of his life two original philosophical concepts took shape in his mind: the concept of the 'Jivan Devata' and his theory on the Religion of Man. The story of the evolution of these ideas is given below:

It has been already mentioned that Rabindranath's poetical starts with his first intimacy with nature, the beauty and power displayed in different phenomena of

2. Religion of Men, The Vision.

nature would attract his attention. The breeze playing with the fronds of cocnut palms, the dark could hanging heavy with rain, the red ball of fire appearing in the morning sky would deeply move his sensitive heart. What, however, specially catches the eye is the fact that his attention was not confined to the physical aspect of the beauty it indicated to him in addition the presence of a hidden spirit beyond. The fluffy clouds moving across the autumn sky not only pleased his eyes but also reminded him of the unseen spirit that set adrift these rafts of cloud in the sky. So that pointedly raises the question 'who is he that floated the rafts of white clouds in the blue sky ?'. When the monsoon sky becomes packed with rain clouds his heart yearns for an unknown beloved.

Ultimately, like his Vedic ancestors, he discovered one day that the different phenomena of nature reveal the presence of an unseen pervasive spirit which comprehends all nature and the entire universe. The life that unfolds itself in trees, creepers and flowers on the bosom of the earth represents herds of cattle grazing in the sun and the countless stars that illumine the nights represent another herd of cattle in form of cultural bodies. The herds are visible but the cowherd that looks after then remains unseen, his presence being betrayed by the music of his flute :

> These are thy luminous cattle
>
> these groups of suns and stars
>
> From what hidden corner
>
> them playest thy flute and
>
> Grazest them under the
>
> endless celestial sphere .[3]

A new stage is indicated in the spiritual life of Rabindranath in the poems of the Chitra. At that stage, he felt the presence of two opposite pulls within himself which, he compares to 'twin spirits'. One represents the attraction for the external manifestation of the supreme

3 . Gitanjali.

spirit in nature; while the other represents the yearning for the establishment of a personal contact with it in privacy. It is in the poems of the Chitra that these opposite yearnings make their presence felt for the first time. As they have been dealt with already in detail there is no point in repeating the process here. It is, however, necessary to refer to an observation made by the poet himself to bear out our proposition. A quotation in translation is given below:

" The realisation which found expression in the poems of 'Chitra' is of a different class. I felt that there were twin souls within me comparable to binary stars which constitute my personality and exert equal influence on me.... The twins souls should equally participate in the worship of the supreme deity. One will inspire me from inside and the other will occupy itself in altruistic activities outside." [4]

This concept of the twin souls within him carried within it the seed of the concept of the 'Jivan Devta'. The twin souls of the poet have different fields of attraction. The world outside is one of them. The supreme spirit in the role of Viswadevta (The Lord of the Universal) manifests itself in a variety of forms and invites the poet to enjoys its charms. The other field is located inside the mind of the poet, where the poet wants to enjoy the company of the supreme spirit as a person in the privacy of the dark chamber of his heart. Very likely, this yearning to meet the supreme spirit alone in privacy led to the decision that the meeting place should be the temple of the mind within.

It appears that the concept of the 'Jivan Devata' did not remain in the form of a seed only at the time the poems of the 'Chitra' were composed, but had also sprouted into a sapling. 'The Chitra' was published in 1896 A.D., when he was living in North Bengal to look after the family estates under the direction of his father. His headquarters were located at Shilaidaha on the south bank of the Padma. He had to go about by boat to inspect

4. Chitor Suchanã.

the different collection offices of the family estates situated in different parts of Nadia, Rajsahi and Pabna districts. It was in course of one of those journeys that the idea of the 'Jivan Devata' flashed in his mind through a vision. He has described the incident in detail in the 'Hibbert Lectures' delivered by him at Oxford University, subsequently published as a book under the title 'The Religion of Man'. He has mentioned there that the concept of the 'Jivan Devata' first made its appearance in his early life drawing nourishment from his mental attitude. It is not a product of philosophical deliberation, but was discovered in a flash through a vision. It is comparable to the experience which provided the inspiration for the poem entitled 'Nirjharer Swapnabhanga' (The awakening of the cataract.) During this period he used to tour about in North Bengal to inspect the particular estates of the family. After working in the office of the estate, he had returned to the attached rest house and on his way to the bath-room was standing near a window overlooking a market in front. Close by flowed a river made lively by the first monsoon showers. Suddenly a vision flashed upon his mind. He felt that he had arrived at his own home groping through a dense barrier of fog. It appeared to him that the detached facts of his life held a significance of their own. He felt the presence within him of a being who seeks fulfilment through the poets activities. He elaborates the idea in his own way thus:

"On that morning the facts of my life suddenly appeared to me illumined us unity of truth. The events that had seemed like vagrant waves were revealed to my mind in relation to a boundless sea. I felt sure that some Being who comprehended me and my world was seeking his best expression in all my experiences". [5]

It is this Being whom he named 'Jivan Devata'. Evidently, the concept of 'Jivan Devata' not only appeared as a seminal idea during the period when the poems of the 'Chitra' were composed but also germinated. He also named the poem composed on this occasion to express his relationship with

5. The Religion of Man, Viswa.

this mysterious being 'Jivan Devata'. It is included in the 'Chitra' It is noticeable 'however' that for a long time after this he composed poem that drew inspiration from this theme. Even in the collection of poems named the 'Naivedya' which are deeply spiritual in content, there is no poem on 'Jivan Devata'. The theme, regained its seats in the poet's mind a long time after. The 'Jivan Devata' reappeared in full glory when he gave up his connection with the anti-partition movement and returned to the life of his choice, devoted entirely to teaching and literary pursuits. Death had knocked at his door many a time before that. It was in this atmosphere, clouded by disappointment and bereavements, that he got back his 'Jivan Devata.' This is, why he said:

If in the darkness of sorrow glows
Thy benign light
Let it be so.

When the "Jivan Devata" came this time he filled the poet's heart entirely and came to stay there. For a long time, he became the principal source of inspiration of the poems that Rabindranath wrote during this period. These poems constitute the material of three books of verse written one after another namely the Gitanjali, the Gitali and the Gitimalya. The 'Gitanjali' was first published in 1910 and the other two books in 1914. The poems occupying the first few pages of the 'Gitanjali' were published in 1906. These facts would suggest that a single theme provided the inspiration for his poems for as long as eight years, a phenomenon hardly repeated in the history of world literature. These three poetical works present us with a complete record of the history of the growth of the poet's spiritual life to maturity in verse.

This chapter of Rabindranath's life was as interesting as it was romantic. The poems composed during this period reflect three broad themes, namely, the poet's yearning for union with the 'Jivan Devata', the pangs of separation felt by him, and their ultimate union. The poet's heart was fortified by a firm belief that he had been born to find out his 'Jivan Devata'.

"It is destined that Thou shalt

realise yourself within me.

Indeed that is why I was born.[6]

But the Beloved does not come to meet him. The poet's anxious waiting is not rewarded by His arrival. This disappointment fills his heart with sorrow. The unbearable pang of separation has filled the entire world a round him. So he says :

" The pang of Thy separation has

become incarnate

And taken shape all around me.

It manifests itself in diverse forms

in forests and mountains

In the sky and in the ocean".[7]

After a long period of suffering, a time came when it dawned on the poet that the 'Jivan Devata' was not to be found in the world outside, because He takes His seat within the mind of a man. He releases that 'Jivan Devata' has no visible form, He is the king of the dark chamber, He loves from behind a veil and, therefore, is not visible in the outside world. So the poet observes:

" I could not realise that

Thouhadst remained hidden within

my heart ;

I had looked for Thee in the

outside world,

But did not look inside my heart".[8]

Then, at last, union came but in a strange relationship. The Vaisnava poet has conceived of four kinds of relationship with God on the basis of different conceivable attitudes. From the servant's points of view, the relationship becomes dominated

6. Gitanjali.
7. Gitanjali.
8. Gitanjali.

by the emotion of servitude, from the child's point of view, it becomes dominated by the emotion of filial affection and from the point of view of a friend it becomes dominated by the emotion of friendly love. He assigns the place of honour to the relationship where the deity and the devotee met on a footing of equality. That is why he calls it the Madhu Rasa. (The sweet sentiment). Rabindranath's relationship with his 'Jivan Devata' passed through the then other forms before it attained the stage of Madhura rasa in its mature form. At the initial stage, he had some hesitation in treating God on a footing of equality.

So he says :

> " I stand apart from Thee treating Thee as a God,
>
> I do not fondle Thee as a dear one,
>
> I bow down to Thy feet treating them as my Father;
>
> I don't hold Your hands as a friend". [9]

When, however, he was able to accept without reservation the relationship conceived in the 'Madhura Rasa' he felt elated to find that the 'Jivan Devata' had as much need for him as he for the 'Jivan Devata' himself. His elation finds a joyous expression in the following lines:

> " That is why Thou takes delight in me
>
> That is why Thou has come down to my level
>
> Without me, oh Lord of the three worlds
>
> Thy love would not have found
>
> fulfilments".[10]

The growth of Rabindranath's spiritual life, however did not step with the God on the personal love manifest as 'Jivan Devata'. It found fulfilment in a richer realisation, the history of which has been also recorded in the poems of the Gitanjali. Evidently, his union with the 'Jivan Devata' swetened his life, but it failed to give him complete satisfaction. He found close access to his beloved but he was denied the pleasure of seeing his beloved, as the 'Jivan Devata' was a disembodied spirit which had no physical manifestation. Consequently, the poet

9. Getanjali.

10. Getanjali.

got access to him within his own heart, but could not reach him through his work. His desire to give personal service to his beloved remained unrealised.

So, the poet started out again in quest of a solution which could fulfil his yearning to serve his God. In the process, he found his own personal religion. He argued that since God pervades the entire universe of He has to be served at all, He should be served in that form of manifestation which is closest to man, He is manifest most intimately to man as man and so he realised that service to man is the best way to serve God. So service of mankind in general amounts to service of his 'Jivan Devata'. A woman is best accessible to a child as a mother. Similarly, God is best accessible to man as man for the purpose of service. So he observes as follows :

"Just as a mother is most intimate to and most directly in contact with her child in her relation as mother, while other diverse relations with the world are unknown and unusable to him, God is manifest to man in the truest and most intimate form in humanity. It is through such relation that we know Him, love Him and after service to Him".[11]

Rabindranath's pilgrimage in sacred of spiritual self-realisation thus found fulfilment, in thus humanising God. This represents his view of the religion of man.

The Hibbert lectures he delivered under the auspices of the Oxford University deals with this subject. In substance, he holds the view that service to mankind is service to God and constitutes the best form of religious practice. A devotee inspired by this ideal would say God cannot be found in temples, traditional religions cannot give access to God and service of mankind in general is the best form of worship. So he says :

"Come out of thy meditation and leave aside the flowers and incense. What harm is there if thy clothes become tattered and staied? Meet him and stand by him in toil and the sweat of thy brow". [12]

This same thought assumed towards the end of the Gitanjali a more refined form. As God is mainfest in all men, service of

11. Jharna.
12. Gitanjali English Version.

mankind is undeniably service of God. But he felt that God is specially manifest in men who are burdened with poverty and subjected to neglect. God takes special delight, in being with people who have been deprived of all they possessed and have been insulted :

> " Here is the footstand and there
> rest Thy feet where live the poorest
> and lowliest and lost ". [13]

It is here that we come across both the poetry and the religions thought of Tagore in their maturest form. The poet who yearned at one stage for union with God in privacy, ultimately attained spiritual satisfaction by dedicating himself to the welfare of mankind. He realised God within his heart in the form of 'Jiven Devata' but rediscovered Him among men in general and the poor and the underprivileged in particular, to serve Him. That is how his religious thoughts culminated in a broad-based humanism. Rabindranath himself admits that it was this concept of religion that provided him the inspiration for his educational and rural welfare activities at Santiniketan and the neighbourhood. The following observation of his becomes relevant in this connection:

" I am sure that it was this idea of the divine Humanity unconsciously working in my mind which compelled me to come out of the seclusion of my literary career and take my part in the world of practical activities. The solitary enjoyment of the Infinite in meditation no longer satisfied me and texts which I used for my silent worship lost their inspiration without my knowing it. I am sure I vaguely felt that my need was spiritual self-realisation in the life of Man through some disinterested service". [14]

Small wonder, the poet who at one stage yearned for union with his 'Jivan Devata' in the dark chamber of his heart declared that he craved for union with God not in the seclusion of forest nor within his mind, but where He is among the multitude". [15]

---

13. Gitanjali 10 English Version.
14. Religion of Man The Teacher.
15. Gitanjali.

This story of his spiritual self-realisation is recorded in the poems of the Gitanjali.

Rabindranath's poetry attained its mature form in the poems of the Gitanjali. That was, therefore, the most suitable time for him to be introduced to the outside world. This happy event was brought about by a combination of circumstances. It may be assumed that people abroad hardly kept any information about the person who was preparing himself for recognition as an international poet unseen, in a corner of Bengal. Even his nephew, Abanindranath, had acquired an international reputation which he did not match. People outside India knew Abanindranath better than him. Then all on a sudden, the combination of certain circumstances focussed the attention of the people of the world on him. It is now time to record that interesting story.

After the death of Mrinalini Devi, there was nobody in the family to look after Rabindranath. The eldest daughter had left the family after marriage and the second daughter died soon after. The eldest son left for the United States for higher education. The youngest daughter Meera was too young to discharge domestic duties. So Rabindranath had to look after himself. Prone to be absent minded and absorbed in his work, he had, however, little capacity to take care of himself. The political agitation raging in the country and the affairs of Santiniketan occupied all his time. Evidently, the body was subjected to many excesses. His robust health enabled him to stand them for a considerable time . But a time came when the body failed and he became seriously ill in 1912. He also developed piles. The doctor advised surgical treatment in the United Kingdom. This advice was prompted by two considerations. For one thing, the long voyage by sea would ensure enough rest for the health to recuperate. Secondy, the best available treatment will be possible.

So a trip to the United Kingdom was arranged for and all necessary preparations were made in due course. He was to leave by ship from Chandpalghat, in Calcutta, and passage was booked accordingly. Ashutosh Chaudhuri gave a big farewell party at his residence at Ballygunge the previous night. Rabindranath returned home late in the night after attending the same. The luggage had been despatched to the ship in the meantime. Rabindranath, however, became indisposed in the morning. Consequently, he had to cancel his voyage and bring back to the luggage from the ship.

Though the journey was thus cancelled. The doctors did not give him permission to resume his activities. They insisted that he must take complete for sometime. So according to his desire, Shilaidaha associated with the memory his days of his youth was selected as the place for him to rest. That is how the prospect of the publication of the English version of the Gitanjali was opened up. The doctors had strictly forbidden all work involving either physical and mental exertion. So creative writing was banned. In these circumstances, Rabindranath decided to engage his spare time in the translation of his Bengali poems into English. In the meantime the translation of some of his composition had been published in the Modern Review and appreciated both by Ananda Coomerswamy and Jagadish Chandra Bose. This acted as an incentive. So he started spending his lovely days at Shilaidaha, in translating his Bengali poems into English.

The English Gitanjali contains 103 poems in translation. Most of them have been selected from the Bengali Gitanjali. The remaining poems were selected from eight other books of poems. A table is placed below to show how many poems were selected for translation from which books:

Gitanjali..........55, Gitimalya...........16
Naivedya..........14, Kheya...............11
Shishu...............3, Chaitali..............1
Kalpana..............1, Utaara.................1
Smarana.............1

Total : 103

The poems in the English Gitanjali do not give a literal translation of the original Bengali composition. The metre of the Bengali poems is together missed in the translation as it had been done in prose. There can be no question of reproducing the euphonic beauty of the original composition in the translation. These are all factors which prevent a perfect literary translation. Rabindranath did not want this either. His main objective was to give adequate expression to the thoughts contained in the original in the translation. In consequence, the translation has assumed a shortened form in one place and an expanded form elsewhere as the circumstances demanded. The translation assumed a literal form only where this could be achieved without sacrificing the sense. They should not, therefore, be treated as translations so much as new compositions inspired by the original poems.

Rabindranath returned from Shilaidah when his health improved. His passage to the United Kingdom was again booked for his treatment. He boarded a ship of the' 'P-O-Company', in the Bombay harbour on 27th May, 1912 accompanied by Rathindranath and Pratima Devi. The manuscript of the English version of the Gitanjali also accompanied them. Rabindranath wanted to show the manuscript to the sculptor Rothenstein who happened to be a friend of the family. Rathindranath was entrusted with the custody of same. They reached London in due course. Thomas Cook had booked their accommodation in Bloomsbury Hotel. They came there by the underground. Rabindranath was due to call on Rothenstein next morning, but, unfortunately, when he asked for the manuscript his son could not deliver it. Presumably, it had been lost during transit. We may conveniently hear how this problem was dramatically solved directly, from the son. He records it in his reminiscences as follows:

"The manuscript of the translation of the poems of father which were subsequently published in two separate collections under the name 'Gitanjali' and 'The Gardener' had been placed in an attache case and made over to for safe custody. When the me attache case was found missing the next day, I rushed to the left luggage office and to my great relief traced it out there. Presumably, it had been left behind in the tube train by which we travelled to the hotel.

One can imagine my relief when at last I discovered the lost property there. Since then I had often wondered what shape the course of events might have taken if the manuscript of Gitanjali had been lost through my negligence". [16]

Very likely, if the manuscript of the English Gitanjali had not been recovered. Rabindranath's literary career might have taken a different course. Would he have had the enthusiasm to translate them over again. If not, he would have remained undiscovered to the people of the West, and the cultural history of India would have been the poorer for the absence of such contact.

Be that as it may, with the manuscript thus recovered Rabindranath called on Rothenstein at the appointed time and made it over to him to read. Though an artist by profession Rothenstein had a wide interest in all branches of aesthetic activities. He took a keen interest in creative literature and was acquainted with many prominent literary figures of the time. He liked Rabindranath's translation and enthusiastically introduced him to English writers.

It was decided that a number of selected writers would be invited to assemble in the drawing room of Rothenstein to listen to a reading of Rabindranath's manuscript. The assembly included Ezra Pound, May Sinclair, Charles Trevelyn and C.F. Andrews. The Irish poet Yeats gave a reading of the poems. The reaction was wholly unexpected. The listeners were so deeply impressed that they turned into Rabindranath's admirers and decided to publish the manuscript

16. Rathindranath Tagore, on the Edges of Time.

themselves. We are familiar with the development that followed leading to the addition of a unique chapter to the history of international literature. His admirers founded the India Society and under its auspices the English 'Gitanjali' was published. Work proceeded at a fast pace. The reading of Rabindranath's rooms was given at Rothenstein's house of 7th July, 1912. His admirers arranged for a reception for him only three days after at the Trocadero restaurant. The observations Yeats made in that reception about the merits of the poems bear out how deeply they impressed English readers. Yeats said:

"In all his poems, there is one single theme : the love of God ......Tagore loves nature; his poems are full of the most beautiful touches showing his keen observation and deep love. He does not count beads but flowers. In this book. There is a ceaseless abundance of beauty" .

What Rabindranath said in reply also deserves our attention. The significant part is quoted below:

"East is East and West is West. God forbid that this should the otherwise but the twin must meet in amity peace and understanding; that meeting will be all the more fruitful because of their difference; it must lead both to holy wedlock at the common altar of humanity".

This observation of his gives a clear indication of the line along which his thought worked. He wanted that he should build between the different cultural groups of the world a bridge to unit them despite their diversity. His desire found the Viswabharati at a later stage stemmed from this thought.

Soon after the India Society founded by his admirers arranged for the publication of his English 'Gitanjali'. The introduction written by Yeats for this book is dated September 1912. The book was published soon after. It introduces Rabindranath's poetry to the people of the West. The poetry which charmed the hearts of his English admirers by the excellence of its literary quality thereafter started its expedition of conquest in a wider area. The people of the continent fell in love with his poetry. In due course, it attracted the attention of the authorities of the Nobel Prize foundation. Its merit was appreciated by them and it was awarded the Nobel Prize on literature the following November.

In between these events centring round the Gitanjali Rabindranath left for the United States accompanied by his son and daughter. In his itinerary he covered New York, Havana, Chicago, Rochester and Boston delivering lectures at selected places. After spending six months, there, he returned to the United Kingdom for his treatment. In the meantime the Gitanjali had been published and warmly appreciated in reviews published in different journals. He was admitted to hospital in June, 1913. The disease yielded to treatment and he left for home in the following September after discharge.

Rabindranath was at Santiniketan when the news of the awards of the Nobel Prize reached India. His people felt highly honoured by this award. What is more important, they became better aware of the literary quality of their poet. There is a Bengali proverb which says that 'immediate neighbours refuse to recognise' talents, which reflects a good deal of worldly wisdom. There is no denying the fact that discerning men with sympathetic hearts had duly appreciated his talents. On reading his 'Sandhya Sangeet', Bankim Chandra did not hesitate to give expression to highly appreciative remarks. When his playet the 'Valmiki Pratibha' was staged, Gooroodas Banerjeer went to the length of composing a poem to sing its praise. It is, however, a fat that a large section of the people of his country did not feel kindly disposed towards Rabindranath. They subjected him to severe hostile criticism. The people of his country were agreeably surprised to find that the literary quality of his poems had been found good enough for the award of the highest honour accessible to writers in the international field.

When a man, refused recognition at home, receives the highest honour abroad, people at home learn to appreciate his merit through the appreciation accorded to him by outsiders. His people thus discovered his talents afresh. It dawned on them that he was a poet who deserved international recognition.

Small wonder, therefore, that his own people became very eager to give him a special reception. It was decided that a reception would be held at Santiniketan, on 23rd November, 1913. Most of the distinguished men of Calcutta and his admirers arrived at Santiniketan by a special train to attend the function. The reception was held in the famous mango orchard. Different institutions and groups read out to him valedictory addresses. Even his erstwhile critics joined the reception. Unfortunately, the function ended with a jarring note. A rankling pain hidden within the heart of the poet suddenly found expression. The man who had so long maintained the utmost restraint in speech, who strictly avoided hurting others feelings, used some hard words in his reply. Evidently, this outburst was prompted by a sense of being hurt. He had formed the impression that it was the recognition given him abroad which had given his people inspiration to come forward to honour him. The following quotation will bear this out:

" The insult and hostile criticism heaped on me by my own people is considerable. I have suffered them, so long in silence.

I have not yet been able to find out why in this situation, recognition came to me from the outside world. I never knew that the deity to whom I gave my offering of flowers on the eastern shore of the ocean, would extend his right hand to receive the same from across the western shore.

"Be that as it may, whatever the reason Europe has given me the garland of honour. If it carries any value, it lies in the aesthetic sense of the men of culture of that country. It has no vital connection with my people. The award of the Nobel Prize does not necessarily enhance the literary or aesthetic quality of any composition." [17]

---

17. Probhat Kumar Mukhopadhya Rabindra Jivan Vol : II.

9

RABINDRANATH-V

Rabindranath had now become an international figure. His extraordinary talents had found recognition not only at home but abroad too. Following this, his countrymen as well as his Government took prompt action to confer on him a new honours. The University of Calcutta gave him the honourary degree of Doctor of Literature in 1914. This was followed next year by the British Government giving him a Kinghthood on the occasion of the Emperor's birthday, an honour never extended to any Indian for literary works by this alien Government.

In his early age Rabindranath had once regretfully observe: "After maintaining silence for long years, Bengal is overfilled with thoughts. Allow her to speak out her thoughts in her own words; the chorus of world music will be the sweeter by the voice of Bengal participating in it." [1]

After a long period of preparation he had now acquired the competence to speak to the world on behalf of the Bengali. The English translation of his original writings in Bengali impressed readers abroad. The voice of the Bengali thus enriched the international chorus of music. The award of the Nobel Prize to a Bengali amounts to a recognition of this fact. Rabindranath thus acquired the qualification to function as the spiritual ambassador of India. It appears that Bal Gangadhar Tilak, a distinguished

1. Vichitra, Prabhandha.

scholar of those days, became congnisant of this fact. He was then a leading political leader also. He made a personal request to Rabindranath that he should undertake publicity for India abroad. Rabindranath was rather surprised to find that Tilak had selected him for such work in preference to a political leader of distinction. Tilak, however, did not hesitate to assure him that lack of such distinction makes Rabindranath the better suited for the discharge of such function. The following observation of Rabindranath will bear this out :

"Lokmanya Tilak was then alive. He despatched to me a sum of rupees fifty thousand through messenger and communicated the wish that I should visit Europe. The non-cooperation movement had not yet started; but the political agitation had assumed the intensity of a storm. He told me that it was not his desire that I should involve myself in political affairs. The message that I could carry on behalf of India would be the proper work for me and I could serve India truly through such work". [2]

Rabindranath also got a call from within for such an excursion abroad. A desire was taking shape in his mind that he should know intimately other people and tell them about his own people. He felt that it was for him an obligatory duty that he should work for exchange of cultural wealth and building up friendly relations with other people. Small wonder, he gladly accepted all invitations extended to him from abroad. This forced him to undertake repeated tours abroad and spend long periods away from home. His enthusiasm for such journeys abroad did not slacken till old age and failing health robbed him of his capacity for such exertion.

After his recognition as a world figure, the first invitation to come was from Japan. Simultaneously, an American gentleman named Pond who ran an institution which organised lecture tours by distinguished men extended to him an invitation to undertake a lecture tour in the United States. Though purely, a business deal, Rabindranath did not hesitate to accept it. It was decided

2. Pashim Jatrir Diary.

that Rabindranath would first visit Japan and then sail for America. Andrews, Pearson and Mukul Dey accompanied him in this voyage.

He reached Tokyo via Kobe and Osaka where he became the guest of his family friend, Taikan, the famous Japanese painter. He was given a fitting reception there and then taken to the village home of the painter to enable him to pick up an intimate acquaintance with the people.

After a stay of three months in Japan he left for America. Andrews had in the meantime returned to India; Mukul Dey and Pearson continued to keep his company. On basis of the contract agreed to before, an itinerary had been drawn up which involved a long tour across the United States from the Pacific ocean on the west to the Altantic occean on the east. He conformed to the programme for two months but then lost patience. In the meantime, he had covered San-Francisco, Los Angeles, Chicago, New York and Boston. He cancelled the remaining part of the contract and returned home the way he came via Japan. He had left in May, 1916 and returned home in March, 1917. The First World War was then being fought in the continent of Eurpoe and so he had to undertake the crossing of the Pacific Ocean twice over.

Rabindranath took care to put on record invariably his experience in form of letters, essays or entries in his diary whenever he went abroad. Through his observations made in these records it is possible to find out how a particular country impressed him. It appears that he showered praises where he felt they were due and he did not hesitate to make adverse comments about what he disliked, never bothering about the consequences to follow. His only concern was to be truthful. Not unoften, the reaction had been unfavourable to him; but he never cared.

His experience in course of the journey referred to above was recorded in the book bearing the title 'Japan-Jatra'. Though the journey involved a tour of the United States also this book deals exclusively with his experience acquired in Japan. One possible explanation is that he had visited America before this already and this was his second visit to the place.

Though he disliked Japan's imperialistic ambition, he appears to have appreciated her culture. Two qualities of the Japanese people excited his admiration. One of them was their aesthetic sense and love of beauty. In his view, love of beauty was such a strong passion that the Japanese would gladly sacrifice claims of the body and endure poverty to seek aesthetic satisfaction. The following observation of this will bear this out :

"We have seen that it is possible to increase the power of one particular sense at the cost of another. Sense of beauty and emotion are both affairs of the heart. Ever since coming here what has struck me is this: It is also possible to develop the sense of beauty and the capacity to give it expression to a considerable degree by delimiting the field of emotion and its expression. I have come across numerous cases of emotional exuberance both in our country and elsewhere but that is missed here. I see evidence of the enjoyment of beauty so abundantly and extensively that it becomes clear to me that it is a phenomenon which we cannot quite understand. Even a man who is very poor goes to the length of denying himself his daily food to be able to buy a penny's worth of flowers. The hunger of their eyes is no less keen than the hunger of their stomach ". [3]

The other thing that excited his admiration was the Japanese style of dance. He had recorded the highest word of appreciation for it. Its decency impressed him as much as its artistic quality. We may hear his view on the subject form him:

"I attended a demonstration of Japanese dance one day. It seemed to me that it was like the music of bodily movements. It compares to the music that is raised in our country by the playing of the Veena. There is no break between two units. There is no gap between two different poses nor is there indication of the joining together of parts; the entire body appears to sway like a creeper in

3. Japan Jatri, 13.

blossom and showers flowers of beauty. Japanese dance is pure dance. Its dress does not premit the least exposure of the body. In dances of other countries there is a mixture of sex appeal with beautiful bodily movements. In this dance, not even a suggestion of lust could be stepped".[4]

Rabindranath's fifth journey abroad started in May, 1920. He reached the United Kingdom in June, but the people there did not show much interest in him, a sharp departure from what had happened in 1912. He was accorded only what formal courtesy demanded. The reason is not far to seek. The Englishman does not take kindly to a person who discards an honour given by the king himself. Whether such attitude is justified is not the question; what is pertinent here obviously is that the British people are incapable of judging a matter dispassionately where their own interest is at stake.

Then he went to France where a rich gentleman extended to Rabindranath his hospitality. Then he went to the Netherlands on a lecutre tour. On his way back to France he paid a visit to Brussels the captial of Belgium. After that it was decided that he would pay a visit to the United States accompanied by Pearson.

They reached New York towards the end of October. Some lecture tours were gone through; but Rabindranath's message heavily burdened with spiritual idealism did not impress the American mind. Having acquired considerable technological skill, they were so much engrossed in producing consumer goods and enjoying material comforts that they had lost the capacity to appreciate anything that does not promise physical enjoyment. He then went to Chicago and then undertook some lecture tours in the State of Taxas which had been arranged for by Major Pond. After that, he returned to the United Kingdom.

His tour of the United States this time proved to be a bitter experience. For one thing, their materialistic outlook pained him. Of this more will follow hereafter.

---

4. Japan Jatri, 14.

Even the darkest could has, however, a silver lining, which prove to be true on this occasion also. He picked up acquaintance with an idealistic young man named Leonard Elmherst. He had gone to the United States for higher study in Agronomy and became intimate with a rich American widow named Mrs. Stuant. Evidently, both bacame admirers of Rabindranath and extended considerable assistance to his rural reconstruction work. But more of it hereafter.

On the journey back home a visit to the continent was arranged for. Rabindranath passed through France to Switzerland. From there he proceeded to Germany and ultimatley to Stockholm, the captial of Sweden, via Denmark. He was accorded a hearty welcome at different places in Europe. On his way back, he passed through Germany to Vienna, the captial of Austira. Ultimately, he retuned home in July, 1921.

His sojourn abroad thus lasted for the duration of thirteen months. One rewarding fatigue of such journeys abroad is the opportunity they offer to pick up acquaintance with the leading intellectuals of other countries. During his stay in Paris Rabindranath became intimate with Romain Rolland, the distinguished Frence writer. Similarly, he picked up acquaintance with Count Keyserling of Darundtadt during his stay in Germany. During his stay at Vienna he was introduced to Professor Winternitz. At a subsequent stage, he picked up acquaintance with Professor Lesney who visited Santiniketan on a later occasion. The journey this time was partially marred by some unfavourable developments as has been mentioned already. As he renounced his knighthood as a protest against the repressive measures of the British Government in India, he was denied a hearty welcome in the United Kingdom. Nor did the people of America accord him a hearty reception. Rabindranath formed the impression on basis of his own experience that the same factor operated against him in America also. The following observation of his will bear this out :

"When I had just stepped into the sixtieth year I had once visited America carrying a lot of responsibility over my head. The war in Europe was already over; even so its intoxication made its presence felt through the red colour of America's eyes to a degree not witnessed in Europe. Moreover, the Biritsh were then in complete possession of her ear by devious methods.....They were then making American democracy think of Britain's own problems. Their propaganda machine was set against me. The British were afraid. I might speak ill of then. The Jallianwala Bagh incident had already taken place". [5]

Rabindranath had started disliking one aspect of the technology-based culture of the West. The mischief started when the people of Europe initiated the mass production of consumer goods by the application of their newly acquired technological skill. This brought about such a rapid transformation of society that the expression industrial revolution as coined to signify this. Evidently, this brought about unprecedented material prosperity to the people of Europe; but they had to pay a heavy cost for this. A gigantic production system was brought into being in which the diffierent social groups were absorbed to play different roles. In consequence, the rythm of life was so much accelerated that people had no leisure of their own to spend in the way they would have liked.

This idea plagued Rabindranath as early as the last decade of the ninteenth century when he paid his second visit to England. This is the observations he made on that occasion:

"In this ceaseless effort to carry on the struggle for life, the voice of peace and misgiving raises a feeble protest to say, 'Go a little slowly brother, take a little rest, take heed, take a little time to ponder'. Man was not born to carry on ceaseless struggle. Some thought should be given to this". [6]

When he visited America in 1920, the mechanised system of production had been firmly established there.

---

5. Pashim Jatri Diary.
6. Europe Jatri Diary Parisitha

The degree of mechanisation was far ahead of the industrially advanced countries of Europe like Germany, France and the United Kindgom. The United States had become the richest country in the world. While huge wealth had been amassed on the credit side, poison had infiltrated into life on the debit side, the ugliness of which shocked Rabindranath's sensitive mind. The following observations of his becomes significant in this connection :

"The tempo of life in the Western continent is increasingly gathering speed because demand for consumer goods has become more desirable than fulfilment in life. Residential houses were destroyed to make room for markets because time is money".[7]

To a culture based on mechanised production, the problem of marketing manufactured goods becomes difficult to tackle. Moreover, the demand for raw material to feed the machines assumes gigantic proportions. Two evils follows. On the one hand, forcible methods have to be perforce applied for the collection of raw materials, while on the other, artificial demands for in essential goods has to be created. In consequence, demand for consumer goods is artificially increased. Man's activities becomes restricted to only the discharges of two functions; to produce goods and to consume them. This was an intolerable situation to Rabindranath. No wonder, he bitterly made the following observation :

"When the entire people of a country work towards transforming inessential needs into essential ones, an organised system of worldwide robbery becomes inescapable..., to meet such a huge demand sound moral conduct has to go; man has to be the exploiter of man. Such exploitation starts with alien people in distant countries. The danger lies in the fact that fire set on a specified area does not remain confined to it. The cruelty that the exploiter practises never knows where to stop; egotism has never learnt to say 'this is enough'. The culture that adopts an intemperate growth of material needs as its objective is bound to be cannibalistic".[8]

7. Pashim Jatri Diary, Parisitha.
8. Ibid

Excessive production of consumer goods not only incites nations to acquire empires but works against people's interest in other ways also. The craze for consumer goods turns men into its slave. He digs up the earth to extract minerals to use them for the production of consumer goods. In the process it complicates man's life to such a degree that man becomes entrapped in the coils of his own greed. He becomes alienated from his environment and misses the joy of life. No wonder, the wealth acquired by the technology-based culture of America did not at all impress Rabindranath; on the contrary disappointed him. He recorded his view on the subject not only in the form of direct criticism, but also in symbolic dramas and poems. Immediately after his return from the United States in 1920, he wrote the drama 'Rakta Karabi' (The Red Oleander). In this book, he has shown what the voracious greed of the American culture leads to and also indicated the way to escape from the chain of bondage built for man by it. This will be borne out from the following observation of his, quoted in translation :

"I have given expression to this thought in the 'Rakta Karabi'. 'In the castle of the Yaksha', man extracts from the bowels of the earth huge quantities of gold. Under pressure of his greedy efforts for acquisition of wealth, the joy of life has been suppressed. Man himself has became alienated from the world by entangling himself in the coils of self-created complication. So he fails to appreciate that joy of life is dearer than gold, he forgets that power does not give fulfilment which can come only through love. Under the elaborate system for his enslavement organised by such a culture man immolates himself." [9]

He wrote the collection of poems entitles 'Shishu Bholanath' to give expression to the same idea. In fact, it was written before 'Raktha-Karabi' immediately after his return from the United States. He has named the power that runs the Universe , the Nataraj (The Master Dancer). In this book of poems, the child has been painted after

9 Paschim Jatri Diary.

the image of the 'Master Dancer' giving prominence to his unconcern for worldly possession. In this role, he is Bholanath (The Unconcerned one) who holds no worldly wealth. He is indifferent to gains and so feels no compunction to destroy what he creates. The child exhibits the same spirit of unconcern and detachment. The concept of the Shishu Bholanath high-lights this aspect of the character of the Nataraj. According to the poet, this attitude of detachment carries great significance; if acquisitiveness got the upperhand the flow of creations will stagnate due to accumulation of materials prompted by greed. The cultural group which overlooks this fact and enslaved by greed packs his store house with material gains misses his freedom and joy and is to be pitied. So he observes as follows:

"The power that works behind the word is subject neither to greed nor attachment; it is averse to acquisitiveness. It does not allow any thing to accumulate as the debris of past acquisitions tends to impede the stream of creations; it keeps itself unburdened and free to maintain its enternal drive for continuous creation. The greed of man collects garbage from all possible sources and builds up large storehouses for them by enslaving countless number of men". [10]

It is with reference to the same topic that he observed with reference to his visit to America in 1920. "I had occasion to spend some days stifled by the poisonous environment of inhospitable hostility, imprisoned in close proximity to a mechanised system of blind mass production".[11]

Next came an invitation from the new democratic Government of China. He responded to the call with enthusiasm accompained by Kshitimohan Sen, Nandalal Bose and Leonard Elnhirst. The party embarked on 21st March, 1924. His intinerary included Sanghai, Hanchow, Nanking and Peking. It was reported that the reception accorded to him by its citizens on his arrivals at Peking

10. Pachim Jatri Diary.

11. Ibid.

falls seldom in the lot of foreign visitors. On the way back, he paid a short visit to Japan and returned home four months after on 21st July.

He got another invitation shortly after his return from Peru, the western most country of the South American continent. It was constituted into an independent state on 9th December, 1824 after breaking away from the Shamish empire. Rabindranath was invited to attend the centenary celebration of that happy event. Being disposed to look upon all people as his kith and kin and subject to wanderlust like his own father, he enthusiastically responded to the invitation.

So the journey started in September of the same year from Calcutta via Colombo. This time he was accompanied by Rathindranath, Pratima Devi and the artist Surendranath Kar. In the first stage of the Journey, they went to France. From there, Rabindranath took another ship to Buenos-Aires. Leonard Elnheirst joined him as his private secretary. Unfortunately, he fell ill during the voyage and had to pass his days confined within his cabin. When he reached Buenos-Airse, he had become too weak for his stranuous journey to Peru. The doctors, therefore, advised him to cancel his journey to Peru. So his journey to Peru did not materialise and after spending a few weeks in Argentina, he returned home, in February, 1925.

Luck, however, was not altogether unkind to him. A lady named Victoria Okampo took over his charge and nursed him with devotion and care to restore him to health. In the process, a sweet relationship grew up between them. The poet dedicated his next book bearing the title 'Purabi'. To mark this happy development.

By the turn of the year, another invitation came from Italy. Professor Farnici, who had come to Santiniketan the previous year as a visiting professor, invited him on behalf of his Government Rabindranath embarked in May, 1926. He was accompanied on this occasion by a big team which included Rathindranath, Pratima Devi, Prasanta Chandra Mahalnabis and his wife Nirmal Kumari Mahalnabis. The party disembarked at Naples and proceeded to Rome. Then it left for Turin in the north via Florence. Rabindranath picked up acquaintance with Benedetto Croce the writer on aesthetics there. He then proceeded to the health resort Villeneva where he met with Romain Rolland.

He then visited Zurich, Vienna and Paris before reaching London. While staying there, he received an invitation from Elmhrist to visit his place of work. Rabindranath had picked up acquaintance with this idealistic young man in 1920, during his visit to the United States where he was studying agronomy. This acquaintance ripened into such strong mutual attraction that Elmhirst came over to India to help Rabindranath in his experiments in rural reconstructions at Santiniketan. He not only gave his personal service to the cause but also collected funds for it from his American friend. Mrs. Strait. The experiment over, Elnhirst returned home. In the meantime, his friendship with Mrs. Strait culminated in their marriage. The lady came over to the United Kingdom to live with her husband. They bought an estate at Totnes in Devonshire and started an institution for research and teaching on agriculture. It was to this institution the Rabindranath was invited to pay a visit. Evidently, he enjoyed the hospitality of this friend and well-wisher.

Then started another tour through the European continent. Rabindranath first went to Norway at the invitation of Professor Stein Konow. Then he passed through Sweden and Denmark to Central Europe. Then started a lecture tour covering Hamburg via Vienna. Unfortunately, he became indisposed under the strain of the continuous movement from place to place. After taking rest for some days, he proceeded to Yugoslavia to visit Belgrade. Then he went to Sophia, capital of Bulgaria and then Bucharest, the capital of Rumania. From there, he went by ship to Istambul. Then he went to Greece to pay a visit to Athens. The long journey terminated in December, 1925 with the poets return to Santiniketan.

Wanderlust, evidently, established full command over Rabindranath in his old age. He partly inherited this from his father who was also very fond of travelling. This was prompted partly by his desire to know other people and partly by economic consideration. The Viswabharati had by then been raised to the status of a University and consequently its monetary needs had increased. The Government was then being run by a foreign power which felt little interest in the activities at Santiniketan. On the contrary, Rabindranath's recent conduct had turned them hostile. They could not be expected to think of extending assistance to a poet who had renounced the title conferred by their king. On the other hand, how could he extend a begging hand without hurting his sense of self-respect? So he had to find money to meet the expenditure. Lecture tours abroad fetched money and helped to solve the problem of funds for the Vishwabharati. So these repeated tours abroad were not dictated exclusively by his fondness for travel but partly by the need for raising funds.

Next time, the invitation came for a visit to the East Indies at the initiative of Professor Bake and his wife. They were Dutch and had spent a few days at Santiniketan. They went ahead of him to accord him a fitting reception on his arrival in Java. He was accompanied by the famous linguist, Suniti Kumar Chatterjee and Surendranath Kar, the teacher of painting of Santiniketan. Rabindranath reached Singapore in July, 1927. After touring round the Malay Peninsula, he sailed for the East Indies. He visited the famous Bara-Buddur, temple in Sumatra, and then passed through Surabaya and Djakarta to the island of Bali. The entire people of Indonesia had at one time adopted the Hindu religion and culture but at a subsequent stage they embraced Islam, but did not give up their Hindu culture. This has led to a synthesis of both the cultures. The people of Bali have not, however, given up Hinduism. The dance style of the Balinese girls charmed Rabindranath. He also liked the Batik techinque of colouring cloth developed in this country. Surendranath Kar mastered the techinque during his stay there and introduced it at Santiniketan thereby enriching the cottage industry of Bengal.

On his way back, he paid a visit to Bangkok, the capital of Siam and reached home on 27th October, 1927.

Then an invitation came from for away Canada. This invitation had a distinctive character of its own as he was called to participate in a conference to discuss problems of education to be held under the auspices of an institution called the National Council of Education of Canada. He was invited to deliver a speech on education and leisure. Evidently, he was invited on the footing that he was a specialist on education.

The conference was to sit at Vancover situated on the eastern shore of the Pacific Ocean. He took a ship in March, 1929 which was to sail to North America via Japan. He was accompanied this time by Professor Apurba Kumar Chanda and poet Sudhirindranath Dutta as well as by Professor Tucker, a clergyman belonging to the Methodist Church of America, then a visiting lecturer at Viswabharati.

After a stay of ten days in Canada, he spent a whole month in Japan on his way back. In Japan, his admirers demanded autographed poetical compositions to be inscribed in his own hand on fans and paper handkerchiefs. In the process of obliging then the produced a number of sparkling couplets which were published in a collection under the title 'Spulinga' (Sparks). On the way, he passed a few days at Saigon, capital of Indochina and reached back home in July.

The next journey undertaken by Rabindranath was significant in many ways. It started in March, 1930 and terminated in December of the same year. The itinerary extended over a wide area covering the United States, the United Kingdom and the European continent. A visit to Russia was also in the programme. He took keen interest in picking up acquaintance with the new Russia built up after the Communist ideology. His appreciative remarks on the achievements of the new system created considerable sensation all over the world. Moreover, this journey was marked by two other distinctive features. For one thing, the Oxford University invited him to deliver the

Hibbert Lectures. There had been occasions in the past when he delivered lectures even under he auspices of Universities but this was the first occasion that he was asked to deliver lectures under a foundation by one of the leading educational institutions of the world. The other distinguishing feature was that Tagore wanted to introduce his paintings to the outside world through this tour. The person who was intrinsically a poet suddenly fell in love with the language of lines and colours in his mature age. Pursuant to his desire, exhibitions of his painting were organised in different places to introduce them to foreigners. The exhibitions were held in Paris, Berlin, Moscow, England and America.

Thus the painter in Rabindranath made his appearance for the first time before the people of the West. Before taking up the detailed account of the tour. The story how Rabindranath turned into a painter may be conveniently narrated.

After stepping into the sixties, Rabindranath developed a strong urge for painting, which was quite natural for a person who was intrinsically an artist. Having exhibited his skill in creative literature, he sought for a new medium for artistic expression. The language of words which had been his medium of expression so far found a new rival in the language of lines and colours. Not that, this rival had not tried to assert its rights earlier. His life long aesthetic pursuits rendered Rabindranath so fastidious in his tastes that he could not tolerate ugliness or break of rhythm in any field. His lovely handwriting, lustrous like rows of pearls, gives ample evidence of his taste. When there was occasion for correction of poetical compositions, he could not remain satisfied with penning them through or smudging them with ink, unlike other writers, he would ply his pen in such a way that the correction assumed a distinct shape of its own. The shape would not necessarily imitate real object but the correction were always so manipulated by the poet that they formed a configuration which would please the eye. That is how Rabindranath picked up his acquaintance with the language of lines.

It was thus that the medium with which he used to have only occasional contact in course of his poetical activity claimed a share of his affection as its rival when he crossed into his sixties. It is comparable to the rivalry between Ganga and Uma for the love of Shiva. Despite the fact that, Uma had been occupying the position of the mistress of his home, Ganga suddenly claimed a seat on the head of Shiva as her rival. Rabindranath has frankly confessed that initially the advances of this new lover were very attractive to him. Moreover, he felt that it was much easier to keep her pleased them to satisfy the humour of his other love which was poetry. His confession is recorded thus in one of his poems:

I have been trapped by the charms of painting.
Literature is a rich man's daughter
And brings a lot of money with her;
Given to talking a lot, a good deal
Of thinking is necessary to keep her pleased.
Painting, on the other hand, is reticent
And carries no meaning.
My dealings with her is not
Motivated by a purpose. [12]

The above confession appears to indicate that the attraction of painting was stronger which is only natural. Rabindranath admits that a new love exerts a stronger full:

A great turmoil is going on inside the mind;
Part of it finds expression in words of mouth,
Part in painting;
So long, I have been trapping these ephemeral objects.
In the language of words. [13]

And now in his mature age, he started trapping them in the words of lines and colours. Like the literary compositions of his early age, his paintings which made their appearance in old age also created considerable sensation among art critics. The

12. Shesh Saptak, 16.
13. Shesh Saptak, 14.

main reasons were that in most cases they neither reflected the shape of objects as found in nature, nor did they carry any idea. Nor did Rabindranath want to give expression to any ideas in his poems as the above quotation confirms. He has sought to distinguish his poetry from his paintings by observing that lines are 'not long winded nor do they carry any meaning.' His own comments on his paintings will bear this out :

"People often ask me about the meaning of my pictures. I remain silent even as my pictures are delivered. It is for them to express and not to explain. They have nothing ulterior behind their own appearance for the thoughts to explore and words to describe and if that appearance carries its ultimate worth then they remain; otherwise they are rejected and forgotten even though they may have some scientific truth or ethical justification". [14]

Rabindranath left for the United Kingdom in the beginning of March, 1930 accompanied by Rathindranath and Pratima Devi. The Hibbert Lectures were to be delivered at Oxford in May. These lectures proved to be significant in more than one sense. The Oxford University ordinarily extends invitations to persons who have distinguished themselves as philosophers to deliver these lectures. Rabindranath had not been academically trained as a philosopher. He distinguished himself primarily as a poet. There is no denying the fact, however, that he had formulated a philosophy of his own in his literary works on independent lines through lifelong contemplation. As he has given his views on the basic problems of reality it will not be justified to refuse him recognition as a philosopher. The invitation extended to him by the Oxford University to deliver the Hibbert Lectures carries the implication that a distinguished educational institution recognizes him as a philosopher and honours him as such.

It carries another significance which is weightier. A poet by nature, Rabindranath was not used to placing his thoughts in a methodical manner. The thoughts are attended to at random as they come. On the other hand,

14. Introduction to Chitra, Life.

a systematic presentation of philosophical thoughts is essential to facilitate their understanding. An idea of his philosophical views is essential for the proper understanding of Rabindranath's literary works. It has not, however, been placed in an integrated form anywhere by him. On the contrary, his philosophical thoughts lie scattered about in his writings. It was the invitation to deliver the Hibbert Lectures which compelled him to some degree to collect his philosophical ideas and present them in a methodical form. Not that the presentation has been satisfactory to the extent it was desirable; the language is too emotionally surcharged for use in philosophical dissertation. Even so, the book which embodies these lectures has made it easier to understand his philosophy. Without this book, his philosophy would have been difficult to follow.

After the delivery of the Hibbert Lectures, Rabindranath went to Paris to organise an exhibition of his own paintings. The leading art centre of the world, this city was worthy of such a compliment. Luckily, a rich lady named Countesse du Nuoy extended to him her patronage. His South American friend Victoria Okampo agreed to finance the exhibition. Small wonder, it proved an impressive show. After that Rabindranath went to Berlin, the capital of Germany. He was introduced there with Einstein. Here also the major attraction was the exhibition of his paintings. A German lady named Dr. Selig came forward to help him and bore the entire expenditure of the exhibition. Dr. Amiya Chakravorty accompanied him during his tour of America.

From Germany, he proceeded to Denmark where he attended a students' conference at Elsino. He then went to Geneva via Berlin. It was here that he received an invitation to visit Russia. He accordingly proceeded to Moscow in September.

He was accorded a hearty welcome in Russia. The Russian writers and the members of the Cultural Relations Organization organised a reception for him in Moscow. From there, he was taken to a pioneer commune, where he mixed freely with the boys and girls living there. Then he visited a farmers' colony. Towards the end of September, he delivered an address at the Central Trade Union Office, in Moscow.

An exhibition of his paintings was organised in Moscow. The Russians warmly appreciated his paintings. Professor Chritie published a critical appreciation of them.

From Russia, Rabindranath proceeded to America and stayed for a long time in New York. He was given the formal courtesy that was due to him, but no reception was organised, nor was he invited to give any public address. An exhibition of his paintings, however, was duly organised there. Then he returned home via London in December, 1930.

It is easy to explain why the Americans were cold to him on this occasion. A giant experiment was being carried on in Russia, at the initiative of Linen, of the socio-economic theories of Marx at the time, after the collapse of the administrative system of the Czars. The communistic system introduced by Lenin was anathema to the Americans. Rabindranath's visit to Russia, followed by his warm appreciation of their achievements in diverse fields, made him unpopular to them.

Rabindranath's observation on Russia, based on his personal knowledge, became relevant in this connection. This appraisal was basically appreciative, but not blindly so. Rabindranath said what a sympathetic man gifted with a detached attitude would have said. To help the reader to verify the corrections of this proposition, a brief account of his observations on Russia is placed below:

In substance, the achievements of the new political system in two fields existed his warm admiration. One of them was the extensive provision for imparting education to the entire population; and the other was restoring the self-respect for the underprivileged classed by establishing them in their rights. Judging impartially, both of them deserve appreciation. But in both cases the new attitude which worked behind them did not escape his notice. Society is constituted by two elements-the individual and the group; a system that has failed to reconsile their conflicting interests is bound to fail. On the other hand, general welfare of the community depends on a proper and just adjustment of their claims; because, they are linked together by a symbiotic relationship. Unfortunately, in the capitalistic system born out of the industrial revolution, the interest of the individual dominated to the detriment of the interest of the community and the wealth that was generated was accumulating in the hand of the capitalist class without being equitably distributed. On the other hand, the new system has reacted to this and taken all the care to safeguard the interest of the community to exclusion of the interest of the individual. Evidently, this also created imbalance which is detrimental to the interest of both parties. Therefore, this is not desirable either. In substance, this is what Rabindranath wanted to communicate in his different observations scattered in his letters on Russia. Some relevant quotations are given below to substantiate this proportion.

With reference to the educational system introduced in Russia, he observed as follows :

"What I see at present strikes me with wonder. Education is the biggest of all our problems. So long the majority of the people had been denied full facilities for education which in India is almost wholly denied. One cannot help feeling amazed to see how education is being spread at all levels of society with surprising enthusiasm. What impresses is not only the number covered by education, but its comprehensive character and its speed". [15]

The extensive arrangement made for the spread of education evidently, impressed Rabindranath, but the method employed did not wholly satisfy him. He noticed that the system had been so devised that the originality of the pupil is destroyed; it aims at producing a specially approved type after the pattern of manufactured goods. He did not like this feature as the following quotation will bear out :

15. Russia, Chitra.

"I do not say that there is no defeet in this system. On the contrary, there is a serious defect for which they will have to face trouble some day. Stated briefly, the defect lies in the fact that through the methods adopted for imparting education; they have moulded a die. But personality moulded to a die is not durable. If the theory of education cannot reconcile itself to a living mind, one day either the die will be shattered to pieces or the mind will wither away through constriction or be reduced to a machine-driven tool". [16].

The new economic system has abolished capitalism and thereby generated a sense of self-respect among that class of people who had been subjected to neglect and exploitation under the previous system. Rabindranath did not fail to notice this and showered praise on them without reservation. He said:

"What I liked most here is the complete disappearance of the coarse pride in wealth. For this single reason, the sense of self respect of the common man has developed without impediment. All under privileged groups like the farmer and the labourer have been able to stand up with an erect head after shaking off the crushing weight of the pride of the privileged. I have been as much surprised as pleased to notice this". [17]

In the capitalist system, the individual enjoys freedom of action, of which the proprietor of a factory takes full advantage to monopolies its profits. This is because man is by nature greedy and greed encourage one to be selfish and claim an undue share of wealth. In the Russian system, the individual has been derived of his liberty of action to uproot greed. He felt that this system is also vitiated with internal contradiction. His observation of this issue is quoted below:

"I do not think that there is a solution of this problem other than by way of a compromise. In other words, individual ownership of property should be retained, but a limitation should be imposed on the individual's right

16. Russia, Chitra.
17. Russia, Chitra, 2.

to enjoyment. The surplus outside this limit should come to the use of the community. That alone can prevent ownership of property from culminating into cheating inspired by greed or cruelty.

"In its effort to solve this problem Soviet Russia has defined its existence. There is no end of correction to fulfil that purpose. It cannot be said that the individual man should have no freedom of action. What I mean is that the individual should have what he essentially needs, but everything beyond that should come to the benefit of the community. The solution lies in admitting the claim of both the individual and the community".[18]

Rabindranath reached the age of three score and ten at this stage. Still invitations continued to come. In the second and the third decades of the twentieth century he had gone abroad as many as nine times and spent as much as sixty months abroad. He was then, however, comparatively young; but now the weight of years was telling on his health. On the other hand, it was difficult to turn down invitations from all quarters.

An invitation came at this stage, from Reza Shah Pelhavi, the emperor of Persia, which the poet had to accept. It was decided that the journey would be by air to avoid the strain of voyage by sea. Pratima Devi, Amiya Chakravarty and Kedarnath Chatterjee accompanied him on this occasion.

He was taken to Siraj, the birth-place of Hafiz and given a reception in the garden where the tomb of Sadi is located. At a subsequent date, he paid a visit to the mausoleum of Hafiz. Elaborate arrangements were made for his reception in the capital, Teheran. He was also given an audience by the Emperor. The reception was highly ordeal for obvious reasons, which have been specifically mention in Rabindranath's memoirs. The relevant parts of the same are quoted below :

"To them, I am not merely a poet but a poet of the orient. This prompted them naturally to honour me at their own initiative; they could claim a share of the honour bestowed

---

18. Russia Chitra, 5.

on me. To the Persians, I carry an additional significance as I happen to be an Indo-Aryan. The Persians have taken pride of being ethically Aryans right from the ancient historic times; and recently this feeling appears to have intensifies. They are conscious that I am linked with them by blood. Moreover, a rumour has gained currency that my writings bear close similarity to the works of the mystic poets of Persia". [19]

The address given to him at Ispahan gives an idea of the feelings the people of Persia bore towards him. They contain these observations:

"Tagore, he is the unique, the philosopher who knows what is past and what the future holds.

"Let his arrival be blessed and fortunate is the land of the great Cyrus an august descendent of whom today fortunately wears the crown of persia". [20]

An invitation came to visit Iraq the nourishing state while Rabindranath was still in Persia. He had, therefore, too accept it. He visited Baghdad and then returned home in June, 1932.

Before stopping tours altogether, Rabindranath had to respond to another invitation which came from Ceylon. He left by ship in May, 1934. The people of Ceylon are our close neighbours and have intimate culturalties with us. Besides delivering speeches and staging his dramas, he also held an exhibition of his paintings in Ceylon. He returned home next month.

---

19. Parasye, 5.
20. Ibid.

10

RABINDRANATH-VI

The problem of education assumed importance in the life of Rabindranath. In fact, he spent half of his life in pursuit of educational affairs. It is not for nothing that he was called Gurudeb by the people, it is not a title conferred by any institution. It gives the stamp of recognition of one of the major achievements of his life. Indeed, the story of his involvement in educational affairs leading to his assumption of the role of a teacher is very interesting.

During his boyhood, he was admitted to a school and private tuitors were engaged to coach him at home. He hated being confined within the four walls of the class-room which denied him contact with nature. The teachers were incapable of showing affection. They were more eager to discipline the student than to teach him, in a rigid manner in an artificial atmosphere. No wonder, he felt little attraction for the educational system of his days in his boyhood; on the contrary, he looked upon it as nothing short of torture . He talks of the experience of this chapter of his life as follows:

" During my boyhood, I was subjected to bitter suffering under the system of school education. This system inflicted such pain on me and hurt me so much that I carried its memory even when I grew up. For, under this system, the child is separated from the bosom of nature and society and placed in the factory that goes by the name of school. The irritation of its abnormal environment subjects the child's mind to daily torture. We used to read in the Normal School......... There was no trace of trees, there, the courtyards being paved with marble slabs and the high compound wall appeared to stare angrily at us. The exuberance of life we, children, felt within our hearts received a rude shock in this environment. Removed from contact with nature and missing emotional ties with our teachers, own soul would dry up. The teachers used to strike terror in our minds".[1]

This bitter experience actuated him to revolt against the prevailing system of education and discontinue attending school at the age of thirteen and to educate himself in his own way. While living with his family at Shilaidaha he felt the need for providing education in an institution for his son Rathindranath, when he attained the proper age for school education. He was very keen to protect his son from the bitter experience of his student life. He, therefore, decided to open a residential school where he would introduce a system of education which fitted with his own ideas on the subject. He was mainly motivated by his desired to build up a model school for his son in taking over the charge of his education.

It appears that there was an additional reason which was prompted by his heart. The traditional ritual practices of his faith ceased to carry any significance to him. He felt an urge to undertake some work which would contribute of the welfare of men in general. Pure literary pursuits or contemplation in solitude no longer gave him spiritual satisfaction. He felt a strong urge to engage himself in welfare activities. The following observation of Rabindranath is quoted for confirmation.

"The solitary enjoyment of the infinite in meditation no longer satisfied me and the texts which I used for my silent worship lost their inspiration without my knowing it. I am sure, I vaguely felt that my need was spiritual self-realisation in the life of Man through some disinterested service. This was the time when I founded an educational institution for our children, in Bengal....... The necessity was my own, for I felt impelled to come back into a fulness of truth from my exile in a dream world".[2]

These are the two inspirations that simultaneously encouraged him to take over the role of a teacher. He

1. Viswabharati, 4.
2. The Religion of Man, The teacher.

decided to open a school which would be different from the type of schools introduced by the British Government, because he felt that this system could not adjust itself to Indian society, culture and tradition. He thought seriously of adopting the model evolved in the forest settlements of ancient India. The account available about them in Sanskrit literature and particularly in the works of Kalidasa excited his utmost admiration. He felt that the Ashram of the ancient forest settlements should be adopted as the model for the proposed school. His father had set up a hermitage at Bolpur which he named 'Santiniketan'. He decided, therefore, to locate his school there.

This plan nicely fitted with Maharshi's own ideas. He had earmarked the income of a specific landed property, for the maintenance of his Ashram, which assured an annual income of Rs. 1800/- He embodied these terms in a trust deed executed in its favour in 1887. This trust deed contained three directives: A school together with a library should be opened there; an annual fair should be organised on 20th Pous to commemorate the date of his initiation into the Brahmo religion. So Rabindranath's proposal to open a school there was readily accepted by Maharshi.

The question that engaged Rabindranath's attention first was the method to be adopted for teaching. In finding his own solution, he was more or less guided by the ancient system of India. As has been already mentioned, the model of the forest settlement, where teaching used to be imparted in the bosom of nature had deeply impressed him. He desired that as in the ancient model, the teacher should live with his family in the campus and the student receives his education living in lose proximity with his teacher and both developing a relationship of mutual affection. He also desired that the student should live a simple life of discipline. There is need for practising utmost self-control as it is essential to keep the mind untouched by all kinds of perversities at the beginning of life. The object of Brahmacharya should be to keep the stage of adolescence in state of tranquality by shielding it from the excitement and irritation of luxury and preventing awakening of the dormant sexual urger".[3]

---

3. Shiksha Samasya.

He also insisted on two other conditions. For one thing, the student should be placed in charge of some specific duty to help him develop his sense of responsibility and to allow him to participate in creative activities so that he can get a taske of aesthetic joy. Not that, this calls for elaborate arrangements. The students can be entrusted with the work of building up a healthy and beautiful environment round them even in their boyhood. Such activity not only develops their sense of responsibility but also initiates them into the principles of cooperative endeavour. With this end in view, he used to give the students of the school some assignment with a directive that he should run it himself. He believed that such provision encourages constrictive efforts. In substance, he desired that these students should build up their own environment at their own initiative.

The Brahmacharya Ashram at Santiniketan was opened on 7th Pous, 1308 of the Bengali calendar corresponding to 22nd December, 1901 with only a few students on the role, one of whom was his son Rathindranath. The teachers who were appointed to run the school included Pandit Sibahandra Vidyaranta, the private tuitor of Rathindranath, and a Sindhi gentleman named Rewachand. Brahmabandhab Upadhya also worked of a short time as a teacher. It is reported that it was he who introduced the custom of addressing Rabindranath as Gurudev. When Rewachand left, Subodh Chandra Majumdar succeeded him as the teacher of English. After a few years Haricharam Banerjee, Bhupendranath Sanyal, Ajit Kumar Chakrovorty and others joined the staff. Monoranjan Majumdar was appointed the headmaster of the school. It was at a still later date that Kshitimohan Sen and Bidhusekhar Shastri became members of the establishment.

What started as a special type of an educational institution slowly developed into an institution of distinction. In due course, Rabindranath felt the need for elevating it to an institution capable of discharging higher responsibilities. He had visited many parts of the world in course of his extensive tours and noted that he had to meet a growing demand from people outside India for more information about India. He spoke to them on such occasions about that aspect of India's culture which would be respectfully received by these people. This experience made him strike upon the idea that Santiniketan could be developed on such lines that it could take over the function of acquainting the people of the world with such achievements as would be respected on behalf of India. Indeed, his desire to found the Viswabharati stemmed from this thought. An observation made by Rabindranath is quoted below in support of this proposition :

"By Viswabharati, I mean that part of Indian culture which has a universal appeal. Our school is too small to represent that culture. Shiva appeared in the garb of a beggar; but that did not prevent the leakage of the fact that he is the source of all wealth. Viswabharati staged its first appearance in the garb of an insignificant school in this Ashram. But that marked only the beginning of its way to glory; it did not give out its latent powers. It was then a beggar collecting alms. Today it is poised to distribute its bounty which is the cultural wealth of India. Representatives of the world have assembled here to announce that they have come. If we say to them by way of rebuff ," We are too busy with our own problems, we have no time to think about giving you anything, it will be a great shame indeed". [4]

One day he trained himself to be a writer to be able to carry some message to the people of the world on behalf of the Bengalis. Today his hands itched to give something to them on behalf of India. He wanted to present them that part of India's heritage, which deserves to be respectfully received. That is why he named his institution 'Viswabharati' on the lines of the Vedic phrase 'Yatra Viswam Bhabati Ekanidam' (the place where the entire people of the world nestle together). His object was to build up the Viswabharati as the centre for the dissemination of knowledge of India's immortal spiritual wealth.

So the Viswabharati was born on 8th Pous, 1325 Bengali era at Santiniketan corresponding to 23rd December, 1918.

---

4. Viswabharati, 12.

As the work load increased considerably in consequence, Rabindranath brought over his son Rathindranath to Santiniketan to assist him. Slowly the Viswabharati assumed a definite shape. Three ideas dominated Rabindranath's thought at this stage. At the first instance, it is necessary to comprehend the nature of Indian culture, for which purpose it is necessary to find out our heritage trace its growth through diverse streams of culture. So he directed that "India's curriculum for teaching should include the Vedic, the Puranic the Buddhist; the Jain and the Islamic cultures in an integrated form. It has to be found out how these different streams shaped the main stream of Indian culture".

Secondly, he thought the primary function of a university should be to create knowledge while the imparting of education should be relegated to a secondary function. The best way to achieve this objective is to invite the scholars with international reputation to visit the institution. He observed: "Invitation should be extended by this institution to scholars who are engaged in research discovery and creative activities with serious application. Fountains of new knowledge will spring up wherever such men assemble to work. A university worthy to bear the name can be founded only in close proximity to the source of such a spring.[5]

"Thirdly, he felt that an educational institution should interest itself with the well being of its country. It follows that provision should be made for teaching economics, agronomy and allied subjects and for the application of technical knowledge thus acquired to the problems of the neighbourhood. The idea of founding the Sriniketan stemmed from this.

It was under the inspiration of these objectives that the Viswabharati was founded. The Viswabharati was formally opened three years after during the Pous festival, to be specified on 8th Pous, 1324, Bengali era, corresponding to 22nd December, 1921. The opening ceremony was presided over by Brajendranath Seal and was attended by

5. Viswabharati, 1.

two distinguished scholars of the West. One of them was Sylvan Devi under whose supervision elaborate arrangements were made for research in Chinese language and literature. The other was Elmhirst with whom Rabindranath picked up acquaintance during his American tour. This idealistic youngman came to organise the rural reconstruction programme at Sriniketan. So long Rabindranath had looked after the institution all by himself. On the occasion of the opening ceremony, he formally made a gift of the institution built by himself to the nation. Simultaneously, he made over to this institution all the landed and other properties acquired for it together with the copyright of all his books published till then.

Rabindranath had been looking for a suitable worker for giving shape to his rural reconstruction project at Surul. He discovered the man he wanted in course of his tour of the United States, in 1920. He was then studying agronomy there. Rabindranath met him in New York and asked him whether he could accompany Rabindranath to Surul. Elmhirst had previously visited India in 1915 and had been attracted to Rabindranath after reading the English 'Gitanjali'. He, therefore, readily agreed to go. Rabindranath felt so enthusiastic that he wanted to take Elmhirst with himself to India; but Elmhirst could not agree and said that he would go after completing studies.

On completion of his study Elmhirst returned to his home in England and then sent a wire to Rabindranath to say: "Study is finished. Can I come"? Unfortunately, Rabindranath's financial resources had dried up in the meantime and so he could not ask him to come to fulfil his wish. So he sent a reply by telegram which said: "Do not come. No funds available. " This negative message could not stifle the enthusiasm of this idealistic young man. He got the backing of his friend Mrs. Strait who had agreed to marry him. So he wired back to say that he would finance his own expenses and reported his arrival to the poet at Bolpur.

Sriniketan was built up at Surul under the leadership of Elmhirst, Rabindranath giving him only broad guidelines. Elmhirst wanted to resuscitate the life of the Moribund villages. Luckily, he got a band of enthusiastic workers to help him, which included Kalimohan Ghosh, Santosh Majumder and Dhinanando Roy.

The work at Sriniketan did not start with a planned programme, as Rabindranath desired that the programme should take shape in the light of experience gained in course of the experiment. When it did take shape in slow stages in the manner desired, it assumed a comprehensive character. An elaborate programme for rural reconstruction had to be drawn up in consequence which the following subjects: agriculture, animal husbandry, cottage industry, literacy drive, cooperatives and rural health. Rabindranath gives the following reasons for the multi-purpose character of the programme:

"Welfare of the community is a combination of many components. They are intimately linked up with one another. If any one of them is kept separate we miss the result. Only when health, intellect, knowledge work, and the feeling of enjoyment are combined together, man's welfare attains fulfilment". [6]

It is due to the lack of vitality that life in villages stagnates. It is natural, therefore, for people to extend help to them from outside to deliver them from this misfortune. Such external aid, however, is not conducive to the welfare of the village folk, as it tends to cripple them further. External assistance makes a man lose his sense of self-respect and tends to make him dependent on others and in consequence, he can never acquire the strength to stand on his own legs. Rabindranath was fully alive to such dangers. He, therefore, observed:

"I have been sounding the warning from the beginning that any effort to enrich a village from the outside is artificial. It amounts to being charitable to the present by robbing the future. It is possible even in a desert to strike a fountain that can replenish itself. Such a fountain never dries up. We have to search for such fountains in the minds of the village folk. The first step towards that is to teach

6. Kalantar, Swaraj Sadhan.

them to have faith in their own capacity and the power behind their cooperative efforts".[7]

The programme for rural reconstruction as evolved by the workers of Sriniketan under the guidance of Elmhirst with the blessings of Rabindranath anticipated to a remarkable degree the community development programme introduced by the Government of India after independence. In fact, what goes by the name of extension service was introduced as a method of rural reconstruction at Sriniketan forty years before that extension service bears two distinctive features in the sense that it is a two-way traffic. It involves an exchange of ideas between those who serve and those who are served. At the one end a solution to a problem faced by a farmer is communicated to him and on the other, the news of appearance of a new problem is brought to the notice of the extension workers. The laboratory takes over the problem to find its solution, through scientific experiments. When such efforts lead to the discovery of the solution, the farmer is not forced to adopt it but persuaded to accept it by convincing him about its merit; so that the former can adopt it voluntarily. These are the broad features of the extension service.

The experiment carried on at Sriniketan led to the formulation of this method also. The work programme adopted by Elmhirst will bear this out:

"To assist them (Villagers) in solving the most pressing problems: To take the problems of the village and the field to the class-room for study and discussion and to the experimental farm for solution: To carry the knowledge and experience gained in the class-room and the experimental form to the village".[8]

---

7. Speech delivered at the opening.
8. Viswa Bharati Quarterly, Education Number, 1947.

11

RABINDRANATH-VII

"We are now on the threshold of the last chapter of Rabindranath's life. The story of his new love in old age which is painting, has been already told. His interest in his old love which was poetry, however, never slackened. He, devoted most of his time in this stage of his life to poetry. He, however, wrote three novels during this period. 'Dui Bon' (Two sisters) was published in 1930 while the 'Malancha' (The Garden) and the 'Chār Adhya' (the Four Chapters) were published in 1933 and 1934 respectively. After that he wrote only books of poems for the rest of his life.

Admittedly, the poems written during this period, differed in style as well as choice of subjects from his earlier poems. In fact he himself became aware of this change. Figures of speech and the rhythmic charm of metres the present in abundance in the early writings slowly disappeared. They were replaced by a simple style unembellished by ornaments. In conformity with this change of outward form, the nature of the content also underwent a change. The emotional content decreased and thought assumed a dominant role. That is why Rabindranath has compared these compositions to the fruits of autumn as distinguished from the flowers of spring. In his earlier poems, the emotions engendered in his heart by the diverse experience of his earlier life found expression is exquisite rhymed words. So they are comparable to the flowers of spring; they attract us by the beauty of their form. In contrast the profound wisdom churned up in a lifetime of experience found voice in the poems of his old age. So he says : "These are not flowers of spring; they may by the fruits of the autumn of my life; they do not care to charm the heart by a show of outward beauty. They are saturated with the wisdom of inner contemplation [1].

During this stage, the urge to avoid decorating the language became so strong that Rabindranath was persuaded to adopt the prose style. It made its first appearance with long before, as early as 1922, when he wrote the 'Lipika. This book deals with short stories carrying symbolic meanings. Even before that, he had acquired some experience in the use of the prose style in poetry when he translated his Bengali poems into English for the English version of the 'Gitanjali.' This book contains translation of poems selected from the 'Gitanjali', the 'Kheya', the 'Shishu' andother books of verse. These, however, are not literary translation, but have been composed to carry the thought contained in the original in an effective way. Secondly, they have been written in the prose form. These translations have the soul of poetry but the body of prose. Inevitably, they assume the features of prose poems even though they have not been cast into the shape of poems.

The style adopted in the 'Lipika' was based on this experience. Here also the subject matter is poetical while the style is prose and the arrangement takes the form of a prose composition as in the English 'Gitanjali'. This can, therefore, be taken as the first specimen of Rabindranath's prose poems.

This was followed by more than one collection of porse poems composed by him in his old age. In this group may be included 'Punascha' published in 1932, 'Shesh Saptak' published in 1935 and 'Shymali' in 1938. They all contain peoms written in prose style but arranged in the form of verses.

A sizable portion of the poems composed in old age record reminiscences of boyhood. This is as should be expected, since boyhood memories are sweet to recall.

1. Nabajatak, Suchana.

Reminiscing them in old is, therefore, an enjoyable pastime in old age. Such poems have found place in the collections bearing the titles 'Punascha', 'Shesh Saptak', 'Shymali' and 'Akashpradip'. Some may be referred to in this connection. There is the story of tamarind flower in 'Shymali' in 'Akashpradip' there is a story of playing truant from school.

Rabindranath's thouhts are dominated by two main streams. For one thing, he was a lover of life; he called the world of forms, tastes, scents, touch and sound a 'festival of joy'. His writings echo the immortal voice of the Rishis of the Upanishads who hailed the created universe as' the incarnate form of divine joy'. His faith in the truth of this pronouncement remained unshaken till the last days of his life, despite contrary experiences. We get repeated affirmation of this faith in the poems composed in his old age. Two examples may be cited in this context. 'Bithika' contains this passage :

My thirst is unquenched,
    my hunger unappeased;
Despite which I have tasted boundless joy.
    Obeisance to the mount of sunrise

The following is a quotation from a poem written at almost the terminal point of his life which finds a place in the collection called 'Arogya':

When I shall bid adieu to this earth
I shall proclaim, with the dust
    I have painted any forehead,
Have spotted the eternal light
    behind the veil of evil days.
Truth as joy has taken shape in
    the dust of this earth;
With this profound realisation
    I salute this dust.

The other major stream of thought traceable in Rabindranath's writings is to link life and death in a comprehensive view. When they are looked at separately, the destructive quality of death looms large in our mind but we miss its constructive aspect. We forget that death helps the stream of life to maintain its freshness by relieving it of the burden of the dead past. This echoes another elevating word of wisdom of the Upanishads which says: "He suffers the horror of death who takes an isolated view of it. But where is the illusion of sorrow when a comprehensive view is taken? " This thought has found expression again and again in the different poems and symbolic plays of Rabindranath. He has visualized the supreme power that controls the universe as the 'Master Dancer,' it is his dance of joy which sustains the stream of creation. This dance is marked the two fold rhythm of birth and death. He has said in one of his poems that he can hear the cadence of this rhythmic dance in his inner mind; like the sound of the drum its rhythm is echoed by laughter and tear, the good and bad, birth and death. He has observed that the bath of death inviogorates life; otherwise the stream of life would have stagnated in the accumulated morass of what is obsolete.

This message has been voiced again and again in new language in the last chapter of his life. That confirms that the philosophy which evolved in his thoughts remained unmodified. Some observations may be referred to for confirmation. In poem No. 39 of 'Shesh Saptak' he observes as follows:

I am death the cowherd
    Shepherding my herd which I lead
From age to age
    To new fields of pasture.

The same thought has been echoed in another poem of 'Senjuti' from a new angle. Everything is in a flux in the universe, death accompanies life eternally to keep it flowing. So in his view, creation is something which somehow keeps ongoing in spite of facing destruction constantly:

The joy of what is abiding is showered
    By the dance of what is fleeting,
The carnival of creation faced

Constantly with destruction
Somehow keeps on going.
Those who raise walls on strong foundations
Transgress the degree of the creator;
They do not follow that eternity
Is the linking together of fleeting events enshrined in time.

Not that no wind of change was noticeable in the writings of his old age. This is in evidence in two distinct but closely linked forms. One of them is the 'Chharrã' a style of composition which is an indigenous form of Bengali folk poetry. Comparing it with the sophisticated style, he observes : "The sophisticated style is comparable to waves while the Bengali folk style is comparable to drizzling rain". [2] The poems of the collection called 'Chharãr Chhabi' (picture in the Folk style of Verse) are written in this chharã style.

The other departure was the composition of what is called non-sense worse in English. The putting together of disconnected ideas is the soul of its wit. There are many poems of this variety in 'Khãpchhãrã'. The poet, however, reminds the readers that this is not an easy style to execute in the following lines:

It is not at all difficult to write
on difficult subject
But writing non-verse
is not easy. [3]

The political turmoil all over the world disturbed his mind seriously towards the end of Rabindranath's life. Towards the end of the fourth decade of the current century, the rapacity of some imperialistic powers led to Wanton acts of cruelty and devastating war on many fronts. Japan could not rest satisfied with the annexation of a part of China and started a protracted war for expansion at her cost. In Italy, the fascist dictator Mussolini, wanted to build up a new Roman empire. Unable to penetrate elsewhere, he subjugated Abyssinia in the African continent thereby depriving the only independent state of that continent of its

2. Charr Chhabi, Introduction.
3. Khapcharra

political freedom. In central Europe, Germany submitted to the dictatorship of Hitler to efface the ignominy of the defeat sustained in the First World War. He dogmatically believed in the superiority of the German race and so started a bitter war in the European continent to establish Germans as the masters of the entire world.

This crisis confronting the entire world and the barbarity of the technically advanced powers deeply shocked Rabindranath's sensitive heart. Out of sheer despair and indignation he could not help recording some harsh words of protest against their barbarity in his poems. Two examples are proposed to be cited in this connection. In a poem included in the collection called the 'Prantik', he said :

The serpents are poisoning the atmosphere
 with their foul breath everywhere;
It is useless to talk of the sweet words of peace,
Therefore, before I depart
 I sound this word of warning
To those who are preparing themselves
 in every house
To fight these devils.

Another poem voicing the same thought was composed much later . The poem quoted above was written in 1937, when the Second World War has not yet started. The other poem was composed much later and is included in the book of verse entitled 'Janmadine' (on the day of the Birth Anniversary). He observed there in desperation that man was probably atoning for his misdeeds by committing suicide:

Men in their hordes have destroyed
 the dignity of man,
Have transgressed the degree of
 God repeatedly,
Throughout history.
To atone for this sin,
Through the curse of suicide,
Man is bringing about his
 own destruction.

12

RABINDRANATH-VIII

We now enter into the last chapter of Rabindranath's life. The significant events of this stage are briefly narrated below.

Rabindranath completed the seventieth year of his life in 1931. The event was celebrated with a reception worthy of the occasion. The homage paid to him and articles written on him by distinguished personalities from all over the world were compiled in a book published by Ramananda a Chatterjee, the editor of 'Prabasi' under the title 'The Golden Book of Tagore'. Enriched by contributions from eminent men, it is worthy of preservation as a valuable book dealing with his literary achievements. The Irish poet, Yeats, is one of those distinguished literary giants who sent their homage to Rabindranath. He was the man who introduced Rabindranath to the West. He wrote a letter to Rabindranath to say that his admiration had not been dimmed by the lapse of twenty years since their last introduction. The relevant part is quoted below. "I, therefore, want to tell you that I am still your most loyal student and admirer. Your poems, as you know, came to me as a great excitement and of recent years I have found wisdom and beauty or both in your prose".

In between, he had passed some adverse criticism on Rabindranath. These remarks can, therefore, be taken as his last words on Rabindranath. In 1932, Mahatma Gandhi became involved in a serious controversy with the British Government on a political issue which had far-reaching consequences. That provided an occasion for

Rabindranath to be brought in close contact with him. Some introductory remarks are called for by way of introducing the subject. The British Government was then engaged in considering what new concessions should be given to India to advance her progress to self-government on the basis of the recommendations of the Simon Commission. The labour leader Ramsay Macdonald was then leading the British cabinet. The British Government had already introduced separate electorates for the Hindus for and the Muslims for the purpose of dividing the communities. Despite Mahatma Gandhi's strong protest the British Prime Minister, Macdonald, gave the award that under the proposed new constitution caste Hindus and scheduled castes should have separate electorates.

Mahatma Gandhi, therefore, took the decision that he would fast to death to register his protest against this decision expecting that the British government should bow down to his wish and withdraw that award or face the consequence of his death. The decision had far-reaching implications. No wonder, Mahatma Gandhi felt the need for advice from a person whom he respects and whose advice he could rely on. The only person who could be worthy of such trust appeared to him to be Rabindranath.

So, he addressed a letter to Rabindranath seeking his advice on the subject before implementing his decision, which was fraught with dangerous possibilities at that critical stage of the history of India. The whole letter can be quoted here with advantage. It ran as follows:

"Dear Gurudev,

This is early morning, 3 O, clock of Tuesday, I enter the fiery gate at noon. If you can bless the effort, I want it. You have been to me a true friend because you have been a candid friend after speaking your thoughts aloud. I shall look forward to a firm opinion from you one way or the other. But you have refused to criticise. Though it can now only be during my past, I will prize your criticism if your heart condemns my action. I am not too proud to make an open confession of my blunder, whatever the cost of confession, if I find myself in error. If your heart approves of the action, I want your blessing. It will sustain me."

The letter was dated 20th September, 1932. The contents of the letter indicate that he had previously asked for Rabindranath's advice on this issue and not receiving any reply, he wrote this letter early that morning to say that even he would still welcome It. In fact, however, Rabindranath had duly responded to the earlier letter and posted his reply on 19th September, by wire. The telegraphic message reached Mahatma Gandhi, at 10.30 A.M. of the 20th, after he had posted his letter. The telegraphic reply runs as follows:

"It is worth sacrificing precious life for the sake of India's unity and her social integrity. Though we cannot anticipate what effect it may have upon our rulers, we feel certain that the supreme appeal of such self-offering of our own countryman will not be in vain.

I fervently hope that we will not callously allow such national tragedy to reach its extreme length".

The letter of Mahatma Gandhi quoted above carries great significance. It clearly indicated how much he respected Rabindranath and how much he valued the latter's advice. He not only addressed Rabindranath as Gurudev (Revered Teacher) but also asked for his blessings.

Luckily, the fast did not end in tragedy. The British Government was forced to change their decision by the rigid attitude of Mahatma Gandhi and the prospect of furious popular upheaval if the fast took its natural course. The news of the withdrawal of the award reached Poone the place of fast on 26th September. So, it was decided to break the fast in the afternoon of the same day. In the meantime, Rabindranath had arrived there under the pull of the affection he bore for the Mahatma. Rabindranath entertained Gandhiji by singing a song while the latter broke his fast.

The tie of affection that grew up between these two great men has a long history behind. They first met as early as 1915, when the movement led by Mahatma Gandhi for securing some rights of Indians settled in South Africa ended in a settlement. Consequently, Gandhiji decided to return to India. He wanted to bring the students of the Phoenix Residential Institution, founded by him there along with him. On the advice of C.F. Andrews who had in the meantime picked up acquaintance with him, it was decided that they would be sent to Santiniketan. In far, they did come to Santiniketan and Gandhiji followed them there. He did not, however, like the system obtaining there. He insisted that the students should manage their affairs exclusively by themselves; they should even cook for themselves. Rabindranath agreed to experiment with the idea. But after four months, Gandhiji removed his students to another place. The friendship that was established between them on this occasion continued till they were parted by death. Mahatma Gandhi paid a second visit to Santiniketan in 1924 and spent a few days there. They, however, stuck to their own ideas and opinions so that they could not influence each other. That does not mean that they did not respect each other's views; they would pay due respect to their opinions. The letter of Mahatma Gandhi quoted above will give some indication of this.

Rabindranath was invited to deliver the 'Kamala Lectures' by the Calcutta University in 1933. This is provided for by an endowment created by Sir Ashutosh Mukherjee as a memorial to his deceased eldest daughter Rabindranath chose a similar subject to the subject selected for the Hibbert Lectures delivered earlier . The lectures had been delivered in English at Oxford; but here they were delivered in Bengali. It was, however, comparatively short.

At about that time, the institutions of Santiniketan were confronted with financial difficulties. As Rabindranath lost his capacity to tour abroad due to old age, the income from such tours ceased to come. It was too much to expect financial assistance from the alien

Government which had little sympathy for them and had been prejudiced by his renunciation of the knigthood conferred by them. Not that, no contribution was forthcoming from the native states; but they were not adequate the income from the landed property had also gone down. The financial problem of these institutions, thus became a source of worry during his old age. Forced by the circumstances, Rabindranath devised a new way out. He created a new style of dance by trans forming some earlier works into dance dramas and staging them with the help of the students of Santiniketan. He started raising funds for his institutions by touring all over India and staging dance dramas at different places, the students playing the roles of artists. Thus the lyrical drama 'Chittrangada' was transformed into the dance drama 'Chittrangada'. A story in the collection of narrative poems named the Katha-O-Kahini' was rewritten as the 'Shyma' and the 'Chandalika' was written on basis of a Buddhist anecdote. He started collecting funds by staging these dance-dramas with the help of his students, in different parts of India.

It was in this connection that he had another contact with Mahatma Gandhi, in 1936. He was then on a tour in North India staging his dance-drama 'Chitrangada' with a troupe of his students. After staging shows at Patna, Allahabad and Lahore he had reached Delhi. That is when the information reached Gandhiji that Rabindranath was engaged in collecting funds in this manner despite age and a breakdown of health. He could not stand this plight of his Gurudev. So he compelled Rabindranath to return to Santiniketan after collecting a purse of Rs. 60,000/- and presenting it to him for his expenses. This gives an indication of the deep bond of love between them.

Mahatma Gandhi paid another visit to Santiniketan on 17th February, 1941. Rabindranath's health had then broken down altogether and so he felt worried about the future of the Viswabharati which had engaged his attention for as long as forty years. He could not find a man who was equal to the task of taking over its responsibility and so he asked Mahatma Gandhi to take it over. The request did not go in vain. After independence, the Central Government gave it the statue of a Central University and took over its charge.

During the last days of his life Rabindranath came in intimate contact with Subhash Chandra Bose. This spirited young man entertained profound respect for this old man of genius. He would frequently meet Rabindranath to be near him and to seek his advice. Rabindranath hailed him as the symbol of youth power of the country and behaved very affectionately with him. The founding of an institution in Calcutta bears clear evidence or the sweet relationship between them. The Corporation of Calcutta had made a gift of a plot of land on Chittaranjan Avenue. A name to Subhash Chandra who in his turn decided to build a house on it and dedicated it to a national cause.

Rabindranath who was asked to give it a name named it the 'Mahajati Sadan' (The House of the Great Nation.) He had also to lay the foundation stone of the building as requested by Subhash Chandra. So he performed the part assigned to him in the ceremony held on 18th April, 1959 in spite of his invalid condition.

Rabindranath had no house of his own in Kalimpong. He used to stay in the house of a friend when he would visit the place. Close to it was situated the cinchona plantation of the Government of Bengal located at Mangpu. Maitreyai Devi, wife of Manmohan Sen, the chemist attached to the plantation was one of the ladies who had attracted his affection. She was , therefore, able to persuade him to come over to Mangpu and spend about two months there. He was so deeply impressed by the beauty of the place and the devotion of the hostess that he paid more visits to the place. He came for the last occasion in the summer of 1940. His birth anniversary was celebrated at Mangpu that year. Thanks to Maitreyi Devi this small place was thus able to secure a place of honour in the literary map of India. Maitreyi has presented another treasure to the Bengali reader in form of his book on Rabindranath's stay at Mangpu. It skilfully records Rabindranath's days in the homely atmosphere at Mangpu replete with humorous anecdotes.

The last notable event in Rabindranath's life was the investing of Rabindranath with an honorary doctorate degree by the Oxford University. As his health had broken down, he was not in a position to undertake journey to the United Kingdom to receive it. In the circumstances, the Oxford University decided to hold a special convocation at Santiniketan. It was attended among others by Dr. Saruvapalli Radhakrishnan and the diploma was made over by Sir Maurice Goyer, the then Chief Justice of the Supreme Court of India.

Gradually, Rabindranath's health deteriorated further. As he had lost the power of movement he had to be pushed in a wheel chair. His power of sight also deteriorated and hearing also was affected. During the Pujhas, he came to Calcutta and expressed a desire to visit Kalimpong. Having regard to his physical condition, Dr. Bidhan Chandra Roy advised against this; but his urge was so strong that he did not listen. While at Kalimpong, he became seriously ill and had to be brought down for treatment. It took him a full month to recover after which he returned to Santiniketan, in November.

His last birth anniversary during his life time was celebrated on the 8th May, 1941. By then, the Second World War had spread all over the world. The crisis that entire humanity was facing occupied a place of prominence in the address. Rabindranath delivered on this occasion. It was published under the caption. 'The crises in civilisation'.

Towards the end of July, Rabindranath became indisposed. On the advice of the local doctors, he was brought to Calcutta on 25th July, 1941 for treatment. This was followed by a surgical operation five days after on 30th July, which he did not survive. In the noon of 7th August, the flame of his life was extinguished.

13
THE LATER GENERATIONS

There is a saying in our country which runs as follows:

The son of a father and the horse of a sepoy
Imbibe at least to some extent
the quality of their masters.

Evidently, its wisdom cannot be disputed. It is not too much to expect that the later generaticn of a family whose founders were men of uncommon talents and achievements would also give evidence of inheriting some of their ancestors' qualities. It is only natural that members of a family which had occupied for the duration of a century the seat of leadership in diverse fields, generation after generation would also distinguish themselves. Indeed, many members of this family belonging to later generations helped to maintain its prestige by establishing themselves in prominent positions. In fact, one of them acquired a reputation which revived the glory of the old days, so to say. The account may consicutively start with him.

Girindranath was the second son of Dwarkanath. He left two sons, Ganendranath and Gunendranath. Ganendranath was very enthusiastic about the development of indigenous industry. These facts have been mentioned before. Unfortunately, he died young without any issue. His younger brother Gagnendranath also died young leaving three sons named Gaganendranath, Samarendranath and Abanindranath. Both Gaganendranath and Abanindranath had a natural aptitude for painting to which they applied their minds seriously. There was a spacious verandah in the first storey of their ancestral house facing south which they used as their studio. In later life, Gaganendranath distinguished himself as a cartoonist. In fact, he was the pioneer in this field, in Bengal.

His youngest brother Abanindranath was a really gifted painter. In his early years, he went through the traditional training prescribed for acquiring skill in painting. He practised the Western technique under the supervision of a British painter. The Western style, however, did not quite satisfy him, as it used to put too much emphasis on the realistic aspect of art in those days. That is why students are taught to paint with the help of a model. As this technique did not satisfy him, Abanindranath turned to the Indian technique. He was deeply impressed by the principles enunciated by Yasodhara in his comments on Jayamangal's book on art. Painting has been analysed here into six component elements one of which is the emotional element. It pointed out that without the emotional content a painting is incomplete. The Hindu concept of six elements of paintings has adopted this principle which Abanindranath considered to be logically sound. So he decided to look for the technique that suited him in Indian Art.

Luckily, in course of his search, he came across a specimen of Moghul painting. He liked the technique, but found the emotional content missing which according to him was an essential element. He thought a perfect Indian style of painting could be developed if the missing element was added to the technique adopted in Moghul painting. His observations on the point may be quoted below in this connection:

" I realised for the first time what treasures lay hidden in the medieval art of India. I saw too what was lacking in the motiff: the emotional element. And this I determined to supply. That I realised to be my mission".

His observations on the ideal of ancient Indian painting contains an explanation of what he meant by the element of emotion in painting. We have already referred to the six constituent elements of Indian art of which the element of emotion is one. Abanindranath defines this as 'what we give expression to in painting by the different gestures and postures adopted by a man under the influence of a particular emotion.'[1]

This theory of Abanindranath has been reflected in his art. Evidently, he was profoundly influenced by the medieval art of India. Efforts to give expression to emotion are clearly discernible in his paintings. He appeared to have a preference for water colour than oil paintings. His intimate contact with the Japanese painters, Okakura and Taikan might have contributed to this. The technique of 'colour wash' used in his paintings might have stemmed from the same source. Evidently, Japanese painting exercised more influence over him than Western painting. The main elements of his technique, however, were taken from the Indian style.

It was Abanindranath's efforts to evolve a new technique of painting which gave birth to the new Bengal school of painting; no mean achievement for him. He was thus able to restore to Indian painting it former prestige. No wonder, he earned a reputation as an international painter. Many young promising Indians flocked to him to be initiated in his technique, many of whom found recognition at a later stage. Nanda Lal Bose was one of them. Abanindranath also became acquainted with some famous artists of other countries two of whom have been mentioned already. The famous British artist Rothenstein was another. It was through his good offices that Rabindranath was introduced to British writers in 1912. We quote below the homage paid to Abanindranath by Rothenstein:

"He became the natural leader of the Indian school of Bengal; indeed his influence extended far beyond his province. His name became a standard; no other name has stood so high as his in association with the painter's art in India".[2]

Sudhirindranath the fourth son of Dwijendranath distinguished himself as a writer. He had developed a keen

1. Viswabharati Quarterly, Abanindranath Number.
2. Ibid.

interest in literature from early life. It was through his initiative that a new literary journal which was named the 'Sadhana' was introduced by the Tagore family. He ran the journal as its editor for three years, after which Rabindranath himself took over the editorship. Ultimately, it was merged with the older magazine Bharati. Sudhirindranath was the author of a few books of poems, novels and short stories.

Another member of this branch of the family distinguished himself as a musician. He was Dinendranath, the son of Dwijendranath, eldest son of Dwijendranath and, therefore, a grand-nephew to Rabindranath. He was a distinguished musician with a prodigious memory for tunes. Rabindranath became very fond of him for this extraordinary talent. Rabindranath was very particular in setting to tune his own songs; but he had, a bad memory for tunes. This is where Divendranath's assistance became indispensable. Whenever, he would set to tune a new song the services of this grand-nephew would be requisitioned, whose function was to listen as Rabindranath would sing and follow it up by recording the notation of the same at his convenience. He was thus instrumental in preserving the tune as applied to Rabindranath's songs by himself. That is why Rabindranath used to call him 'the store-keeper of all his songs'.

Satyendranath was survived by a son and a daughter both of whom were gifted and distinguished themselves in life. They were educated in the United Kingdom in their childhood under the care of their mother. Surendra had commendable mastery over English. He translated into English the novel entitled 'Char Adhyay' (The Four Chapters) written by Rabindranath. He also wrote a condensed version of the original Sanskrit Maharbharata in Bengali at the behest of Rabindranath. He carried on some experiments in the field of business and commerce. Though he did not prove a successful businessman, he became the founder of the Hindustan Insurance Company.

Satyendranath's daughter Indira became very intimate with Rabindranath in her girlhood. No wonder, she became the first lady to have the distinction of regularly corresponding with Rabindranath Tagore. The letters Indira Devi received from him were carefully preserved by her and subsequently published under the title 'Chhina Patravali'. She was married to Promatha Chaudhuri who was a distinguished contributor to Bengali literature. She spent her last days at Santiniketan and officiated for sometime as the Vice-Chancellor of Vishwabharati. She was an admirer of Rabindranath's songs and became a specialist in them. She has left a valuable book on Rabindranath as composer.

Hemendranath had three sons : Hitendranath, Ritendranath and Kshitindranath who distinguished himself most. He wrote books on diverse subjects. It appears that he took keen interest in collecting materials throwing light on the history of his family. He has left behind in a well preserved condition old letters, documents, important cuttings from newspapers and other papers related to the house of the Tagores. His daughter-in-law Menaka Tagore made a gift of the whole collection to the Rabindra Bharati University. As the materials are considered to be important source materials for research in the affairs of the Tagore family, they have been made over to the custody of the museum attached to the Rabindra Bharati University.

It appears that Kshitindranath also made use of the materials thus collected by himself. He entertained profound respect for Dwarakanath Tagore the first distinguished member of the family, which inspire him to write. Dwarakanath biography. Unfortunately, he could not publish it during his life time. Menaka Devi made over the manuscript of this book also to the Rabindranath Bharati University which has since published it.

Balendranath was the only son of Birendranath, the fourth son of Maharshi. He was exceptionally good-looking and distinguished himself as a writer; Rabindranath became very fond of him and took interest in his literary activities. Unfortunately, he was over taken by death at the early age of 29. He was the author of a book of essays entitled 'Chitra O Kavya' (painting and poetry) and two books of poems named 'Shrabani' and 'Madhabika'. His writings bear promise of a future of distinction which unfortunately was not to be realised.

Jyotirindranath had no issue. We therefore, came to Rathindranath, the son of Rabindranath. Having lost his mother in early age, he was both brought up and educated by his father. In fact, it was to provide for his education in an academic atmosphere that Rabindranath founded the Brahmacharaya Ashram at Santiniketan. When he passed the Matriculation Examination from this school, Rabindranath sent him to the United States of America for study of agriculture in 1906. He passed the B.Sc. degree of the Illinois University in 1909 and returned to India. As Rabindranath wanted to introduce a programme for rural reconstruction, he made his son qualify as an expert in agriculture. Accordingly, it was decided by his father on his return that he would live at Shilaidaha to look after the family estates and start a farm of his own to apply his newly acquired technical knowledge to agricultural activities. This forced him like his father to spend part of his time at Shilaidaha and part in Calcutta, alternately. It was during this time that he established the 'Vichitra' club in the family house at Jorasanko with the help of his cousins, Gaganendranath and Abhanindranath under the patrona of his father. Some years after, when the work-load at Santiniketan increased considerably Rabindranath brought him to Santiniketan to relieve him of a share of his burden. The rest of Rathindranath's life was thus spent mostly at Santiniketan. After his father's death, he had to take over the charge of the institutions at Santiniketan. At a subsequent stage, when the Central Government took over charge of the Viswabharati he functioned as its Vice-Chancellor for some years.

To be born the son of a famous father is not an unmixed blessing; it entails serious responsibilities also. What excites ones admiration is the fact that Rathindranath never shirked from such responsibilities. He had the option to avoid this and shape his life in this own way; but he never thought of this. On the contrary, he always gave priority to his father's wishes. It appears that he made it the mission of his life to devote his energy whole heartedly towards the fulfilment of his father's desire. His father refused to educate him according to the traditional system and put him in the first batch of students to be taught in the Brahmacharya Ashram of Santiniketan. He willingly submitted to this. Subsequently, when his father decided to send him to America for study of agriculture he complied with his father's wish. When he returned home after completion of his training, he took over charge of the administration of the family estate from Shiladaha as decided by his father. Again, when his father wanted that he should come over to Santiniketan permanently, he joyfully complied with his father's wish. This quality of implicit submission to his father's wishes is worthy of admiration.

Rathindranath was potentially an artist. He did not allow this talent to rust despite his many preoccupations. He devoted his spare time to painting and handicraft under the inspiration of his artistic urge. As raw materials for handicraft, he would use wood and leather and produced many five specimens of handicraft. He also distinguished himself as a painter. Two subjects dominated his paintings: flowers and the hills. He has left many paintings on flowers the silent grandeur of the hills. It appears that he developed a style of his own.

The observation made by Stella Kramarisch, the distinguished art critic may be quoted in this connection. She says that his paintings did not follow any school; it is a simple style spontaneously evolved which follows the basic principles of painting which has been applied with unerring skill to handicrafts and paintings.

14

THE ROLE OF THE TAGORE FAMILY IN THE CULTURAL HISTORY OF BENGAL

The glorious history of the Tagore family of Jorasanko is more or less well known to the people of Bengal. The birth of many outstanding men in the same family is a rare event. The Tagore family is extremely lucky in this respect. Their record remains unbroken throughout India. For a full century, different members of this family led the Bengali society in different fields. The example set by Dwarakanath in the beginning of the nineteenth century in trade and commercial enterprise has no parallel. He was the special object of respect and admiration of both the Indian and European communities of Calcutta for his numerous qualities of the head and the heart. A rare event indeed! His son, Debendranath, repeated this example in the second half of the same century by giving leadership to an extensive religious movement. His piety, saintly character and concern for imparting to his newly founded religion a national character endowed his life and work with special significance.

His personal conduct and indirect supervision made it possible for an atmosphere to be created in the family which enabled his sons to engage in nationalistic and cultural pursuits. They lived a life which was utterly different from the style pursued by the sons of landed property owners. When the tradition was to waste time in idle luxury, his gifted sons engaged themselves in distinguishing themselves in different fields with the fervour of a devotee. His eldest son was attracted to philosophy and poetry. His second son, Satyendranath, not only distinguished himself as a meritorious student but also seriously interested himself in the education and emancipation of women. His third son showed enthusiasm in physical culture as well as female education. He voluntarily undertook the responsibility of educating the female members of his family. Moreover, he was a keen advocate for using Bengali as the medium of instruction. The fifth son, Jyotirindranath, specialised as a playwright, composer and actor. Maharshi's nephew, Ganendranath, engaged himself in the development of the Bengali stage. All of them were without exception imbued with deep patriotic feelings long before the Indian National Congress was born. Satyendranath and Ganendranath started the institution of the Hindu Mela in the seventh decade of the last century with the assistance of Babagopal Mitra, for inculcating patriotic feelings among their people and promoting indigenous industries. In an age, when it was the fashion to the top members of the society to talk in English and dress in Western clothes, the members of this family dressed in national clothes, talked in Bengali and undertook to enrich the Bengali literature. Despite his long sojourn in the United Kingdom and his membership of the Indian Civil Service Satyendranath wrote books, letters in Bengali and had the distinction of composing the first nationalistic song in Bengali for the inaugural ceremony of the Hindu Mela. His preoccupation in a life of piety and indifference to worldly affairs did not prevent Maharshi from giving encouragement to his sons, and nephew in diverse noble pursuits. When his nephew, Ganendranath, interested himself seriously in the

Bengali stage, Maharshi sent him a letter of encouragement.

This atmosphere prevailing in the family of the Tagores produced an impact on our national history in two ways. For one thing, it helped to direct the movement born out of the impact with Western culture with our old moribund society to a channel conducive to our national interest. Secondly, it helped the development of the genius of Debendranath's youngest son Rabindranath. It is not seeds alone which ensure a good harvest. The proper condition has to be created to achieve good results like adequate ploughing, manuring and care. Similarly, a favourable atmosphere is necessary for the blossoming of even a genius all by himself. The favourable atmosphere, his elder brothers created in the family, helped considerably towards the development of Rabindranath's talents. The point is so patent that it hardly calls for proof. In fact, Rabindranath himself draws our attention to this fact in his reminiscences. We can, therefore, dispense with a detailed treatment of this subject.

A close look is necessary to realise how strongly the activities of the member of the Tagore family reacted to the impact produced by contact of western culture with our society in the nineteenth century. Evidently, a detailed treatment of the subject is called for. Some facts should be placed here for a better understanding of the subject.

When the East India Company first established its empire in India they did not show any interest in the spread of English education. On the contrary, they patronised the indigenous system of education. They opened the Calcutta Madarsaah in 1781 for encouragement of education in Arabic and Persian. This was followed by the opening of the Sanskrit College at Benaras as in 1792, for encouraging education in Hindu Shastras. It was the Christian missionaries and the

Indian leaders who first showed interest in English education. It is not without reason that the Company adopted this policy. The imperial interest of the British Government had received a severe setback recently in their North American colonies which revolted and after wresting freedom from the parent state set up an independent sovereign state for themselves. This rebuff made the British people think that people of India would imbibe western ideas of preaching political freedom if English education was allowed to spread in India and start a movement for political independence. Small wonder, they did not like that Indians should be brought in close contact with Western culture.

This negative policy, however, could not prevent such a contact. It was the Indian leaders that took the lead. A Scottish merchant named David Hare joined them. Through their efforts, funds were raised and the Hindu College came into being in 1817. William Carry opened the Serampore College at Serampore the following year. These are the two oldest institutions imparting English education in India. So the Bengali youth did receive English education and through the medium of English language picked up acquaintance with this new culture. This is a culture which replaces dogma by reason, which has acquired scientific knowledge and by developing technological skill produced some wonderful results.

This has endabled the Englishmen to use power-looms driven by steam-engine to produce textiles and to navigate ships driven by steam power. This culture does not practise image worship; on the contrary, condemns it and hates it. They said that the shastras of the Hindus, which are filled with empty rituals and rules for securing redemptions from sins committed and carry no sense.

To the Bengali youth of those days who has received English education the very novelty of the new culture was a tremendous attraction by itself. Its vitality contrasted with the morbid old Hindu culture burdened with age, charmed their hearts. In this unfair contest between a senile old man and a vigorous youth, the old man was easily defeated. Under the leadership of their young teacher Derozio, the Hindu youth decided to destroy Hinduism. They founded an institution which they named 'Young Bengal' and formulated the slogan 'Down with Hinduism'. Many of the young men who graduated from the Hindu College embraced Christianity. There were indications that this new culture might displace altogether the old indigenous culture of India.

The possibility made Macaulay, the education member of the Governor General's Council rejoice as he thought that these developments would promote the imperial interest of Britain. He noted that English education turns educated young Indians hostile to their national culture and religion and in some cases even made them embrace Christianity. He felt that the conditions were favourable to the British interests of which they should take full advantage. If the Indians thus became alienated from their own culture and exchange it for the Western culture, conditions would be created which should be considered favourable to British imperial interests. So he advised his Government to change their educational policy and provide for large-scale education in English. His recommendation was accepted and under the new policy Zillah schools were opened in districts to impart English education. If Macaulay's dream was realised the new awakening that took place in Bengal by the impact of Western culture which historians label as 'Renaissance' would have never come into being. The entire Bengali Hindu community would have rejected Indian culture and adopted Western culture: This is what happened in the Phillipines when Spain occupied it. Their indigenous culture was completely replaced by Spanish culture. There were, however, many forces which worked against this possibility in Bengal. A major one was the strong leadership of the Tagore family in this critical stage of our history. The head of this family Debandranath was also a product of the Hindu College but he did not follow the course adopted by Krishna Mohan Banerjee. His role call for special reference in this connection. He lost faith in image worship; but he did not, for that reason, give up his own culture. He adopted the course laid down by Rammohun Roy and evolved a form of worship without image in conformity with the ancient scriptures of India. That is what actuated him to resuscitate the Brahmo Samaj establised by Rammohun and take the lead in introducing the Brahmo religion.

It was he again who started a movement to protest against the misdeeds of the Christian missionaries. He was highly mortified to receive information that minor daughter-in-law of the brother of one of his employees had been forcibly converted to Christianity. He called a meeting to protest against this outrage. He arranged for the publication of a series of articles in the Tatvabodhini Patrika, to support the cause of the Hindus. To keep boys of Hindus families away from the contact of Christian missionaries, he set up a new primary school for them like the missionaries. Bhudeb Mukherjee functioned as the first honorary teacher of that school.

In fact, he was keen on maintaining his link as well as that of the Brahmo Samaj with the Hindu religion. He strongly desired that Indians should maintain their national character. He never wanted that Indian culture should be entirely replaced by a foreign culture. That is the reason why he continued to look after his old Brahmo Samaj even when the radical section of his own community left him and set up a new samaj under the leadership of Keshab Chandra Sen.

The renaissance was born in Bengal because Indians refused to part with their own culture. What the contact with Western culture led to was not the extinction of Indian culture but its regeneration. In fact, the impact produced a new culture which is neither like Western culture nor like Indian culture. A richer culture was brought into being by the fusion of both these cultures which is now our heritage. That is how Macaulay's dream remained unrealised.

The Tagore family not only took an active part in the religious movement of the nineteenth century but also contributed to the development of the Bengali culture by taking the leadership in different areas of our national life and encouraging progressive movements. In fact, all progressive movements that eventually enriched Bengali culture were initiated from this family. Several members of the Tagore family played prominent parts in these movements. As our attention has so far been monopolised by a few stalwarts among them, we fail to notice the contribution of others. We miss the fact that a sizeable number of the members of the Tagore family have contributed towards the enrichment of our culture. That is the reason why a brief account of their contribution should be placed here. If this involves some repetition can be justifiably excused.

It has been already mentioned that the Company's government was against the spread of English education in India and whatever was done for this was done at the initiative of the people. Two prominent Bengalis took the lead in the matter and a Scottish gentleman extended to them his help. Of them, David Hare has been already mentioned. The two Indian leaders are Rammohun Roy and Dwarakanath Tagore both of whom had distinguished themselves by their personality, high intellectual calibre and achievements. Rammohun was senior in age by as much as twenty years despite which they became very intimate by sharing same values. When Rammohun opened a school for imparting English education Dwarakanath got his eldest son Debendranath admitted to it. His efforts also contributed to the founding of the Hindu College in 1817. Dwarakanath was not merely interested in the spread of English education but also encouraged the spread of scientific and the technological knowledge. He desired that in addition to the indigenous medical system the Western system of medicine should also be introduced to India. There was then a provision for the teaching of Ayurveda in the Sanskrit College in Calcutta. Dwarakanath proposed that a medical college should be opened in our country for teaching Indians the allopathic system of medicine. His desire was fulfilled in 1835 by the establishment of the Medical College of Calcutta. Next year, he announced some scholarships to encourage Indians to learn the Western system of medicine and allocated an annual contribution of Rs. 200/- from his own funds.

The Calcutta Sanskrit College used to teach the Ayurvedic system of medicine as already stated; but it did not provide for dissection for acquisition of intimate knowledge about the anatomy of the human body. It was through his insistence that dissection was made a part of the curriculum and Madhusudan Gupta, teacher of Ayurveda, was entrusted with the work of supervision of dissection. Dwarakanath's interest in the spread of the Western system of medicine attracted him to take some additional measures. To ensure a high standard of medical treatment in India he desired that some Indians should go over to the United Kingdom to learn the Western system of medicine. With this end in view, he undertook to take two young men with him in his second visit to the United Kingdom and bear their expenses for medical training. He selected Bholanath Bose and Gopal Chandra Seal for this purpose and took them with himself in this second voyage to England.

Dwarakanath did not lack interest in social reforms either. The incidence of the practice of burning widows on the funeral pyre of their husbands registered a sharp, in the beginning of the nineteenth century. Rammohun repeatedly drew the attention of the British Government to this custom and suggested its abolition by legislation. Lord Amherst declined to intercede on the plea that it would amount to interference with the religions practices of the Hindus. When Lord William Bentinck succeeded him as Governor-General the suggestion was repeated to him. On this occasion, Dwarakanath strongly supported Rammohun's suggestion. What weighed more in the mind of the British administrators was the impression that their rite of suttee had been prescribed by the Hindu scriptures and so preventive measures by legislation would amount to interference with their religious practices.

Against this, both Rammohun and Dwarakanath asserted that though the rite of suttee had a long history behind it, was merely sanctified by custom; it was neither prescribed by the Hindu scriptures nor approved by them. When this information was communicated to Lord Bentinck, he did not hesitate to prohibit it by legislation. This is how this barborous custom was exterminated. That both Dwarakanath and Rammohun were responsible is acknowledged in a letter written by lady Bentinck to Dwarakanath.

The first Bengali journal was brought out by the Baptist Mission Press of Serampore, in 1818. It was named the 'Digdarshan' but was of the nature of a newspaper. To the Tagore family goes the credit of starting for the first time a Bengali literary journal of quality dealing with literature, religion, philosophy and other allied subjects. Debendranath started the Tatvabodhini Patrika in 1843 for carrying on publicity on behalf of the Brahmo religion with Akshoy Chandra Dutta as the first editor. Besides religion it published philosophical and literary subjects. It was in this magazine that Rabindranath's poetical compositions of his early age were first published.

The example set by Debendranath by starting a journal to serve the cause of Bengali literature was followed by his successors. In 1877, Joytirindranath mooted a proposal that the family start a magazine devoted exclusively to literature which received the blessing of his eldest brother Dwijendranath. When asked to give it a name Dwijendranath named it the 'Bharati'. He also became its first editor, which responsibility he continued to discharge for as long as nine years. He was succeeded by his sister Swaranakumari Devi. In 1896, her two daughters Hiranmayi Devi and Sarala Devi were appointed joint editors of the journal. They continued till 1899 when Rabindranath himself took over the editorship. Many compositions of Rabindranath made their first appearance in print in the pages of this magazine. In fact, he started contributing to it from his early age. He published the experience he had gained during his sojourn in the West in form of letters in the Bharati under the title 'Europe Prabasir Patra'. The 'Bharati' continued to be published till 1926.

A third magazine named the 'Sadhana' made its appearance in the family in 1891, at the initiative of Sudhirindranath, son of Dwijendranath who became its first editor. Three years after, Rabindranath took over its editorship. The next year it was discontinued. But during its short life, it enjoyed the privilege of introducing to the reading public many contributions for Rabindranth's pen. It may be mentioned in this connection that many stories of the 'Galpagucha' were written to fill the pages of the 'Sadhana'.

To the Tagore family goes the credit of bringing out first children's magazine in Bengali; it was Jnandanandini Devi, wife of Satyendranath who was particularly fond of children, who mooted the idea. It has been reported that this lady introduced the practice of celebrating children's birthdays and giving them presents on the occasion in this family. She started the magazine 'Bālaka' in 1885 to develop among children a taste for literature and became its first editor. The family could boast of sizeable number of youngsters at the time who included Dwijendranath's fourth son Sudhirindranath, Hemendranath's three sons Hitendranath, Kshitindranath and Ritendranath and the three sons of Gunendranath, Gaganendranath, Soumendranath and Abanindranath. After a year, the children's magazine was merged with the 'Bharati'. This was the magazine which provided the inspiration to Rabindranath for writing poems suitable for children; a sizeable number of poems included in the collection named the 'Shishu' were written to feed this magazine. His novel the 'Rajarshi' was first published in the 'Balak' in instalments.

The first movement for the development of the Bengali stages was initiated by the members of this family. Gunendranath, son of Girindranath, was deeply interested in writing and staging dramas. Failing to get a suitable drama for staging, he announced a prize for the author of the best drama in Bengali. In the competition that followed the drama named the 'Nabanatak', written by Ramnarayan Tarkaratna was adjudged the best and awarded the prize. Gunendranath staged it in the drawing room of his residential house at No. 5 Dwarakanath Tagore lane. After that his cousin Jyotirindranath undertook to write plays for him. He followed this up by writing a play named 'Sarojini' based on a story current in Rajasthan. This was staged on the roof of the Maharshi Bhavan with great enthusiasm. When Rabindranath returned from the United Kingdom his lyrical drama 'Valmiki Pratibha' was staged in the courtyard adjoining the 'Thakur dalan' of the Tagores. Both Jyotirindranath and Rabindranath used to take part in them. In those days, it was customary for men to play female parts; but when 'Valmiki Pratibha' was staged history was made by making a departure.

Pratibha Devi, daughter of Hemendranath appeared in the role of goddess, Saraswati, disguised as girl. This was a new example set by the family of the Tagores. This was the first instance when a female character was played by a girl in an amateurs' performance.

The movement for inculcating patriotic feelings and encouraging indigenous industries was initiated by the members of the Tagore family. As long as twenty years before the founding of the Indian National Congress, some enthusiastic young men of this family took the lead. Girindranath's eldest son, Gunendranath, and Debendranath's second son Satyendranath enjoyed respectively the status of the Mejda and the Sejda of the family. It was at their initiative that fair Swadeshi Mela, was organised for the first time in Calcutta, in 1867. They were ably assisted by a patriotic young men named, Nabagopal Mitra. Thanks to the efforts of these men, the Swadeshi Mela became an annual festival. It was run with two objectives in view: to inculcate patriotic feelings among Indians and secondly, to increase sale of indigenously produced consumer goods.

It is not a long time ago that there was no system of notation to record in a permanent form a musical composition; a terrible handicap for lovers of music. It was the members of the Tagore family who initiated pioneering efforts to solve this problem. Dwijendranath, the eldest son of Debendranath, was the first to invent a system of notations. As this did not prove wholly satisfactory his younger brother introduced some modifications and the system of notation thus evolved has found recognition as the standard system of recording the time of Bengali songs.[1] It was

1. Two systems of notation are current in Bengali:— (i) The notation called 'Dandamatrik' invented by Keshetramohan Goswami; (2) The notation introduced by Jyotirindranath known as 'Aksharamatrik'. The second system is more popular for the convenience with which it can be printed.

Jyotririndranath again who very probably started the first journal in Bengali devoted to music.[2]

Towards the turn of the century India could claim no particular style of painting as distinctively its own as a break had occurred with the past tradition. Western India could claim the distinction of owning two distinct schools of art, namely the Kangra School and the Rajasthani School. Eastern India could claim none and consequently, the Western style became the model. In South India, Rabi Verma Established his reputation as a painter by following the Western style; but his paintings could not avoid the stigma of being borrowed things. It fell in the lot of a member of the Tagore family to wipe out this stain. The reference is to Abanindranath about whom an account has been given in the previous chapter. By founding the Bengali school of painting he restored to Indian painting its lost prestige. It has been already mentiond that his elder brother Gaganendranath was the first cartoonist of India.

An attempt has been made above to give a brief account of the contribution of the family of the Tagores to the social, and cultural heritage of Bengali. It is amazing that a single family had the distinction of producing so many men of distinction. For over a century, this family functioned as the centre of all progressive activities under the leadership of three srtalwarts endowed with uncommon qualities. The contributions of other members were not insignificant either. Indeed, it is rare luck that Bengal could claim the ownership of such a family. No wonder, the Bengali looks upon the ancestral home of the Tagores, reminiscent of past glory, as a place of pilgrimage. The

2. Gopeswar Banerjee, the famous exponent of music, claims that it was Manamathanath De who first brought the Bengali magazine on music named the 'Alapani'. This is no clear evidence to decide what is the buits.

West Bengal Government discharged its responsibility by acquiring it as a national trust and saving it from destruction. It took the additional step of founding a university there together with a museum to disseminate information about the glorious achievements of the Tagores of Jorasanko. It has been fittingly privileged to be linked with the name of the most distinguished member of this family.

APPENDIX-A

CHRONOLOGICAL TABLE
(Chart I)

- Panchanan
  - Jayram
    - Anandiram
    - Nilmaniram
      - Ramlochan
      - Rammoni
      - Ramballav
      - Kamalmani
    - Darpanarayan
    - Gobindaram
    - Sidhweswari
  - Santoshram

(Chart II-A)

- Ramlochan
  - Daughter (short-lived)
  - Dwarakanath (Adopted son) 1794-1846 Digambari Devi
    - Daughter (short-lived)
    - Debendranath (1817-1905)
    - Narandranath
    - Girindranath (1820-1854)
    - Bhupendranath (1826-1839)
    - Nagendranath (1829-1858)

(Chart II-B)

- Rammoni
  - Jahnabi
  - Radhanath
  - Rasbilasi
  - Dwarakanath (Adopted by Ramlochan and his wife Alaka Devi)
  - Ramanath

(Chart III-A)

- Debendranath 1817-1905, Sarda Devi
  - Daughter (short-lived) 1838
  - Dwijendranath 1840-1926, Sarbasundari Devi
    - Dwipendranath 1862-1922 (eldest son)
      - Dinendranath 1882-1935
    - Sudhindranath 1869-1929 (fourth son)
  - Satyendranath 1842-1923, Jnanadanandhini Devi
    - Surendranath 1872-1940
    - Indira Devi 1837-1960, Pramatha Chowdhury
    - Kabindranath (1875-1879)
  - Hemendranath 1844-1884, Neepmoyee Devi
    - Protiva 1865-1922 (eldest)
    - Hitendranath 1867-1908
    - Kshitindranath 1869-1937
    - Ritendranath 1870-1936
  - Birendranath 1845-1915, Prafullamoyee Devi
    - Balendranath 1870-1899
  - Saudamini 1847-1920, Saradaprosad Ganguly
    - Satyaprosad 1859-1933 (eldest son)
    - Irabati (eldest daughter) 1861-1918

- Debendranath 1817-1905 Sarada Devi
  - Jyotirindranath 1849-1925
  - Kadambari Devi
  - Sukumari 1850-1864 Hemendranath Mukherjee
  - Punyendranath 1851-1857
  - Sarat Kumari 1854-1920 Jadunath Mukherjee
    - Sushila (eldest)
  - Swarna Kumari 1856-1932 Janakinath Ghosal
    - Hiranmoyee 1868-1925
    - Jyotsnanath 1817
    - Sarala 1872-1945
    - Urmila 1873
  - Barna Kumari 1858-1948 Satish Chandra Mukherjee
  - Somendranath 1859-1922
  - Rabindranath 1861-1941 Mrinalini Devi
  - Badhendranath 1863-1864

(Chart III-B)

- Girindranath
  1820-1854
  (vide Chart II-A)
  Jogmaya Devi
  - Ganendranath (1841-1969)
  - Kadambini
    - Jyotiprakash (1855-1919)
      - Jamini Prakash
  - Kumudini
  - Gunendranath (1847-1881)
    SaudaminiDevi
    - Gaganendranath (1867-1938)
    - Samarendranath (1870-1951)
    - Abanindranath (1871-1951)
    - Benayanee
      Seshendrabhusan Chatterjee
      - Pratima Devi 1893
    - Sunayanee

(Chart IV)

- Rabindranath (1861-1941) Mrinalini Devi
  - Madhurilata (1886-1918) Saratchandra Chakravorty (No Issue)
  - Rathindranath
    - Nandini (Adopted daughter) 1922
  - Renuka (1890-1903) Satyendranath Bhattacharyya (No Issue)
  - Mira 1892 Nagendranath Ganguly
    - Nitindranath (1912-1932)
    - Nandita (1916-1967) Krishna Kripalani
  - Samindranath (1894-1907)

APPENDIX-B

(IMPORTANT EVENTS IN THE FAMILY HISTORY OF THE TAGORES)

1784	Nilmani Tagore founds the Jorasanko branch of Tagore family in Calcutta.
1791	Death of Nilmani.
1794	Birth of Dwarakanath.
1799	Adoption of Dwarakanath by his uncle Ramlochan.
1807	Death of Ramlochan.
1814	Rammohun Roy settled in Calcutta.
1815	Rammohun founds Atmiya Sabha.
1817, Jan.19	Hindu College founded.
1817, May.15	Birth of Debendranath eldest son of Dwarakanath.
1818	Dwarakanath appointed Sheristadar of Twentyfour Parganas collectorate.
1820	Birth of Girindranath second son of Dwarakanath.
1828, Aug.20	Brahmo Samaj started in the house of Kamal Lochan Basu in Chitpore Road Calcutta (observed as Bhadrotsab).
1829	Birth of Nagendranath Youngest son of Dwarakanath.
1829	Dwarakanath appointed Dewan of the Custom, salt and opium Board.
1829, Aug.1	Union Bank founded.
1829, Dec.4	Abolition of the Suttee rite.
1830, Jan.23	Brahmo Samaj shifts to its own house (observed as Maghotsab).
1834, July	Dwarakanath resigns from his post under Government and opens the Carr-Tagore & Co.
1835, June1	Medical College founded in Calcutta.
1835	Death of Alaka Sundari Devi, mother of Dwarakanath.
1838	Dwarakanath founds the Bengali Land holders, Association.
1839, Jan.21	Death of Digambari Devi wife of Dwarakanath.
1839, Oct.6	Tattwabodhini Sabha founded by Debendranath.

1840, Mar.11	Birth of Dwijendranath eldest son of Debendranath.
1840, Aug.20	Dwarakanath executes his trust deed.
1841	Birth of Ganendranath son of Girindranath.
1842, Jan.6	Reception of Dwarakanath at the Town Hall of Calcutta on the eve of his departure to the United Kingdom.
1842, Jan.9	Dwarakanath leaves for the United Kingdom.
1842, June1	Birth of Satyendranath second son of Debendranath.
1843, Jan.	Dwarakanath returns from the United Kingdom.
1843, Aug.	Tatvabodhini Patrika started by Debendranath.
1843, Aug.16	Dwarakanath executes his will.
1843, Dec.22	Debendranath is initiated into the Brahmo Dharma (observed as Pous Utsab).
1844	Birth of Hemendranath third son of Debendranath.
1844	Brahmo Upasana Paddati (a book on Brahmo rites for prayers) compiled by Debendranath.
1845	Birth of Birendranath fourth son of Debendranath.
1845	Dwarakanath founded the Bengal Coal Company.
1845, Mar.8	Dwarakanath leaves for the United Kingdom a second time.
1846, Aug.1	Death of Dwarakanath in the United Kingdom.
1847	Birth of Gunendranath second son of Girindranath.
1847, Dec.27	Union Bank fails.
1848, Jan.12	Carr-Tagore Company declared insolvent.
1848	'Brahmo Dharma Beej' (The Essence of Brahmo Religion, written by Debendranath.

1849	Publication of 'Brahmo Dharma Grantha', a treaties on Brahmo Religion by Debendranath.
1849, May.4	Birth of Jyotirindranath fifth son of Debendranath.
1851, Oct.31	British Indian Association founded with Debendranath as Secretary.
1854, Dec.19	Death of Girindranath second son of Dwarakanath.
1856, July 26	Hindu Widow Remarriage Act passed.
1859	Birth of Somendranath seventh son of Debendranath.
1861, May 7	Rabindranath eighth son of Debendranath was born.
1862	Kesabchandra Sen appointed Acharyya of Brahmo Samaj.
1866, Jan.24	Kesabchandra Sen founds Bharatbarshiya Brahmo mandir.
1867	Birth of Gaganendranath eldest son of Gunendranath.
1869	Death of Ganendranath eldest son of Girindranath.
1871	Birth of Abanindranath youngest son of Gurendranath.
1875, March	Death of Sarada Devi wife of Debendranath.
1877, Aug.	Bharati (a literary journal) started by Dwijendranath.
1878, Sept.20	Rabindranath accompanies his brother Satyendranath to the United Kingdom.
1881	Death of Gunendranath younger son of Girindranath.
1863, Dec.9	Rabindranath married to Mrinalini Devi.
1884, April,19	Kadambari Devi wife of Jyotirindranath committed suicide.
1884, June 7	Death of Hemendranath.
1888, Oct.19	Ashram opened at Santiniketan.
1891, Dec.22	Brahmo Mandir opened at Santiniketan.
1894	Bangiya Sahitya Parishad founded.
1899, Aug.	Death of Balendranath

1901, Dec.22	Brahmacharyya Ashram opened at Santiniketan.
1902, Nov.23	Death of Mrinalini Devi.
1903, Sept.	Death of Renuka second daughter of Rabindranath.
1905, Oct.16	Partition of Bengal.
1905, Jan.19	Death of Debendranath.
1907, Nov.	Death of Shamindranath younger son of Rabindranath.
1912, Jan.28	Reception of Rabindranath at Calcutta.
1913, Nov.15	Award of Nobel Prize to Rabindranath.
1913, Nov.23	Ovation paid to Rabindranath by his countrymen at Santiniketan.
1915, Feb.17	Mahatma Gandhi visits Santiniketan.
1915. June15	Knighthood conferred on Rabindranath.
1915	Death of Birendranath.
1918, May16	Death of Rabindranath's eldest daughter Madhurilata.
1918, Dec.23	Visva-Bharati informally opened
1919, April13	Jallianwalabagh Massacre.
1919, May 29	Rabindranath announces Knighthood.
1921, Dec.23	Visva-Bharati opened formally.
1922	Death of Somendranath.
1923, Jan.9	Death of Satyendranath.
1925 Mar.4	Death of Jyotirindranath.
1926, Jan.19	Death of Dwinjendranath
1932, Sept.20	Mahatma Gandhi started fasting over the issue of separate electorate for Scheduled Castes.
1932, Sep.26	Mahatma Gandhi breaks fast in presence of Rabindranath.
1937, April	Opening of Hindi Bhavan at Santiniketan by Jawaharlal Nehru.
1940, Feb.17	Mahatma Gandhi visited Santiniketan.
1940, Aug.7	Conferment of D.Litt. Degree on Rabindranath by Oxford University in a ceremony at Santiniketan.
1941. July 25	Rabindranath brought to Calcutta for treatment.
1941, July 30	Surgical operation performed on Rabindranath.
1941, Aug.7	Rabindranath died.

APPENDIX-C

CRONOLOGICAL LIST OF RABINDRANATH TAGORE'S IMPORTANT WORKS

1878	Kabi Kãhini	Poetry
1880	Banaphul	A stroy in verse
1881	Vãlmiki Prãtibha	A Play in songs
	Bhagna Hriday	A book of poems
	Rudra Chanda	Playlet
1882	Sãndhya Sãngeet	A book of poems
	Kãlmrigayã	A play in songs
1883	Bau-Thãkurãnir Hat	A novel
	Prabhãt Sangeet	A book of poems
1884	Chhabi O Gãn	A book of poems
	Prakrtir Pratishodh	A drama in verse
	Nalini	A drama
	Saishab Sangeet	A book of poems
	Bhanu Singha	Poems composed after the old Vaisnava
	Thakurer Padavali	Style
1886	Kari O Komol	A book of poems
1887	Rãjarshi	A novel
1888	Mãyãr Khelã	A drama in songs
1889	Rãjã O Rãni	A drama in verse
1890	Visarjan	A drama based on the novel Rajarshi
	Mãnasi	A book of poems
1892	Chitrãngadã	A drama in verse
	Gorãy Galad	A comic play. A revised version was published in 1928 with the title Sheshraksha
1894	Sonãr Tari	A book of poems
	Chhota Galpa	Short stories
	Vichitra Galpa	Short stories
1894	Kathã Chatustay	Short stories
1895	Galpa Dashak	Short stories
1896	Nadi	A long poem
	Chitrã	A book of poems
1897	Baikunther Khãtã	A comic play
1899	Kanikã	A book of poems
1900	Kathã	Narrative poems

	Kãhini	Narative poems and playlet in blank verse
	Kalpanã	A book of poems
	Kshanikã	A book of poems
1901	Naivedya	A book of poems mostly sonnets
1903	Chokher Bali	A novel
	Karmaphal	A story
1906	Kheyã	A book of poems
	Naukãdubi	A novel
1907	Prãchin Sãhitya	Literary criticism
	Adhunik Sahitya	Literary criticism
	Hãusya Kautuk	Comic sketches
	Byãnga Kautuk	Comic sketches
1908	Prãjapatir Nirbandha	A novel.Subesquently named Chirakumar Sabha. A dramatised version appeared under the same name subsequently.
	Sãradotsab	A play
	Mukut	A playlet
1909	Sãntiniketan (parts 1-8)	Lectures on religion and philosophy
	Prãyaschitta	Dramatised version of the novel Bauthakhranir Hat
	Shishu	Child's book of verse
1910	Sãntiniketan (parts 9-11)	Lectures on religion and philosophy
	Gorã	A novel
	Gitãnjali	Poems and songs
	Rãjã	A symbolic play
1911	Sãntiniketan (Parts 12-13)	Lectures on religion and philosophy
1912	Galpa Chãriti	Short stories
	Mãlini	A play
	Chãitãli	A book of poems
	Jibãn Smriti	Biographical remi niscences
	Ãchalãyatan	A symbolic play

1912	Dãjghar	An allegorical play
1914	Smãran	A collection of poems on his deceased wife
	Utsãrga	A book of poems
	Gitimalya	Songs and poems
	Gitali	Songs and poems
1915	Sãntiniketan (part 14)	Lectures on religion and philosophy
1916	Sãntiniketan (parts 15-17)	Lectures on religion and philosophy
	Fãlguni	A play
	Ghare Baire	A novel
	Bãlaka	Long poems
	Chãturanga	A novel
	Galpa Saptak	Short stories
1918	Guru	Revised version of the play Achalayatan
	Pãlãtãkn	Narrative poems
1920	Ãrupratan	A symbolic play. Revised version of Raja Saradotsab
	Pãylã Nambar	A story
1921	Reenshodh	A playlet. Revised version of Saradotsab
1922	Muktãdhara	A symbolic play
	Lipikã	Prose poems
	Shishu Bholãnath	Child's verse
1925	Purãbi	A book of poems
	Grihãprãbesh	A play
	Prãbãhini	Songs
1926	Chira Kumar Sabha	Dramatised version of Prajapatir Nirbandha
	Sodhboodh	A play
	Raktakarabi	A symbolic play
1927	Rituranga	Drama songs
1928	Sheshraksha	A comic play.Revised version of Goray Galad
1929	Yogayog	A novel
	Tapati	A drama. A prose version of Raj O Rani

	Mãhua	A book of poems
	Shesher Kabitã	A novel
1931	Bãna Bãni	Songs and poems
	Shãpmochan	A playlet in songs
1932	Punãscha	Prose poems
1933	Duibon	A novel
	Manusher Dharma	Kamala lectures delivered at the Calcutta University
	Chãndalika	Dance Drama
	Tãsher Desh	A symbolic play
	Bãnshari	A play
1934	Mãlancha	A novel
	Chãr Adhyay	A novel
1935	Shesh sapthak	Prose poems
	Bithikã	Poems
1936	Chittrangada	Dance drama. Based on the original drama in verse.
	Pãtraput	Prose poems
	Shyãmali	Prose poems
1937	Khãpchhara	Non sense verses
1938	Prãntik	A book of poems
	Chãndalika	Dance drama.
	Senjuti	A book of poems
1939	Prãhasini	A book of poems
	Ãkaspradip	A book of poems
	Shyma	Dance drama
1940	Nabajatak	A book of poems
	Sanai	A book of poems
	Chhelebela	Reminiscences of childhood
	Rogshajyay	A book of poems
1941	Arogya	A book of poems
	Janmadine	A book of poems
	Gãlpa Salpa	Poems and stories
	Sãvyatar Sankat	Last birthday Speech translated in English as 'crisis in civilization'

APPENDIX-IV

CHRONOLOGICAL LIST OF WORKS OF RABINDRANATH TAGORE IN ENGLISH (INCLUDING TRANSLATIONS BY HIMSELF)

1912	Gitanjali	Translation from own Bengali poems
1913	The Gardner	Translation from own Bengali poems
	The Cresent	Translation from own Bengali poems Moon
	Chitra	Translation of his drama chitrangada
1914	Sadhana	Lectures in English delivered in the United States in 1912-13
1917	Nationalism	Lectures in English delivered in Japan and America in 1916-17
	Personality	Lectures in English delivered in Japan and America in 1916-17
1919	The Centre of Culture	Lectures in English
1922	Creative Unity	Essays in English
1925	Talks in China	Lectures in English
1928	Fireflies	Translation from own Bengali poems
	Lectures and Address	Lectures in English

1931	The child	A symbolic poem in English
	The Religion of Man	Hibbert Lectures
1932	Mahatmaji and Depressed Humanity	An appreciation of Mahatma Gandhi

INDEX